Simple Lessons
for Change Leaders
and Teams

Simple Lessons for Change Leaders and Teams

Communication ▸ Collaboration ▸ Project Management

Karen R. Brown, MSW
Yvette L. Harms, PMP

CHANGE LEADERSHIP NETWORK

University of Michigan, Institute of Continuing Legal Education

Ann Arbor, MI

© 2010 Change Leadership Network, University of Michigan, Institute of Continuing
Legal Education

ISBN: 978-0-615-40221-5

Library of Congress Control Number: 2010936378

The Institute of Continuing Legal Education, a jointly sponsored institute at the University of
Michigan, provides practical legal education for Michigan lawyers and related professionals. The
Institute is cosponsored by the State Bar of Michigan, the University of Michigan Law School,
Wayne State University Law School, University of Detroit Mercy School of Law, The Thomas M.
Cooley Law School, and Michigan State University College of Law.

Printed in the United States of America

About the Authors

Karen R. Brown is Administrative Director at the Institute of Continuing Legal Education (ICLE).

In her 23 years at ICLE, she has managed many major transitions, including those in technology, business, marketing, customer service, warehouse and shipping, team implementation, strategic planning, corporate reorganization, and Web design.

Ms. Brown has also led training at ICLE to enhance management, team management, and project management skills.

During her time at ICLE, she has been a member of the Association for Continuing Legal Education (ACLEA), winning several "ACLEA's Best" awards and presenting on marketing, change management, and strategic leadership topics.

Ms. Brown holds an MSW from the University of Michigan.

Yvette L. Harms has been a project manager for the past 15 years and was certified by the Project Management Institute in 2006 as a Project Management Professional (PMP).

She has worked at the Institute of Continuing Legal Education (ICLE) for the past 11 years. During her time at ICLE she has been instrumental in managing the Institute's change initiatives. She has managed the development of many products and ICLE's technical infrastructure. Ms. Harms was a co-leader in training the ICLE staff in general project management skills.

Ms. Harms has also served as a consultant for publishers in the development of editorial processes, publishing systems, and digitization projects.

A past presenter on technology and project management for the Association for Continuing Legal Education (ACLEA) and a past chairperson of the Technology Special Interest Group, her IT team at ICLE has won several "ACLEA's Best" awards for product development.

Contents

Foreword

The Institute of Continuing Legal Education (ICLE) at the University of Michigan is delighted to publish our first book on change leadership. Over the last decade our work at ICLE has become increasingly complex. In the past, we simply needed to draw on the legal expertise of our volunteer speakers and authors as well as our in-house expertise on book and seminar production. Now, we also need technical functionality as well as convenient customer support to remain relevant to our customers. To innovate requires expert communication, collaboration, and project management skills, not just legal skills. What a change this has been for us! To cope with this change, we learned a lot of lessons.

This book is an outgrowth of those simple lessons for complex work. Many organizations and workers struggle with completing projects on time and within budget. The real challenge is in addressing the people side of the issue—effective communication and conflict resolution—along with the forms and process side of project management. This is the challenge we took on in "Simple Lessons for Change Leaders and Teams". ICLE has benefited enormously from the lessons learned as set forth in this book. We decided to publish this book and launch the "Change Leadership Network" to share our insights and exchange ideas with others. We hope that our readers will join in the blog discussion at the Change Leadership Network at www.icle.org/cln. Share your own practice tips, time savers, and educational exercises, and keep up with our latest additions to change leadership guidance by visiting our Web site. This book and its associated blog is the first in our line of products and services on change leadership.

I want to thank our authors, Karen R. Brown, ICLE Administrative Director, and Yvette L. Harms, PMP and ICLE IT Manager, for their tireless hours and dedication in developing this book and its invaluable lessons. Their insights have helped many of our own staff members learn to manage projects, to innovate, to communicate, and to lead change effectively. It's my hope that these lessons will be equally helpful for our readers.

I also want to thank ICLE's sponsoring organizations—the State Bar of Michigan, the University of Michigan Law School, Wayne State University Law School, University of Detroit Mercy School of Law, The Thomas M. Cooley Law School, and Michigan State University College of Law. Sponsor representatives reviewed this manuscript and shared how they saw these change leadership principles applied in the legal profession and in the world of education. I thank them for their feedback and encouragement with this endeavor.

Finally, I welcome feedback from our readers. I hope you will share with us, at www.icle.org/cln how you have used this book and approached change at your workplace.

Lynn Chard
Director, ICLE
University of Michigan

Introduction

"Management is about human beings."

~Peter Drucker

Today's change leader must be a master of complexity and have the ability to "read" individuals and groups as clearly as he can assess a project plan. Projects that once could be handled alone are now part of a web of tasks that require timing, collaboration, shared specialties, conflict resolution, organization, and teamwork to complete. *Simple Lessons for Change Leaders and Teams* helps you deal with the human communication issues that underlie this complexity and acquire the "sixth sense" that makes a truly successful change leader.

This book is for

Executives who want to introduce successful change.

Project managers or anyone given a change initiative to manage who want a start-to-finish, practical guide to getting it done successfully.

Seasoned project managers who want pointers on communication and collaboration and how they can make or break the project management process.

Project leaders who are struggling with how to get buy-in for their project or commitment from stakeholders.

Any manager who wants better meetings, meaningful communication, effective supervision and delegation, decision-making skills, time management, problem solving.

Team members who would like a practical reference to the team building and project management process so they can contribute fully to the success of the project.

How to use *Simple Lessons*

Are you new to project management? *Simple Lessons* offers 46 basic Lessons, guided by the *Facilitator*, our experienced management coach, who steps you through the project management process from Initiation through Planning, Execution, and Closing. Use *Simple Lessons* as a complete guide for the communication, collaboration, and project management savvy you need to take charge of your project and complete it successfully. Follow the case study, a real Web redesign project, as you work through your project. Each Lesson introduces a typical problem facing the project manager. The Facilitator shares the key point the project manager should keep in mind and backs it up with what you need at your fingertips: what to do, how it works, questions to ask, what to say, forms and templates, and an exercise to test your understanding. Each lesson ends with "In a nutshell"—a quick summary of how communication, collaboration, and project management are applied to solve the problem at hand.

Are you an experienced project manager? Use *Simple Lessons* as a reference for how to deal with specific situations or to get new insight on communication and collaboration techniques. You'll find brief, practical tips for busy project managers who need more than theory or academic charts and graphs to get back on track.

Are you struggling to get buy-in from top management for your project? Use *Simple Lessons* to hone your leadership skills. Learn to assess and communicate the strategic merit of your project. Develop collaborative management and communication skills that will resolve the conflict and invite support. Recognize the unexpressed concerns—what may really be holding back your project—of stakeholders and address them successfully.

Are you a busy executive who is leading your organization through a change initiative? Use the concepts in the Initiation section to communicate the change and lay a foundation for success. Use the concepts in the Planning and Execution sections to know what your project team should be doing and reporting to you. Encourage your teams to follow our simple yet effective method and use the forms and templates to build the foundation for a shared process and vocabulary within your organization—one that leads to innovation. Recognize the importance of the Closing section activities to launch your teams to tackling the next change with enthusiasm and true collaboration.

Key roles in the change initiative process

There are many roles in project management. Each contributes to the success of the project. *Simple Lessons* explains the functions each role contributes throughout the project, offering communication, collaboration, and project management guidance for how they best work together. These roles include:

Project Manager: The person responsible for the planning, execution, and successful outcome of the project. The Project Manager commits to deliver the project outcomes on time, on budget, and within quality standards.

Project Sponsor: The project champion and funding provider. The ultimate authority on the project.

Stakeholders: Anyone who will be affected by the outcome of the project. Those who have an interest or "stake" in the project deliverables. They are executives who sponsor the project and provide funding. They are partnering organizations that have a shared goal. They are the department heads who manage the work. They are the speakers and authors who will contribute content. They are also the customers who will use the Web site, and the staff members who will design, program, create content for, and maintain the Web site.

Team Leader (also called Subgroup Leader): The manager of a team responsible for delivering specific project objectives.

Team Member: A person assigned to a project team either temporarily or full-time who contributes time and expertise to implementing a project objective.

Subject Matter Experts: Stakeholders providing functional and authoritative direction and support to the project in their area of expertise. Each representative has an interest in the outcome of the project and how their department will be impacted by change. Our Web redesign project included representatives from Information Technology (IT), Marketing and Design, Customer Service, Seminars, Publications, Business Office.

Facilitator: An experienced management coach who is particularly skilled in meeting management, one of the most important skills of the project manager. The Facilitator works with the project leader to prepare the meeting and debrief afterward.

Results—the bottom line

The top three project success factors identified by the Standish Group (see Chaos study http://www.cs.nmt.edu/~cs328/reading/standish.pdf) are user involvement, executive management support, and a clear statement of requirements. This human side of project management, more than flowcharts, timelines, and formulas, makes or breaks most projects.

The project management process alone does not develop the communication and collaboration skills needed to get top management buy-in, engage the end user throughout the project process, or deliver a set of clearly defined project requirements. By combining communication, collaboration, and project management principles, ICLE achieved a consistent track record of meeting these success factors and delivering projects that met or exceeded expectations. Our innovative methods and approach are not secret or mysterious. They are built on simple concepts—mastered—and we share them with you in these pages.

Getting Ready to Collaborate

Unity is Strength. . . . When there is teamwork and collaboration, wonderful things can be achieved."

~Mattie Stepanek

Lessons

1. Manage Organizational Change
2. Communicate Effectively
3. Aim for Collaboration Instead of Cooperation
4. Assess and Build Collaboration Skills
5. Gain Control of Meetings
6. Reach Decisions through Consensus

1

Manage Organizational Change

"I hear there are going to be some significant changes to the Web site," says the Project Manager. "The new technology seems daunting to me. How will I lead a team when I don't even know how to use it myself?"

"Welcome to the ICLE Web redesign project!" the Facilitator responds. "You seem ready for training! We won't focus on the technology—your tech experts will guide you there. Instead, help your team invite, rather than resist, the organizational changes this technology will bring. They will need to trust that they will have some control over what's happening."

Leading change

"It is not the strongest species that survive, nor the most intelligent, but the one most responsive to change."

~attributed to Charles Darwin

The hard part about leading change is not about understanding technology or systems—it's about understanding people. Change means that something will be different than it is now. Up through our teenage years, we are programmed to welcome change. After that, we are more prone to avoid it. A project that is part of a change initiative can be met with skepticism, resistance, fear, anger, and bargaining before it is accepted. These negative reactions have little or nothing to do with the project itself; they are the stages we commonly go through before accepting any change.

We've all had experience with changes and our reactions to them. Very often our reactions can be traced to two major sources of stress: feeling isolated and feeling overwhelmed. These stressors can make the team member who is struggling with a change transition feel

surprised ("Why didn't anyone tell me?");

unhappy ("We have to make changes again? We just went through this.");

confused ("Am I the only one who doesn't know how to do this?");

at a loss about how to get work done ("It was so much easier before."); or

burdened by extra work ("Overtime again?").

When introducing change, it is helpful to demonstrate to people the natural reluctance or resistance they may have toward what will be different. This can be done in a fun activity called the Change Game (directions are given at the end of this Lesson). Participants are asked to change something about their appearance. They may remove a scarf or move a watch to their other wrist to make this change. Once the change has been identified and the game is over, however, the subjects immediately put the items back where they had them in the first place. When this behavior is brought to their attention, they usually say they are not even conscious of having moved things back to their original positions.

Participants discover that they and others have the same reaction to change—namely, the desire to put things back the way they were, the way that was familiar and comfortable. It was efficient and worked for them. They knew what to expect. They felt in control.

Leading a team or organization through a successful change transition is best accomplished when those involved understand the business purpose for the change, know what to expect, and trust they have some control over what is happening to them. Team members who are engaged in the change initiative are less likely to feel isolated or overwhelmed. Their response will be positive rather than negative.

Communication, sharing information—this includes thoughts and feelings—in a meaningful way, establishes a connection between the change leader and others in the organization. Both sender *and* receiver understand the purpose for the change and can then work together to achieve the purpose. Change, then, points to progress and the foundation is laid for collaboration, the yielding of individual interests in favor of sharing and supporting a common goal.

The effect of change on productivity

Here are some typical concerns of employees affected by change:

Will I be able to keep up with the work?

Will I be given time to adjust?

Will I be given training in the way that I need to learn?

Will my job change to something I no longer want to do?

Will I be replaced or phased out by the new system?

Will I have to work in a new location? With different coworkers?

What the worker is really saying is, "I like my job, and I am angry that I am being forced to change." Many of these concerns can be allayed by communicating what the change is going to be and what typically happens to productivity as a result of the change. The following figure represents productivity before, during, and after change.

Effect of Change on Productivity in the Workplace

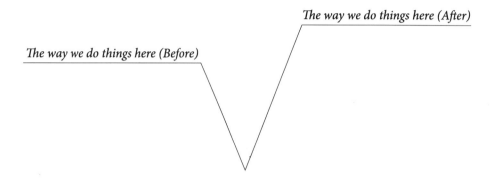

At the point of introducing the change, productivity drops dramatically. Note the sharp decline that forms the V in the figure. Staff are asked to learn new skills, vocabulary, and processes. There are inconsistencies and problems to work out. The organization's data structure may not fit into the new system. Data can be lost or destroyed. It takes longer to complete tasks that used to be routine. The pull to return to the old familiar way of doing things is very strong. Finally, it starts to turn around. Staff begin to use the new vocabulary consistently, and processes become familiar. Technical bugs have been worked out, progress speeds up, and the way to work efficiently becomes more apparent. At the end of the change transition, workers are more productive than before the change and proud of their accomplishments.

The drop in productivity and morale represented by the downward slope of the V can last one to six months or longer, depending on the complexity of the change. Changing a single process may have a mild effect on productivity. More complex system changes may have greater impact.

Using this figure as a guide, the response by the change leader to the typical concerns just listed can be positive.

Will I be able to keep up with the work?

> Probably not at first. All of us will experience a drop in productivity. Here is what we will do to support you: We have lightened your schedule. We will hire temporaries to do routine work while you are learning the new way (especially needed for major systems changes).

Will I be given time to adjust?

> Yes. The period of adjustment is about six months. It may take us more or less time.

Will I be given training in the way that I need to learn?

> Yes. We will provide group training and individual support for a year.

Will my job change to something I no longer want to do?

> Maybe. Here is the vision for how we will be working after the change. Here is *your* place in that vision as we see you working. We see the change as exciting and as a great opportunity to learn new skills that are in demand in the general workplace.

> Some workers may choose to leave the organization rather than accept the changes. This can be a positive response for the person and does not have to be seen as a negative implication of the change. It should be anticipated as a risk of the change and managed appropriately. (See Lesson 28, Identify Risks and Opportunities.)

Will I be replaced or phased out by the new system?

> No. If we had any plans to decrease our workforce we would have already informed anyone who would be affected. We expect the changes we make to increase customer demand or improve efficiency and allow us to develop new services.

Will I have to work in a new location? With different coworkers?

>We don't know. We have not made every decision to this date. We will give advance notice of any change of that nature.

I really like my job, and I am angry that I am being forced to change.

>It's okay to be angry. Everyone feels different about changes. We will give you support, training, and time to help you adjust. We also encourage you to talk to your human resources representative.

Support your team through the transition process by reducing the stress that occurs when people feel isolated and overwhelmed. Be sure to include yourself—leaders and managers must also adjust to the change. Here are some guidelines for handling the typical stressors listed at the beginning of the Lesson.

Changes can *surprise* us.

>Avoid surprises by being a proactive communicator. Tell the team what is happening, what is coming, and what to expect. Provide regular updates that are formal and informal, written and verbal. Make regular opportunities to explain what is happening and why. "Tell and retell," Roger D'Aprix explains in *Communicating for Change*, p. 24.

Changes can make us *unhappy*, even *angry*.

>Encourage the team to acknowledge their feelings about the change. Provide opportunities for team members to share their concerns and frustrations. Help team members recognize that everyone is going through this transition together. Encourage team members to help each other.

Changes can leave us *confused*.

>Help team members understand and value their place in the change transition. Share the vision that is driving the change and make it clear where their work fits in this vision. Be sure they understand the business reason for the change and

what benefit the change brings to the organization. Even if the change transition is being carried out by a selected team, communicate to the entire organization what is happening and how it will affect and benefit everyone.

Changes can leave us *at a loss* about how to get our work finished.

Provide training and support. Identify staff members who are in the front of the change—those who learn quickly and are most positive and responsive to the change. Train them first and enlist their help in training and supporting others. Your change leaders are not necessarily the current supervisors.

Change that alters your core systems can disrupt your operations significantly. While staff are learning the new methods, working out new processes, etc., do not expect them to also keep up with day-to-day routine work. Allow the staff who are learning the new way to reduce their workload to overseeing decisions that need to be made in the current system. Turn over other routine work either to those who are not as involved in the first wave of learning or to temporary help.

Sometimes leaders are reluctant to add the expense of temporary help to their project budget to assist during change transitions. The benefits in reduced overtime, increased morale (providing tangible support), faster learning (allowing staff to leave the old methods and focus on the new), and more quickly building a group of trainers who can help others, often justify the cost.

Changes can require some *extra work*.

Be up front about the extra work that will be needed to make the transition. Try to keep the overload at a minimum by good planning. Celebrate victories along the way!

Positive responses to negative reactions

Change leaders are most effective when they are able to be patient with the emotions their employees are feeling about the anticipated change. Leaders want to act quickly, especially when market forces are compelling the change. As a result, they may expect their staff to act quickly, assuming that they also understand the market forces, and are frustrated when there is resistance to the change. Leaders who recognize and help their staff deal with the underlying conflict behind the resistance are more likely to realize long-term gains.

To deal with conflict, we resort to four mechanisms based on fight-or-flight survival methods—avoid, accommodate, compete, compromise. A negative reaction may be to deny the change will happen and avoid taking any steps to prepare for it. Or, we may go along with the preparations but resent that the change is happening. We may openly oppose the change or try to bargain to keep things the same. These reactions stem from emotions and the desire to keep things the way they are. They do not resolve the conflict.

The following chart shows samples of these negative reactions and how they might be managed with positive conflict-resolving responses.

Reactions to change	Symptoms of reacting	Conflict-resolving responses
Avoid (no action is taken)	Deny it will happen.	Make a plan.
	Procrastinate.	Make commitments and set deadlines: sign up for training.
	Want to leave the job.	Share the vision of the benefits of the change and the steps everyone will take.
	Hold on to rules or complexity (perfectionism).	Be a problem solver; use problem-solving skills.
Accommodate (one side gives in)	Say okay to the change, but resent it.	Be involved in the decisions as well as the training.
Compete (one side must always win, the other lose)	Do your own thing.	Understand the organization's vision and key elements for the change and understand team dynamics.
	Be angry that others are not willing to change as quickly as you are.	Understand the productivity implications of change (the V formation) on most workers. Ask to be assigned as a pilot who helps others along.
Compromise (both sides give up something of value)	Try to keep some of the old with the new instead of totally embracing the new.	Stick with the shared vision. Be willing to drop the old for the new.

Does your organization foster a culture of change?

You can promote an organizational culture that welcomes the idea of change. Develop a pattern of setting and meeting goals and honestly assessing results, acknowledging mistakes, correcting course, and celebrating success.

Look around at how your organization does things now. What do you see?

Does the leader clearly and frequently articulate her vision for the organization?

Are staff involved in setting and meeting strategic goals for the organization?

Do team members trust they can readily speak up to their superiors or in staff meetings without fear of reprisal?

Are staff allowed to fail when new ideas are tried without fear of losing their jobs or advancement in their careers?

Do team members take time to evaluate their project results, meetings, etc., and trust that improvements will happen?

Do staff members have opportunities to work with other staff outside their own departments in collaborative initiatives?

Do supervisors seek feedback from a wide range of coworkers, including the staff member, when performance reviews are prepared?

Are staff members encouraged to set goals and are they recognized when the goals are achieved?

When staff members speak, do they trust that others will listen without interrupting and will respond respectfully?

Is staff training encouraged and supported with time and money?

The organizational culture of change is one of *trust*. If you would like your workplace culture to welcome change instead of resist it, begin by trusting your staff to help you turn things around. Enlist their suggestions for improvement and for how to implement the suggestions. Learn collaborative principles and apply them consistently and persistently. Even small steps forward will begin to foster an atmosphere that responds positively rather than negatively to change.

In a nutshell

Communication: Sharing information before, during, and after a change transition invites staff to be involved and committed to the change. Explain the business purpose for the change. Use formal and informal communication channels and invite feedback. Encourage team members to share their concerns and frustrations.

Collaboration: A collaborative culture counteracts the fear of change. Sharing the vision for the change and helping team members see their value in the new scheme of things builds trust and alleviates fear of the change, a stressor that can lead to feelings of isolation and being overwhelmed. Giving team members a sense of control will encourage them to invite rather than resist the change transition.

Project Management: A common first response to change is the desire to put things back the way they were. This pull is particularly strong when productivity drops right after the change is implemented. Anticipate this drop in productivity and plan to support and train your team. This period can extend for six months or more.

EXERCISE

Describe a time when you went through a significant change, such as a job change or a move, and how it made you feel.

Try this group exercise

Change Game: It works best to have at least four participants. They stand facing each other in pairs (as in the Virginia reel). Ask one row to look at their partners carefully. Have the row who did the "looking" turn around so they cannot see their partners. Then ask the partners to change something about the way they look. For example, one may move a bracelet to her other wrist. Another may take off his tie. Ask the "lookers" to turn back, study their partner, and say whether or not they recognize what was changed.

After they identify what has changed, reverse roles and repeat the process so that each partner in a pair has a chance to both change and identify what was changed.

Throughout this process, also notice what the person who made the change does as soon as the change is identified. In virtually every case, the person will put things back the way they were before the game started. For example, within five seconds she will return the bracelet to the original wrist, and he will put his tie back on. Bring this to the attention of the group, noting that our normal reaction is to put things back the way they were. This is how we choose it to be. This is our comfort level.

Discuss what implications this may have for an organization or team facing a change transition.

RECOMMENDED READING

D'Aprix, Roger. *Communicating for Change: Connecting the Workplace with the Marketplace*, San Francisco, Calif.: Jossey-Bass, 1996.

D'Aprix, Roger. *The Credible Company, Communicating with Today's Skeptical Workforce.* San Francisco, Calif.: Jossey-Bass, 2009.

Kotter, John P. *A Sense of Urgency.* Boston, Massachusetts: Harvard Business School Press, 2008.

Kotter, John P. *Leading Change.* Boston, Massachusetts: Harvard Business School Press, 1996.

Kotter, John P., and Rathgeber, Holger. *Our Iceberg Is Melting.* New York: St. Martin's Press, 1996.

Smith, Douglas K. *Taking Charge of Change: 10 Principles for Managing People and Performance,* Reading, Mass., Perseus Books, 1996.

Thomas, K. W., and Kilmann, R. H. *Thomas-Kilmann Conflict Mode Instrument.* Palo Alto, Calif.: XICOM, 1974.

2

Communicate Effectively

"This next meeting is important," says the Project Manager. "I have planned it so that everyone will know exactly what to do. Here are my flipcharts; they're easy to follow—step-by-step."

"You'll probably reach half the people in your meeting with a step-by-step approach," says the Facilitator. "The other half want to figure out what to do for themselves. Show them the big picture. They want to know how it works—the 'why.'"

Learning and working styles

As projects move along, especially projects that bring change, it's easy to get frustrated with the communication differences of team members and wonder why everyone can't just think the same way you do. Of course, if everyone thought the same way, you wouldn't end up with a very good product. You can create fantastic things if you take advantage of the various perspectives on your team, and one way to do that is to get to know their working styles.

How important is it to know your working style and that of others on your project? Very important. A person's working style influences how he listens and what he will hear. Team members will commit to the project and take action based on their perceptions—what they understand their relation is to the project goals or what they think they will need to do. When you introduce your team members to their own working style and to the styles of others, you help them to understand their differing perspectives and to open channels of communication.

A person's working style is most apparent when he is approaching a new assignment or project. People tend to listen for clues that tell them either "How does this work?" or "What do I need to do?"

> **The *navigator*—"how does this work" style**
>
>> This working and learning approach is exploratory and navigational. The person is listening to find out "how this works." She prefers an overview. She is curious about the possibilities, wants to know the context, and needs to know why it is important. She propels your organization forward.
>
> **The *procedural*—"what do I need to do" style**
>
>> This person's working and learning approach is procedural and systematic. She seeks process, order, directions, and rules. She is efficient and highly productive. She gets your work done.

The goal: Take advantage of both working styles

Individuals and their projects benefit when team members go beyond their comfortable working style and begin to feel more at ease with the style traits of others. *Procedural learners* benefit if they become more exploratory. The graphic interfaces that make word processing, spreadsheet, and database applications more uniform encourage exploration—as do online help functions. *Navigational learners* benefit by breaking down assignments to their component parts and becoming better estimators of their time. To help your team members to feel more at ease outside their comfort zone and to take advantage of both styles, first help them to get to know their own style, and then the styles of others. Start with *yourself.*

Know your own working style

Be aware of the approach you take when giving instructions or explaining something that is new. Do you make a checklist and give step-by-step directions? Or do you give an overview and expect that the listener will figure out what to do for himself?

For example: Imagine that you have arrived at work and a new computer is sitting on your desk. You have never used one before. There is a note from your Information Technology (IT) department indicating someone will be stopping by to introduce you to your new computer. The note has been clipped to the user manual. What is your first inclination?

If you answered that you would immediately look for the on/off switch and figure out how the computer works, ignoring both the note and the user manual, you have a *navigational* working style.

If you answered that you would wait for the IT person to come or would look in the user manual for what to do first—following the instructions—you have a *procedural* working style.

Getting to know *navigators*

In general, *navigators*

▸ listen for the answer to "How does this work?"

▸ take a hands-on approach to learning and are comfortable working independently

▸ are comfortable with change and uncertainty and are creative problem solvers

- ▸ are willing to take risks
- ▸ look for relationships
- ▸ tend to propel the project forward through innovation

Navigators also

- ▸ do not tend to follow or give directions and are uncomfortable asking for help
- ▸ tend to be guided by their own priorities and may miss deadlines
- ▸ blame the system if something doesn't work ("I'll find a better way to do this.")

Communication tips for working with *navigators*

When a *navigator* is the listener

- ▸ give an overview with a clear picture of the end result. Explain why something is happening and give context, the background information essential to understanding the situation or work assignment.
- ▸ communicate priorities. Give clear work requirements and outcome expectations, especially for cost and time allotments.
- ▸ encourage time management skills by giving shorter deadlines and clear expectations. Hold regular status meetings to check on progress.
- ▸ be creative in meetings.
- ▸ engage the *navigator* in problem solving.

Avoid

- ▸ giving new information as step-by-step instructions of what to do and how to do it.
- ▸ vague priorities or deadlines, such as "please do this as soon as you can get to it" and open-ended statements to check with you if help is needed.

- Micromanaging, which is the need to have an assignment look as if you had done it yourself, including the way it was done.
- routine and repetition.

Getting to know *procedurals*

In general, *procedural* workers

- listen to find out "What do you want me to do?"
- learn best by being shown; follow and give directions; and are comfortable asking for help
- are very organized and detail oriented, including creating efficient processes and thorough documentation
- meet deadlines; are highly productive; and get the work done

Procedural workers also

- tend to jump to the task and are slower to build relationships
- are uncomfortable with change or taking risks
- approach problem solving by enforcing or making rules
- blame themselves if a procedure or direction does not work ("I must have done something wrong or missed a step.")

Communication tips for working with *procedurals*

When a *procedural worker* is the listener

- provide opportunities for relationship building.
- give step-by-step instructions and demonstrations; keep an open-door policy and provide help.
- explain where a task or activity fits into the process.
- provide structure in meetings, including keeping minutes, planning documents, and up-to-date status reports.
- encourage the development of problem-solving skills by asking questions that will lead them to discover their own answers.

Avoid

- ▸ ambiguous directions, such as "This project is strategic, so make sure it's up there on your priority list."

- ▸ wasting time.

- ▸ unnecessary rework. Support the efficiency that results from following standard procedures.

Is one style better than the other?

One style is not better than the other. Organizations and teams need both to be successful. Collaborative projects benefit when both working styles are represented and members easily communicate with each other to bring out different perspectives. Here are some tips to facilitate communication.

Provide overviews, as well as step-by-step procedures in documentation.

Allow time in meetings for both relationship building and getting to the task. Spend more time on relationship building when the team is new and members are getting to know each other's working style.

Be alert to the styles of your team members. Encourage them to recognize their working and learning styles and to respect the styles of others on the team.

Present the goal of the project or assignment clearly. Show what is to be achieved (the vision) and how it will be achieved in broad terms. Ask team members to share what they think they will need to do to achieve the goal or how they think it relates to the larger purpose of the organization.

Define expectations clearly. Ask team members to rephrase their understanding of the task, including the due date and how long they estimate the work will take.

Establish clear priorities that are understood by the team.

Be alert to issues between members with the same working style. *Procedural* workers may struggle over who has the best procedure or what the rules should be. *Navigators* may struggle over what the priority should be.

The Time-Saver resource, "Be a STAR!," at the end of this Lesson, has tips on bringing out the best of both styles.

In a nutshell ▶ ▶ ▶

Communication: Listening is the most important communication function. Make certain your communication reaches your listeners. Tune in to their learning styles and provide what they need. Are they listening for "How does this work?" or for "What do I need to do?" Help your team to take advantage of both styles and hear both perspectives.

Collaboration: Providing time to build relationships and helping team members recognize their own and others' working/learning styles will foster understanding and, ultimately, trust. Trust is needed to commit to a shared goal and to work together to achieve it.

Project Management: Recognize the working styles of team members when planning meetings and giving assignments. Give *navigators* the big picture, shorter deadlines, and clear expectations. Provide *procedural workers* with directions and an open-door policy if help is needed.

EXERCISE

The expressions "New" and "How-To" are two of the most important messages used in advertising. They traditionally get very high response rates from potential customers. Advertising experts recommend these expressions be used in headlines and titles to attract attention. Analyze them in terms of working and learning styles. Why do you think they are so effective?

Exercise answer

The expression "New" would capture the attention of the person who has the *navigator working style.* This person is looking for what is novel or unfamiliar and would be curious to find out what it was. "How-to" would capture the attention of the person who has the *procedural working style.* This person seeks the directions, structure, and guidance that how-to would signal.

TIME-SAVER

Handout: Be a STAR! Guides for Procedural and Navigational Working Styles

---

Be a STAR!

For *procedural* workers

Stop	Don't immediately ask someone else. You may be able to find the answer.
Think	Take time to think about what the problem is. Can you clearly describe it? Have you encountered a similar problem before?
Assess	Assess the urgency of the problem. Do you need an answer right away?
Resources	Recognize the resources available to help solve the problem. Is there any documentation? How was a similar problem solved previously? Can you look on the Internet to find the answer? Is there an example from last year to look at?

For *navigational* workers

Set your watch	Be clear about deadlines and priorities.
Tell	Tell others how you will proceed. What basic steps will you follow? Don't assume others know what you know.
Ask	Ask for help from others. And report your progress before you are in danger of missing a deadline.
Relate	Help others relate to the big picture and see it as you do.

© 2010 Change Leadership Network, University of Michigan, Institute of Continuing Legal Education

Aim for Collaboration Instead of Cooperation

"Isn't collaboration just another word for cooperation?" asks the Project Manager. "Don't you have to cooperate to succeed in collaboration?"

"Cooperating isn't the same as collaborating," responds the Facilitator. "To collaborate is to commit to achieving the same goal. This is the basis for resolving conflict."

The distinction between collaboration and cooperation

In *collaboration,* members work together to achieve a common goal. Both sides identify and agree on this goal and work from a shared vision of what the result (or outcome) will be. *Cooperation* does not require a shared vision. Two parties can cooperate by sharing resources, data, facilities, etc., but keep their own distinct goals.

Here are the key characteristics of a *collaborative* project. The parties

- create a shared vision and goals
- define a shared vocabulary
- may share resources
- use the collaborative method of communication
- have shared values
- share information with trust
- work at the level of the whole project, rather than on a piece of it
- communicate and resolve conflict to reach a win-win outcome

Here are key characteristics of a *cooperative* project. The parties

- are contacts
- maintain separate goals and separate visions
- exchange resources and information
- fulfill their own missions, values, and visions
- may work on only a piece of the whole
- often have unique vocabularies and assumptions that are not questioned or clarified
- tend to resolve conflict by compromise or accommodation

Teams often assume they are collaborating when they are only cooperating. Cooperation may be an effective short-term solution to get parties over a hurdle or to complete a one-time arrangement. Collaboration is more effective in achieving long-term results and establishing long-term relationships because it requires that the parties agree upon and accomplish shared goals.

Conflict resolution

When conflicts arise that threaten the project, the parties will often compromise, accommodate, compete, or avoid the conflict entirely to keep the project moving forward. (See the Strategies and Outcomes of Conflict Styles table, pg. 30.) Ultimately, these are win-lose or lose-

lose conflict resolution styles that build resentment over time as parties begin to feel their voices are not being heard and their concerns are not being met. When parties are cooperating, these conflict styles usually come into play and create an obstacle to actually resolving the conflict. They leave a winner or a loser and both parties will eventually revisit the conflict.

In *collaboration,* the parties use a win-win style of conflict resolution. They work together to achieve solutions that allow both sides to fully succeed.

Conflict can arise at any time in the project. It is often evident at the beginning when the proposed project outcomes signal the need for change in current processes or products. Stakeholders—those affected by the outcome of the project—may feel an ownership stake in a current process they use and not be able to let go of it. Or, they may fail to see the importance of this piece of the project to the success of the overall endeavor and be unwilling to support it.

A conflict conversation illustrated

Imagine an organization about to undertake a major change in their work processes to meet their strategic goal of introducing Web technology into all of those processes. They will also significantly redesign their Web site. Their desired end result is to have "Web First" be the core of their operations.

Here is a conversation between a team leader, who has explained the redesign with its new processes, and a team member who does not support it. The team leader has a collaborative win-win style. The team member has a competing style. The goal is to get to a win-win outcome for both the leader and the team member:

Team leader: "We will know when we have reached our goal of changing our processes and products to Web First when all of our content is developed using Web technology and we can deliver it using any channel the customer wants: print, MP3 download, Webcast, read online, mix and match features, etc. The product content is developed in shorter pieces and the customer chooses which pieces he wants and how he wants to see it." *The team leader is describing the desired goal.*

Team member: "We are not ready to take that step. It will throw out all of our efficient processes that we have worked years to perfect. We are so efficient at going to print first that it is still faster to create content for print and then convert it to the Web. We will not meet our production deadlines if we have to switch. We will miss our budget targets." *The team member is competing to keep her production methods in place to meet her deadlines and budget targets. She may not envision herself working successfully in the final system. Her remarks may seem unsupportive of the project outcome.*

Team leader: "Help me understand how you see yourself (or your department) working when the redesign is finished." *The leader is encouraging the team member to express her goal for the project outcome—to describe a picture of the outcome with herself in it.*

Team member: "I see me writing and editing our content to our excellent print standards and then displaying it on the Web site electronically. We quickly put in the tags and—voila!" *The team member is now describing her goal. She is no longer competing to be heard.*

Team leader: "Help me understand why you feel it is important to develop the content first for print." *Team leader is placing importance on the team member's goal: listening for the path to a win-win outcome.*

Team member: "It's very efficient for the production crew. It is much more difficult to go from Web to print. We must do a lot of extra work to get an online product to look good in print. It is a snap to post our print files to the Web." *Team member is engaged in explanation and team leader is listening.*

Team leader: "I see your important goal is to make the print product look good and the process to make it be efficient. Let me show you the latest technology that makes that very easy. The content is actually produced online and the order to print in the format you need is a one-step process. I have samples of results. Look at them and see if they pass your quality standards." *Team leader is offering the win-win: use the technology, change the process to Web First that meets the project goal, and assure the quality and efficiency that meets the stakeholder goal. She is giving the team member a degree of control by asking if the product will pass her quality standards.*

Here are some phrases to use to help bring a conversation to a win-win outcome:

- ▶ Help me understand.
- ▶ How do you see it working?
- ▶ What is important to you?
- ▶ Here is the goal I am trying to achieve. What is the goal you are trying to achieve?
- ▶ Let me repeat what you said so I am sure I heard it correctly.
- ▶ Where does your goal fit within the overall vision?

Strategies and outcomes of conflict styles[*]

Strategy	Outcome
Avoid: No opportunity to resolve the conflict (I am unwilling or unable to resolve the conflict).	You lose/they lose.
Accommodate: One gives in to the other at the expense of her own needs. Useful goodwill gesture. Leads to resentment if we accommodate all the time.	You lose/they win. or You win/they lose.
Compete: The survival of the fittest creates one winner, many losers. Winning the competition takes precedence over finding a fair solution to the conflict.	You win/they lose. or You lose/they win.
Compromise: Both parties give up something of importance. Ultimately they will address the same issues later. Temporary gesture, but no one is happy.	You lose/they lose.
Collaborate: Both sides express their needs and get their needs met. Sounds simple, but this is most difficult because it requires both parties to articulate, prioritize, and satisfy their own needs as well as the other's.	You win/they win.

[*]Adapted from Stephen Dent, *Partnering Intelligence: Creating Value for Your Business by Building Strong Alliances,* pp. 180–182.

In a nutshell

Communication: The collaborative communication style is win-win. Both sides openly express their goals, concerns, and feelings, and work together to define a common vision. This results in a shared understanding and vocabulary. In collaboration, conflict is resolved using the win-win style of communication.

Collaboration: The shared vision agreed upon by both sides is geared toward meeting each party's goals. This is different from cooperation in which both sides may keep their individual goals and try to resolve conflict through compromising, competing, or being accommodating.

Project Management: Collaborative projects begin with a common vision or goal. Until this goal is defined, the project cannot proceed. It is the project manager's responsibility to lead team members and stakeholders in collaborative discussions and steer unproductive conflict resolution attempts toward collaboration.

EXERCISES

1. Four of the strongest instinctive conflict resolution styles are based on "fight-or-flight" defense mechanisms. In the following table mark which they might be. Which one is not based on fight-or-flight?

Conflict resolution style	Fight	Flight	Neither
Avoid			
Compete			
Compromise			
Collaborate			
Accommodate			

2. Describe three recent conflicts you tried to resolve. What resolution style did you use? What were your results? What is your primary conflict resolution style, the one you resort to first?

Try this group exercise

3. Role-play situations of conflict using these different conflict resolution styles: avoid, compete, compromise, and accommodate. Then role-play using win-win or the collaborative style. Which style is more difficult to use? Which style resolved the conflict?

Exercise answer (#1)

Conflict resolution style	Fight	Flight	Neither
Avoid		X	
Compete	X		
Compromise		X	
Collaborate			X (Collaboration is learned.)
Accommodate		X	

RECOMMENDED READING

Denise, Leo. "Collaboration vs. C-Three (Cooperation, Coordination, and Communication)." *Innovating Reprint*, Vol 7, No 3, Spring 1999.

Dent, Stephen M. *Partnering Intelligence: Creating Value for Your Business by Building Strong Alliances.* Palo Alto, Calif.: Davies-Black Publishing, 1999.

Partnership Continuum, Inc. (Stephen Dent, founder). Partnering Intelligence. http://www.partneringintelligence.com/.

Thomas, K. W., and Kilmann, R. H. *Thomas-Kilmann Conflict Mode Instrument.* Palo Alto, Calif.: XICOM, 1974.

4

Assess and Build Collaboration Skills

"The sponsor says it's full steam ahead on the Web redesign," the Project Manager announces. "Top priority. Everyone's on board. I remember the last major design project. Design will be a bottleneck— they're always backlogged. Customer Service will want to keep as much as possible the same so customers won't be inconvenienced or confused. If I show the developer how much revenue we get from online sales, he might inflate his estimate for the programming. Wish me luck."

"You don't need luck," replies the Facilitator. "Maybe you were trying to get everyone to cooperate on the last project and they still pursued their own interests. Learn the skills to manage this project by trusting collaboration."

Are you ready to collaborate?

Collaboration requires defining a common set of goals. It requires hard work in resolving conflicting goals and priorities. But the result is well worth it because both parties' needs are met.

You may determine that you can successfully manage your project without involving others. If, however, you need collaborators to help you reach your goal, then developing collaboration skills will give you a solid foundation to be successful. Take the opportunity at the beginning of your project to assess your readiness to collaborate. To be effective, commit to developing an awareness of effective collaboration skills. If you are not ready to collaborate, commit to learn and develop the needed attributes.

Stephen Dent, in his book *Partnering Intelligence*, notes that there is a strong relationship between the attributes of partnership readiness and success in collaborative initiatives. The partnering attributes identified by Dent include the following:

- ▸ future orientation in decision making
- ▸ comfort with change
- ▸ win-win orientation to resolve conflict
- ▸ comfort with interdependence
- ▸ ability to trust
- ▸ ability to self-disclose and welcome feedback

The following table shows these attributes and the basic elements in developing them.

Attribute	Collaboration skills
Future orientation in decision making	Ask yourself: Do I look to the future with a clear vision? Or do I rely on past history for decision making and have a strong need for control? Develop a planning style and then hold people accountable for doing what they say they will do. Challenge assumptions.
Comfort with change	Ask yourself: Do I welcome change? Or do I maintain the status quo and resist change? Let go of the way things have always been done. Listen to new ideas and try new things.
Win-win orientation	Ask yourself: Do I creatively resolve conflicts and solve problems? Or do I need to win? Move off the win-lose style of conflict resolution based on avoidance, accommodation, competition, and compromise and seek to reach a win-win through collaboration. See Lesson 3 for more information on resolving conflicts.
Comfort with interdependence	Ask yourself: Do I value interdependence? Or do I like to "go it alone"? Recognize that cross-department and cross-organization projects can be complex and require expertise in many different areas. Develop trusting relationships with experts in these areas and make them accountable for decisions and results.
Ability to trust	Ask yourself: Do I create trust through actions and words? Or do I have a low trust of others? Be open, honest, and direct. Walk the talk yourself. Focus on your feelings. Talk it out with others; stop the action and communicate if it does not "feel" right. Hold others accountable.
Ability to self-disclose and welcome feedback	Ask yourself: Do I self-disclose information and give feedback? Or do I keep information to myself? Am I willing to share financial or other data about my company? Share information about yourself, including your feelings, and provide feedback to others. Learn to assess what you need and then ask for it.

A readiness to collaborate is the foundation for successful collaborative projects. Dent provides a thorough readiness assessment at his Web site, http://www.partneringintelligence.com/products_assessments_pq.cfm. It is well worth taking the PQ assessment. Dent also provides detailed guidance on building those important collaborative skills.

Overcome barriers to collaboration

If you would like your organization to benefit from developing collaborative attributes but encounter barriers, take some simple steps to overcome them.

1. Start with yourself. Assess your own readiness to collaborate. Develop the skills and let your own success be an example. Start with one skill and focus on consistently applying it. Then add others. Watch for the ripple effect when those around you take notice of your new, successful approach to resolving conflicts and responding to change. They'll want to know more.

2. Challenge leaders to take the partnering assessment survey. It was the first step we took and the results became a wake up call to our organization. We were not ready to collaborate. Recognizing this helped us to commit to getting the skills.

3. Write a vision for what you would like to see happen. What does it look like when you, or your organization, are consistently using any one of these collaborative traits. Then write the steps to get there.

4. Consider if there are unexpressed concerns held by stakeholders in your organization. See Lesson 30 for tips on spotting unexpressed concerns and dealing with them. Often, it is what is not being said that you need to listen to.

5. Take a long-term view. Be patient with yourself and with others. There may be change initiatives in which collaboration is not the best method to use. Learn to recognize them and use the best approach.

In a nutshell ▸ ▸ ▸

Communication: Collaborative communication builds the foundations of trust. The ability to communicate your needs, self-disclose, and receive feedback from others is key to developing collaboration skills.

Collaboration: Collaborative projects begin with assessing the readiness of each partner to collaborate. If partners collaborate, they will resolve their conflicts by focusing on achieving their shared goal.

Project Management: Collaborative skills can be learned and developed throughout the project. A readiness to learn them and opportunities to develop them can be part of the project management plan.

EXERCISE

Consider the parties mentioned by the project manager from our opening conversation:

"The sponsor says it's full steam ahead on the Web redesign," announces the Project Manager. "Top priority. Everyone's on board. I remember the last major design project. Design will be a bottleneck—they're always backlogged. Customer Service will want to keep as much as possible the same so customers won't be inconvenienced or confused. If I show the developer how much revenue we get from online sales, he might inflate his estimate for the programming. Wish me luck."

Are these parties ready to collaborate? What collaborative traits do each need to develop?

▸ Project Manager

▸ Design

▸ Customer Service

Exercise answer

Where is the project manager's readiness to trust? Is she looking forward in her decision making or back to the bottlenecks caused by Design? The project manager needs to develop future orientation in decision making.

What about Design? Are they backlogged because they are not comfortable with outsourcing or being interdependent? Design needs to develop comfort with interdependence.

What about Customer Service? Are they open to change? Or are they hoping things can stay the same so customers won't be inconvenienced? Customer Service needs to develop comfort with change.

Is the project manager willing to disclose business information to the developer that will give him the volume and value of online sales so his development decisions will be effective? The Project Manager needs to develop the ability to self disclose.

RECOMMENDED READING

Dent, Stephen M. "Effective Partnering: Collaboration for Change." Partnership Continuum, Inc. http://www.partneringintelligence.com/documents/LeadershipExcellence%20Dec%2006%20article.pdf.

Dent, Stephen M. *Partnering Intelligence: Creating Value for Your Business by Building Strong Alliances.* Palo Alto, Calif.: Davies-Black Publishing, 1999.

Partnership Continuum, Inc. (Stephen M. Dent, founder). Partnering Intelligence. http://www.partneringintelligence.com/ We strongly recommend taking the online PQ assessment at http://www.partneringintelligence.com/products_assessments_pq.cfm.

5

Gain Control of Meetings

"I mentioned to Customer Service that I'll be sending a meeting notice soon," says the Project Manager. "She threw up her hands in despair and said, 'No, not another meeting!' How will I get my team members to come to meetings when they clearly dread them?"

"Sounds like she has lost trust in meetings," says the Facilitator. "That can happen quickly if the meeting gets out of control. To stay in control, be clear about the meeting purpose and make sure you achieve it. Your team needs to trust that the meeting will deliver what it promises."

"That was the best meeting I ever attended"

You will spend much time in meetings during any collaborative projects—make it time well spent. Turn "No, not another meeting!" into "That was the best meeting I ever attended. I hope we have more of these." (This is a real quote from a Web redesign team member.) You can improve the productivity of your meeting by following a few simple rules. The most important rule is to be crystal clear about your meeting's purpose. This, more than any other preparation you do, allows you to create a realistic agenda and make sure that time spent at the meeting is productive for everyone who participates.

Collaborative meetings bring together many team members who have their own interests and concerns. However, they must work together during the meeting to describe and achieve the project goal. A collaborative approach to meetings has far-reaching effects beyond the accomplishments in the meeting itself.

A well-run meeting results in good working relationships. It promotes respect, confidence, and trust among team members. Plus, it just feels good to walk away from a meeting knowing that you accomplished your goals—not only the short-term meeting goal, but also the long-term collaboration goal of building trust.

Meeting control points

So often we hear the phrase, "That meeting was out of control." Perhaps the meeting did not start or finish on time. Communication may have been unclear. It might not have accomplished its objectives or requirements. There may have been no agenda or the time frame may have been unrealistic for the agenda. These problems—the inability to control timelines, task requirements, or communication—are also associated with projects that are out of control. The skills that give you control of your meetings will also help you gain control of your project.

Control your meetings by clearly defining the purpose, careful planning, crafting a realistic agenda, and following your agenda.

Purpose—The key control point

The first and most important control point of a well-run meeting is a clearly stated purpose. The purpose for the meeting describes its end result and governs the amount of time allotted for the meeting and how that time is spent.

While it is important to set a regular schedule of team meetings in advance (thus confirming the availability of your team members), it is crucial that you spend time before each meeting thinking through the meeting purpose—what you want to have accomplished by the end of the meeting. A clear meeting purpose controls all other meeting elements: who to invite, decisions to be made, agenda topics, time limits, meeting preparation materials, and meeting minutes. It also governs the planning and execution of the meeting. The meeting purpose is the authority behind a well-run, productive meeting.

Here are some examples of meeting purpose and corresponding results.

An early team-building meeting

Purpose: Introduce team members and agree on rules of conduct. (Lesson 11 provides detailed guidance for this, including how to get agreement on the rules of conduct.)

Result: Initial relationships are built, and consensus is gained on the rules of conduct the team agrees to follow.

Long-term collaboration goal: Team members are given the opportunity to form relationships. The result is that they get to know one another and the rules and processes they will follow. This is the basis of trust.

To introduce the project and its goals

Purpose: Introduce the project charge (requirements) from the sponsor and invite team members to question the sponsor about the project scope and expectations.

Result: List of issues or vocabulary that needs to be clarified or were clarified at the meeting.

Long-term collaboration goal: The meeting provides the opportunity for team members to ask questions, to challenge assumptions, and to hear the questions and answers of others. The result is clarity about the project scope and requirements.

To introduce the team members and their roles

Purpose: To introduce the team members and their roles.

Result: List of role assignments.

Long-term collaboration goal: The team members understand and accept their roles on the team, why they were invited, what they will contribute, and how they will work together. The result is an understanding of the larger goal they will achieve by working together.

To solve a problem

Purpose: To use the problem-solving method to find the root cause and solution for a problem.

Result: A determination of the root cause, options for solution, and how the team will determine that the problem has been solved.

Long-term collaboration goal: The meeting uses the wisdom of the group to get at the cause of a problem. The result is moving past opinions to solving the problem.

To brainstorm

Purpose: Brainstorming.

Result: A list of ideas generated by the group that can be sifted and evaluated at a later time. Quantity of ideas rather than quality is the goal.

Long-term collaboration goal: The meeting provides a positive atmosphere that welcomes new ideas without judgment or criticism. The result is participation from the entire group to generate a large quantity of new and useful ideas.

To gain consensus on an issue

Purpose: To gain consensus on an issue.

Result: The group reaches agreement on a decision that each member says they can support even if they don't agree with it personally or it was not their first choice.

Long-term collaboration goal: The meeting provides the requirement for each person to speak to the group and to support and be supported by the group. As a result, each team member's voice is represented in decisions and the decision is supported inside and outside the meeting. Lesson 6 describes the consensus process.

To train and educate

Purpose: To introduce a new concept or to train.

Result: The team members receive materials and instruction in the new concept or skill. New forms, vocabulary, or processes are introduced.

Long-term collaboration goal: The team participates in learning something new, often to be able to share work, back someone up, or be able to do something new. The result is shared vocabulary, processes, and expectations leading to effective communication, and clarity.

To analyze options and make decisions

Purpose: Analyze options and make a decision.

Result: The decision and agreement on the decision or the development of a new or different goal.

Long-term collaboration goal: Background work has been done. The team has had time to study options in advance. The meeting is spent sharing pros and cons of the options. The decision arises out of the wisdom of the group. The collaboration process may also result in the group reaching its goal by defining and agreeing to a different option altogether. Rather than resort to compromise, the collaborative result of finding the win-win solution is reached.

Purpose is the key control element. When you are crystal clear about the purpose you want to achieve, you will not be pulled off during the meeting to accomplish a different (or someone else's!) purpose. For example, if you are clear your meeting purpose is to brainstorm, you will not waste time problem solving or analyzing options you are unprepared to discuss.

Be as clear about when you *don't* need to meet: Sharing information that does not require discussion or decision making can be done as effectively using e-mail or an intranet.

Plan each step

Planning the meeting helps you identify and control potential barriers to achieving your meeting purpose. Once you are clear on the purpose, consider the steps you need to take before or at the meeting to accomplish that purpose. Who needs to attend? What information will they need beforehand to be active participants in the meeting? What is the best place and time to meet?

Give plenty of notice to any member who needs to present information. Determine what materials need to be prepared, what copies need to be distributed, and don't forget to reserve your meeting room and time.

Assign someone to take notes and someone to be a gatekeeper (a person who keeps the meeting on time and on track, signaling the leader if the agenda is not being followed). If you are brainstorming, assign a scribe (someone to record items on a flipchart). (See Lesson 17 for the discussion of meeting roles.) Inform the gatekeeper, note taker, and scribe of their roles before they receive the agenda.

Craft a realistic agenda

Carefully construct your agenda to achieve your purpose. The agenda is the plan for the meeting. More important, it is the key communication signal to the participants that the meeting is purposeful and will be productive. The agenda lists the purpose, attendees, decisions that need to be made, steps toward achieving the purpose, and the timeline for those steps. To be successful, the agenda must be realistic.

To craft a realistic agenda

> State the purpose of the meeting. Tell clearly what the meeting will accomplish.
>
> Indicate any consensus items or decisions that will be asked for at the meeting.
>
> List the meeting participants. Be sure that you include those who have the authority to make decisions and those whose expertise will be needed to solve problems.
>
> List your agenda topics and include a realistic time limit for each item. Put the most important items first. Place informational items at the end.

Then, do a reality check on the agenda.

> Does the agenda lead to the outcome you need (fulfill the meeting purpose)?
>
> Do all the topics require time spent during a meeting? Can some information be shared by e-mail?
>
> Is the time allowed for each topic realistic? Consider the people attending the meeting, their perspectives, and potential discussion items.
>
> Will the participants be prepared to contribute to the meeting?

If you need input on the agenda, circulate a draft for comment ahead of time.

E-mail or distribute the agenda and any other meeting materials to the members at least 24 hours before the meeting.

Note: A sample agenda is included in Time-Savers at the end of this lesson. The agenda template also has a boxed inset called "Meeting Guidelines" that provides helpful tips to all meeting participants.

Follow your agenda from start to finish

Start and end your meeting on time. This is the most valuable and appreciated commitment you make to your team. Be in the room, with all materials ready, and welcome the participants as they arrive. Call the meeting to order at the time stated on the agenda, even if all the participants have not arrived. Do not stop the meeting to fill in the latecomers about what was discussed before they arrived. You can talk to them after the meeting to give them any information they missed and stress the importance of the meeting start time. Note: This is reinforced only if you end your meetings on time.

Introduce the meeting by quickly reviewing the purpose and agenda so people know what to expect.

Stick to your agenda's purpose, topics, and time limits. Especially avoid the temptation to engage in problem solving when this distracts from your meeting's purpose. If a topic or issue is brought up that seems important but does not support the agenda item, make a note of it and "park" it for discussion at a later time or at its own meeting. You can easily create a "parking lot" by writing the off-topic item on a flipchart. This important technique will allow you to keep within the time allotted for the discussion.

Before you end the meeting, make a plan to revisit parked items. Plan to add them to future agendas or to turn them into action items.

Stop the meeting at your stated end time. When your time limit has run out, the meeting is over. Even if you are in the middle of an agenda item, *stop the meeting*. The participants should leave. After the meeting, work with your meeting facilitator about how to gain control over the agenda or the meeting activity—whichever has caused the meeting to exceed its time limit. This control can only be gained if you commit in advance to stop the meeting when the time limit has been reached.

If you finish the agenda early, end the meeting. Participants are prepared to discuss the items on the agenda and may not be ready to discuss extra items. Reward your team for holding an efficient meeting by giving them back their extra few minutes.

Evaluate the meeting

To improve future meetings, evaluate your current one. Get feedback from all participants at the end of the meeting, and ask for suggestions for how to improve. At the end of the meeting, go around the table and ask each person what went well. When this round is finished, go around a second time and ask what could be improved for the next meeting. It is important that each person be allowed to speak without comment from others. The leaders and members should take note of the positive responses and incorporate those into their meeting planning. Look also into the areas recommended for improvement. Initial meeting comments usually include, on the positive side, "appreciated getting an agenda in advance" or "liked that everyone participated in the discussion." Recommendations for improvement usually include "need to end the meeting on time" or "we need to stay on topic." As the team gets more familiar with evaluating their meetings, basic processes are worked out, members develop trust, and their comments become very insightful.

Prepare the meeting notes and distribute them within 48 hours

Meeting notes provide an essential record of the meeting. They stand as a reference to participants—and nonparticipants who receive them—for what happened at the meeting and what is to follow.

Effective meeting notes include the participants (note who was absent), meeting purpose, decisions made (consensus items), and specific action items to complete. Indicate the date the action item is due, the person assigned to it, and brief discussion notes as needed. List any handouts. It is helpful to start your notes with the date and time of your *next* meeting and include agenda items that were agreed to by the team members or that arose from the meeting discussion itself. This becomes a handy, time-saving reference when you are ready to plan your next agenda and gives the team advance notice if some preparation is needed. Distribute notes within 48 hours of the meeting.

It is important to consistently follow the same simple format. A meeting notes template is included in Time-Savers.

In a nutshell

Communication: Being clear about the purpose and agenda items of your meeting communicates to the participants that the meeting is planned and will be productive. It also sets up how you state the call to the meeting, which handouts and materials you need to distribute, and when team members need to receive them. Participants will know what to expect and will come prepared.

Collaboration: Focus on purpose and make it clear so that during the meeting all participants work together to accomplish that purpose. Introduce the meeting by quickly reviewing the purpose and agenda so people know what to expect.

Project Management: The skills that give you control of your meetings will also help you gain control of your project. The ability to communicate, control timelines, and manage task requirements are associated with projects that succeed. Start and end meetings on time. Keep the purpose in front of the group and park any topics that detract from it. Stick to the agenda items and time limits.

EXERCISE

Create an agenda for your next meeting. Refer to the agenda template in the Time-Savers section.

TIME-SAVERS

Template: Meeting Agenda

Agenda	
Project Name:	**Meeting Date:**
Project Manager:	**Meeting Time:**
Meeting Leader:	**Meeting Location:**
Recorder:	**Timekeeper:**

Meeting participants

Meeting purposes

•

Decisions needing consensus

•

Agenda (with time limits)

1.

Attachments

•

Meeting Guidelines

- *Start and end on time.*
- *Encourage participation.* "Talkers" should try listening more and "listeners" should speak up.
- *Welcome bad news* as an opportunity to do risk management and problem solving. Do not be afraid to identify what is going wrong.
- *Encourage brainstorming.*
- *Use good meeting manners.* Do not make personal put-downs. Do not interrupt the speaker.
- *Use good listening skills.* Try to understand the entirety of what is being said, not just what you want to hear. Ask questions if you don't understand. Do not pre-judge on the basis of past history.
- *Use good speaking skills.* When communicating an idea, use common language so the listeners understand. Give people time to communicate an answer to your questions. Try to be succinct.
- *Reward input.* Celebrate contributions.
- *Keep the meeting focused.*

ICLE thanks Marianne Clauw for permission to reprint this agenda template.

Template: Meeting Notes (Minutes)

Meeting Notes	
Project Name:	**Notes Distributed:**
Leader:	**Notes Prepared By:**
Date of Meeting:	

Meeting participants

Absent

Date of next meeting

Agenda topics

Purpose(s) of meeting

Action Items

Action required	Assigned	Due	Status

Decisions

Discussion

ICLE thanks Marianne Clauw for permission to reprint this meeting notes template.

6

Reach Decisions through Consensus

"I don't see how it's possible to get everyone to agree on project decisions," says the Project Manager. "We can't even agree on what to order for the company picnic! Requiring consensus will hold up decisions. How will I meet my deadlines?"

"Consensus doesn't mean that everyone agrees with the decision," replies the Facilitator. "It means that everyone agrees their voices were heard and they will support the decision—even if it wasn't their first choice."

Consensus is a win-win outcome

What is a team member's most challenging task? Often it is accepting a decision that she does not agree with or feels she has not participated in making. Teamwork is most productive when all members both participate in making the decision and agree to support it. Gaining consensus is the method to achieve this participation and agreement and is an important tool in the success of a collaborative initiative. Consensus occurs when every member of the group says honestly:

"My view has been accurately heard by the other members."

"I will support the decision being recommended even though it may not be my first choice."

Consensus is a win-win outcome. It differs from voting, in which the majority wins but there are also losers who may never support the decision. To achieve consensus, the issue is discussed with full participation by team members. When a decision point has been reached (for example, there is no new discussion), each team member is asked if he or she agrees with or can support the decision. Each person must be asked individually. Each person must speak. Head nodding, silence, or passing is not accepted. If every team member does not agree, the team continues to discuss the issues and possible solutions until consensus is reached, that is, until every member agrees with or can *support the decision.*

Consensus satisfies both the group goal and individual needs. If a team member does not agree, his explanation of why not can set the team on the path to consensus. The process itself may help team members reach a new solution that had not been considered before.

Consensus is a valuable tool for collaboration because it requires that no member give up something of value and that the discussion continues until each other's goals are met. The consensus process works best when

all team members participate fully;

team members explore alternatives;

team members trust and respect each other and are willing to share differing views;

the discussion is based on facts rather than opinions;

the process is not rushed; and

the rules of conduct for team meetings (see Exercise at the end of this Lesson) are enforced.

It is also important that the leader allow each member to speak without comment from either the leader or other team members. Ask whether or not the member agrees, then listen to the answer and move to the next member. If more discussion is needed or if team members have questions, open the discussion *after everyone has had the opportunity to speak.* This will build trust on your team and encourage participation.

Pay attention to team members who need encouragement to voice their opinions. Raising issues and debating a decision is an important part of most projects and leads to better results. Be sure your team members feel it is safe to speak, particularly when their opinion differs from that of management.

There are some drawbacks to the consensus process, however. Reaching consensus can be time-consuming, and it may be helpful to work with a facilitator to gain mastery of this method. Here are some of the problems that arise and some guidance for how to deal with them.

▸ The team may be caught up in what seem like endless discussions with no forward progress. This is more likely to happen when the issue is complex. Break down the issue into smaller components and gain control of the discussions.

▸ One person who does not agree may hold up the progress of the team's work, even though she provides no new information during the discussion. It may be helpful to remind the team that agreeing does not mean that the decision is everyone's first choice or that everyone likes it. Consensus means that everyone will support it. Be sure that the person feels her views have been accurately heard and given fair consideration by the team.

▸ Consensus may be rushed, resulting in a poor decision and lack of support for it later. Prepare thoroughly so that members have plenty of time to review all necessary information before the meeting. Make sure that the issue is adequately discussed and encourage full participation by team members.

▸ Members may experience *groupthink,* saying what they think others want them to say, rather than thinking independently and expressing their own thoughts. Groupthink may result in a group decision that the members do not really trust. To control for this domination through conformity, make sure the participants are diverse and encourage open discussion. Focus on facts rather than opinions and make it safe for individuals to speak freely.

In some situations, consensus is *not* the best method for decision making. The project leader should consider voting or an authority-based decision as the better choice.

▸ A large number of people may be involved in the decision, or the time constraint for making the decision is very short. In these cases, voting may be the better tool for making the decision and moving the project forward.

▸ A person of high authority does not agree. This may indicate that the item is not open for consensus. The discussion, however, may help the person in authority evaluate his decision.

▸ If discussions are largely opinion based, you may not have all the facts you need. Take the time to do fact-finding or problem solving. The issue may require a solution rather than a decision. For example, customers complained that their search results were slow and filled with irrelevant references. Some team members offered strong opinions that the search engine was not powerful enough and should be replaced. When the facts were presented, however, it became clear that replacing the search engine would have no effect on improving the search results. A problem needed to be solved: how to reorganize the data so that the search engine could properly identify it.

▸ Sometimes a team member will compromise or accommodate— agree to support the decision to move the project forward even though he gives up something he values. For example, something he really wants on the project list is dropped. He understands the time constraint required for the decision and the organization's priorities and agrees to the deletion, but the item is still important to him. This fulfills the intent of consensus, but not of collaboration. This is cooperation, and it may be in the best interest of the project at the time. If the members continue to communicate their goals, his issue will probably resurface and there may be another opportunity to satisfy his goal, or he may see that it did not satisfy the vision for the project after all.

Achieving consensus is a skill that is worth mastering. It supports teamwork. Introduce it to the team as early as possible and use it throughout your project. It will improve communication, problem solving, and collaborative skills.

In a nutshell ▶ ▶ ▶

Communication: Reaching consensus builds communication skills among team members. It requires silent members to participate, and it encourages "talkers" to listen. It builds trust by ensuring that each member's view is heard without a retort or question.

Collaboration: Gaining consensus is the primary tool for collaborative decision making because it results in a win-win outcome. Unlike voting, where the majority wins and the minority loses, each team member has participated in the process and agrees to support the decision.

Project Management: Leading the consensus process is a skill that team leaders should master. It builds teamwork and leads to informed decisions. Learn to use it effectively to resolve conflicting ideas. Avoid groupthink and evaluate alternatives, such as voting, that may better serve the project needs.

EXERCISE

Use the Rules of Conduct to teach the consensus method to your team.
Present these Rules of Conduct and gain consensus from the team to
adopt them.

Rules of Conduct for Meetings

Share ownership of the team's mission

Start and end the meeting on time

Listen objectively

Respect teammates and their views

Criticize only ideas, not people

Question and contribute

Share responsibility

Attend all meetings

Handout: Guidelines for Achieving Consensus

Guidelines for Achieving Consensus

Get full participation in the discussion and listen to what others say.

Trust and respect teammates and be willing to share differing views.

Examine all the options.

Focus on actual problems, not symptoms. Clarify issues by exploring differences.

Do not accept the quick fix. Insist on finding the best solution.

Do not avoid disagreement by taking a majority vote, averaging, or tossing a coin.

Do not compete with each other.

Base discussion on facts, not on opinions. Use data to help evaluate an alternative.

Allocate time for discussion and decision making and monitor it carefully. Do not rush.

Enforce the rules of conduct for team meetings.

Avoid groupthink.

TIME-SAVER

Handout: Rules of Conduct for Meetings

Rules of Conduct for Meetings

Share ownership of the team's mission

Start and end the meeting on time

Listen objectively

Respect teammates and their views

Criticize only ideas, not people

Question and contribute

Share responsibility

Attend all meetings

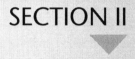

Initiating

We are limited, not by our abilities, but by our vision.

~Unknown

Lessons

7

Build and Understand the Business Case

"Does the sponsor need to write the business case for the redesign of the Web site?" asks the Project Manager. "Isn't that for the MBAs?"

"These are good questions," says the Facilitator. "Actually, good questions are the heart of a business case, regardless of who writes it. Answering them can make the difference between merely having a great idea and seeing it implemented successfully."

Building the business case

The business case is the document that provides high-level justification for making a change in the business—the reason for the project. It steps through the key elements to consider, outlining an objective framework for analysis. The writer, usually the project sponsor, will make the case for the project, including the goals, funding source, the target market, resources to do the work, the timeline, scope requirements, and the risks and opportunities. At the end, the decision to proceed (often called a "go/no-go" decision) can be clearly weighed and discussed.

The following questions provide a step-by-step guide for writing a business case:

Situation:

▸ What is the situation? Why is the project needed?

Strategies and Initiatives:

▸ Is the project related to an organizational strategy or key initiative?

Scope:

▸ What are the project goals and objectives?

▸ What will be produced in products or services?

▸ What are the technology implications?

▸ What are the customer support implications?

▸ What are the maintenance implications?

Market and Competitive Analysis:

▸ Who/what is the target market?

▸ Why would target customers be attracted to the product or service?

▸ What similar products or services are available currently within the organization, other like-minded organizations, or other service providers? Are any planned for the future?

Advisory Committee Recommendations:

▸ If the organization has an advisory committee, was the idea presented to the committee or to any individual members?

▸ If so, what advice was provided?

Risks and Opportunities:

▸ Are there significant risks or opportunities?

▸ Are there high-level mitigation or facilitation strategies? (Detailed risk/opportunity actions will be completed in project planning.)

Budget/Schedule:

> ▸ Does the nature of this project require a target date?

> ▸ Are there fixed constraints related to budget or schedule? (Detailed commitments will be completed in project planning.)

> ▸ Is there a revenue target?

Staffing/Skills:

> ▸ What key roles are necessary for this project?

> ▸ Are unique or important skill sets required?

> ▸ Assign the following key roles:

>> project manager

>> functional or technical expert, content expert

>> project sponsor (writes the business case, provides funding, champions the project; in a small organization, can also be the project acceptor)

>> project acceptor (provides approvals at milestones)

A business case may also be written by the project manager and reviewed by the project sponsor. It is essential for the sponsor and project manager to have common agreement on the goals, scope, and risks of the project. The business case is an important document that is referred to regularly. It guides decisions and continues to be a reference for the scope, prioritization, and other key elements throughout the project process. It determines if the project will be delivered in one or in several versions. See Lesson 46 for an explanation of the agile process.

Understanding the business case

The heart of a business case is the justification for bringing about a change in the organization. To understand the business case is to understand the strategic purpose of this change. What needs to change and why? What are the assumptions? To get an understanding of the business case, go through its components with the author. Then follow through with additional questions until the strategic implications of the business case are clear.

Imagine a conversation with the author of the business case for the project to redesign the Web site. The discussion clarifies the business case and, more important, clearly describes the strategic nature of the change and its implications. The project manager can use this understanding to develop a project plan with a solid foundation.

The following dialogue reveals the expectations of the project sponsor. Without this dialogue, the project manager may simply follow orders without really understanding the project goals.

Q. How does the organization's vision and strategic plan impact this project?

A. Our vision is clear. We need to think Web First. The Web site is core to all our values and operations.

Q. What do you mean by Web First?

A. Right now, our products are developed for print and then posted to our Web site. At the completion of this project, I expect to see our products developed for our Web site *first*. They need to be searchable and easy to use on the Web site. Our printed products will come from our Web site.

Q. What are the project goals and objectives?

A. Here are some specific objectives:
- To support our partnering efforts by supplying subsites for jointly sponsored services.
- To personalize customer self-service and make it available 24/7.
- To tailor advertising to customers based on their needs. Customers are drawn to the Web site for content and see ads for services related to their interests. We can move away from mass produced ads pushed out to the customer.
- To enable our Web site to support high quality content by delivering online subscriptions, individual products, and Web casts.

Q. What will have been produced when it is finished?

A. An up-to-date Web site that exceeds customer expectations. But, more important, the in-house processes and technology that will require departments to think Web First when they are developing their products and policies.

Q. What are the technology and design implications?

A. We want the latest in technology and design, of course. The technology processes and software need to lead our product developers to think Web First when they make product decisions and set up their product policies and processes.

Q. If we want to meet customers' expectations online, we have to offer the latest technologies our users want. Our technology, therefore, must be flexible and easy to change. Is this right?

A. Yes. Flexibility and maintainability are goals.

Q. What are our customers' needs? What do we need to address?

A. Customers tell us they need to save time and get what they are looking for without any delay, 24/7. They need to quickly find *all* that we offer on a particular topic. They need fast, relevant search results. They need to *stay on our site* and not be drawn off to competitor sites.

Q. What is the funding source for the project? Will this impact any decisions?

A. As in the past, we are funding Web development from a combination of past profits and the shift of expenses from print, postage, invoicing, and phone services to staff salaries and software. We also expect continued increases in online subscriptions.

Q. Who are the stakeholders—those you expect to be impacted by the decisions and outcome of the project?

A. The Web site touches decision makers in every department—product developers, legal editors, technology developers, designers, customer service agents, sales and marketing managers. Contributors and customers also are stakeholders. All will influence the project's requirements and design.

Q. What are the risks of doing or not doing a redesign?

A. Ultimately, we risk losing customers. We risk missing opportunities for faster delivery of information in the way customers want to receive it. If we continue to create our products and seminars in the traditional way, we risk losing the power of the Web to transform our products and reduce the costs of production and delivery of information.

In this dialogue, the discussion of the business case made it clear that the strategic nature of the change goes beyond redesigning the Web site to moving the organization to operate with a Web First mind-set for developing both products and processes.

Developing, communicating, and understanding the business case will clarify the strategic goals and benefits of the project. This sets the groundwork for the communication, collaboration, and project management needed to successfully implement the project.

In a nutshell

Communication: The business case provides a focus for communication. The more clearly it is stated, and the more objective its goals, the more those affected by the project will be able to determine how their own goals will, or will not, be met. The business case provides a reference point for conversations about scope, project success, and project completion.

Collaboration: Collaboration is the process of individuals working together to achieve a common, agreed upon goal that meets the needs of all. The business case for the project provides a framework to state the goals and benefits of the project so they can be discussed.

Project Management: The project manager is not an order taker. She must understand the goals of the project to create an effective plan and manage the scope of it. The business case and discussions about it are foundational to this understanding.

EXERCISE

In the preceding discussions, the overriding goal of the Web redesign is more than just updating the Web site. It is to make Web First core to the values and operations of the entire organization. This is a goal for product developers as well as programmers and designers. What would be the risk of starting the Web redesign project without this understanding?

Exercise answer

The risk is spending months of work and thousands of dollars to deliver a new Web site without also changing the way products and processes are developed. The organization mind-set that drives work flow doesn't really change. The organization risks losing out to its competitors who shift wholly to Web technology and processes and are able to produce their products more quickly and at less cost. The risks are overspending, losing market share, disappointing the stakeholders, and not moving the organization forward strategically.

TIME-SAVER

Template: Building a Business Case

<table>
<tr><td colspan="2" align="center">**Business Case**</td></tr>
<tr><td>**Project Name:**</td><td>**Created By:**</td></tr>
<tr><td>**Last Updated:**</td><td>**Approval Date:**</td></tr>
</table>

The following template describes the contents of a Business Case document. The purpose of the document is to establish the business case for the project and define the key elements. The length of the document is usually 1–2 pages, as it is a high-level view of the project. The Business Case is completed by the project sponsor, who is usually a member of the Leadership Group.

Business Case

Strategies and Initiatives: Is the project related to a strategy or key initiative?

Scope

- What are the project goals and objectives?
- What will be produced in products or services?
- What are the technology implications?
- What are the customer support implications?
- What are the maintenance implications?

Market and Competitive Analysis

- Who/what is the target market?
- Why would target customers be attracted to the product or service?
- What similar products or services are available currently within the organization, other like-minded organizations, or other service providers? Are any unavailable currently, but planned for the future?

Advisory Committee Recommendations

- Was the idea presented to the Advisory Committee or individual committee members?
- If so, what advice was provided?

Risks and Opportunities

- Are there significant risks or opportunities?
- Are there high-level mitigation or facilitation strategies? (Detailed risk/ opportunity actions will be completed in project planning.)

ICLE thanks Marianne Clauw for permission to reprint this Business Case template.

Budget/Schedule

- Does the nature of this project require a target date?
- Are there fixed constraints related to budget or schedule? (Detailed commitments will be completed in project planning.)
- Is there a revenue target?

Staffing/Skills

- What key roles are necessary for this project?
- Are there unique or important skill sets that are required?
- Assign the following key roles:
    —Project Manager

    —Functional or Technical Expert

    —Project Sponsor (writes the business case, provides funding, champions the project; in a small organization, can also be the project acceptor)

    —Project Acceptor (provides approvals at milestones)

8

Turn Stakeholder Interests into Strategic Interests

"There's a request to put money in the budget for a new search engine," says the Project Manager. "They said to charge it to the redesign project. How do I go about getting it funded?"

"Sounds like there's an assumption that we need a new search engine," replies the Facilitator. "Before you look for funding, ask some strategic questions. Is the individual request in line with our strategic direction to make our processes Web First? Will a new search engine fix our outmoded processes? Is it a search engine we need?"

What are the interests of the stakeholders?

Stakeholders are those who are impacted by the change that the decisions and outcomes of the project bring about. They are executives who sponsor the project and provide funding. They are partnering organizations who have a shared goal. They are the department heads who manage the work. They are the speakers and authors who will contribute content. They are also the customers who will use the Web site, and the staff members who will design, program, create content for, and maintain the Web site. Their interests need to be clear because they will influence the requirements, priority, and outcome of the project.

At the executive level, the project sponsor will define the interests of the organization and its customers in the business case.

The project manager, project team, experts, and partnering organizations are strategic players. They need to understand and accept the overlap and differences between the organization's interest and their own because they will be making many decisions throughout the project that will affect its outcome.

In the following scenario, the Director (the sponsor of the project) is announcing the project to other executives and end users.

> "It's time to redesign the Web site. I've done the business case and it's a go. The risk of not redesigning the site is stagnation. To keep our customers loyal, we need to stay agile and keep up with technology to gain speed, convenience, and economy. The project has high priority. We really need to get this thing fixed."

Everyone involved, including the Director, is enthusiastic.

> "Not a minute too soon," says the Web designer. "We need to focus on our brand identity. And we need to improve the Web site usability. Customers have to think too hard to figure out how things work."

> "We need the site to be updated so we can use cross-selling to meet our sales targets," Marketing reports.

> "Great," says IT. "Time to get rid of the old technology and rewrite. We can clean up our style sheets and improve security."

> "How soon can we start?" asks Customer Service. "Customers would like easier password access and online ordering."

"Do it right away," say the editors of the legal content. "It's past time to replace the search engine. It's delivering far too many irrelevant results."

"Just what we need," say the course planners. "We need to get our courses offered online so we can compete with other education providers and give our speakers publicity."

Team members are eager to get started and are building a to-do list that meets their individual department interests. Time to get everyone together and get to work! We've done redesigns before. No need to start from scratch.

When everyone agrees about the importance of the project, has experience in the area, and has ideas about what needs to happen, the project manager may be tempted to jump in and schedule the work. Before taking that first step, however, ask: Is there one project with a set of agreed-upon goals? Or is there the potential of multiple projects with individual goals that may not advance the Web site strategically?

A directive to "fix the Web site" invites a list of individual requests that will attempt to correct problems with the current site. Because the requests may not flow from an overriding goal, they will be difficult to prioritize and will soon compete for resources. They are power struggles waiting to happen. Costs will escalate because decisions are likely to get overruled, causing rework, or work will be completed that does not advance the organization.

Here's how a collaborative project manager can begin to shift the approach from individual interests to *strategic interests*.

Strategic partners focus on the goal

Focus first on understanding the overriding business goal (see Lesson 7 on the business case). This will align your work with the strategic direction of your organization and give you a framework for assessing individual requests. You'll become a strategic partner, one who sets strategic priorities and makes good business decisions.

Strategic partners ask strategic questions

Strategic questions encourage the thought processes that bring about change. What is causing the change? How will the individuals be affected by the change? What is their role in implementing the change? How is their role broader than their specialized area of interest? Where do they fit in the bigger picture? Strategic questions encourage a description of the vision and the part the person will play in bringing it about.

Strategic questions might be used to tie the individual self-interests in the scenario to the strategic goal of the Web redesign: Web First. For example,

> In what way does improving or replacing the search engine move the organization to make Web First the core of our operations?

> How will the recommendation to rewrite the code that runs the site cause our customers to think Web First when they want information from our organization?

> What part will Web First thinking play in making our courses available online?

> What needs to change to allow Web First to be the core of operations for the organization?

> We've always done the print books and live (in person) courses first and then posted to the Web. How do you see us producing our print products and live courses using Web First methods?

When those who are working on a project—and those affected by the decisions made throughout the project—understand the strategic nature of the change, individual interests are brought into alignment with the overriding goal. The stakeholders see how their interests will be served by their contribution to the larger strategic goal. As a result, the change is implemented more effectively and accepted more readily.

In a nutshell

Communication: To be a strategic partner, ask strategic questions. This will uncover the goals and expectations of the sponsor and help you define what needs to change.

Collaboration: Collaboration is the result of working toward a shared goal. Individual interests are dropped and a common, strategic goal that meets the needs of the stakeholders is agreed to.

Project Management: Know the goal you must achieve before you work on a plan. Understand the individual interests of the stakeholders and unite them in a strategic goal they all will support.

EXERCISE

A request has come to offer online seminars on the Web site. Identify each question as either an individual interest or a strategic interest.

Question	Individual or strategic interest?
1. Do you want live Webcast seminars or archived seminars available on the site?	
2. Where on the site do you want to put access to the online seminars?	
3. Is there a business case for online seminars? Where do online seminars fit in ICLE's vision for education online?	
4. What are the technical and design implications of adding online seminars to the site? Are there technical implications for our customers?	
5. Who will have access to the seminars? Will they get continuing education credits if they watch them?	
6. What is the funding source for this project?	
7. Who are the stakeholders that will be impacted by adding online seminars to the Web site?	
8. How will you process the registration forms and send out reports showing credit for attendance?	

Exercise answer

Question	Individual or strategic interest?
1. Do you want live Webcast seminars or archived seminars available on the site?	Individual interest
2. Where on the site do you want to put access to the online seminars?	Individual interest
3. Is there a business case for online seminars? Where do online seminars fit in ICLE's vision for education online?	Strategic interest
4. What are the technical and design implications of adding online seminars to the site? Are there technical implications for our customers?	Strategic interest
5. Who will have access to the seminars? Will they get continuing education credits if they watch them?	Individual interest
6. What is the funding source for this project?	Strategic interest
7. Who are the stakeholders that will be impacted by adding online seminars to the Web site?	Strategic interest
8. How will you process the registration forms and send out reports showing credit for attendance?	Individual interest

Questions 1, 2, 5, and 8 ask for specifications on how to map out the design. They represent "order taking" rather than probing to ask the strategic merit of the request.

RECOMMENDED READING

For more discussion on the importance of strategic questioning, see the Co-Intelligence Institute's Web site at http://www.co-intelligence.org/p-strategicQing.html.

9

▼
▼

Select the Project Leader

"How do I know if I have the skills to lead a collaborative project?" asks the Project Manager.

"Imagine this scenario," replies the Facilitator. "It is one month before the rollout of the new Web design. Two members have dropped out of the Web redesign team. The cost of temporary help to replace their work will send the project over budget. The new site design is in the final round of user testing, and the results are negative. The new feature the team was most excited about is confusing the customers. Morale is low, and there is fear that the project will be delayed. What is the first thing you would do?"

How you lead is as important as what you lead

Does it seem as if the project in this scenario is out of control? What kind of leader does it need to bring it under control?

- A *command-and-control* person who would take charge, make decisions, and offer clear directives?
- A *diplomat* who would engage the team and boost morale and productivity?
- A *coach* who would be a teacher and mentor, keep her cool, look for opportunities, and mitigate risks?
- A *visionary* who can steer to the end result and not be phased by bumps along the way?
- A *democratic leader* who will value the expertise of team members and make certain everyone has input toward solutions?
- A *pacesetter* who will lead the way and draw out the best from his experienced team members?

In any collaborative project, the leader will have the opportunity to use all of these leadership styles. Projects, whether they are in trouble or not, thrive when the leader is flexible, has command of several leadership styles, and uses them skillfully, depending on the situation. How you lead is as important as what you lead.

Here are typical responsibilities of the collaborative project leader:

- build a team with members who have differing self-interests
- coach the team through the stages of team development; provide training in collaboration methods of conflict resolution
- challenge assumptions of stakeholders
- lead change initiatives, including managing the uncertainty and discomfort change can bring
- introduce the project to the team
- communicate the vision to the team
- communicate the status to the stakeholders
- gain consensus from team members

- ▸ run effective meetings
- ▸ delegate and give direction
- ▸ prevent problems
- ▸ find problems early, anticipate changes, and provide solutions
- ▸ keep the project on time and on budget
- ▸ negotiate with department heads for resources
- ▸ correct poor performance of a team member
- ▸ motivate team members
- ▸ listen
- ▸ manage stress
- ▸ write plans, reports, memos, and other documents
- ▸ deliver bad news as well as celebrate victories
- ▸ take responsibility, feel ownership for the success or failure of a project

Who is the best person to handle these responsibilities? It is tempting to appoint your most experienced manager (she runs a tight ship, very efficient) or most senior specialist (knows everything there is know about tech—can even do the programming) on the basis of expertise as a manager or specialist. This expertise, however, does *not* qualify him or her as a leader of a collaborative project. Why? Because years of experience may offer efficiency, but ingrain outdated habits and reinforce inflexibility. Years of seniority may support entitlement and cause you to overlook the talent needed to complete the project successfully. Years of being a manager may bring control and authority but can discourage change and vision.

Is the leader a manager? In many important respects, the leader is not necessarily a manager.

- ▸ Leaders are *change agents* charged with bringing about the change called for in the project. They argue for change. Managers are responsible for ensuring efficient operations on a day-to-day basis. Change can disrupt those operations. Managers argue for keeping the status quo.

- Managers are charged with making decisions and solving problems. Leaders are responsible for making sure that decisions get made and that they are in line with the project vision.

- Leaders keep the *long-term view* in sight and make decisions based on the vision. Managers often need to make *short-term* decisions to meet budget constraints or production deadlines.

Leadership traits of collaborative leaders

Managing a collaborative project tests the communication, collaboration, and project management skills of the leader. Here are leadership attributes to consider when choosing or developing a collaborative project leader.

Collaboration:

- Expertise and experience leading cross-departmental teams.

- The ability to resolve conflict as well as coach others in collaboration methods.

- Consensus building skills. The ability to gain consensus when there is a wide range of individual interests.

- Courage to implement change. She is apt to challenge the status quo to drive toward the vision goal and is considerate of the emotional effect the change process has on those it touches.

Communication:

- Flexibility. She is able to adapt her leadership style to the situation. She can speak with authority if needed; she is more apt to persuade, to coach, or to be democratic, depending on what the situation calls for.

- Excellent communication and relationship building skills. She is as comfortable making a presentation to a large group as holding a one-on-one conversation. She effectively uses the appropriate medium: face-to-face, e-mail, written report, meeting, podium, phone.

- Responsibility. She delivers bad news quickly without assigning blame. She explains without being defensive.
- Curiosity. She asks questions and is comfortable speaking to those her senior in both years and experience. She maintains the context.

Project Management:

- Decisiveness. She makes decisions according to the vision of the project, and ensures that the project requirements align with the vision and are relevant to the organization, including the customers.
- Problem solving. The ability to value facts over opinions.
- The ability to conduct productive meetings. She has mastery of the purpose, agenda, and use of time at meetings.
- The ability to delegate. She does not attempt to micromanage technical work but is able to integrate it within the project.
- Respect for the talents of team members. When she needs to follow, she does. When she gives direction, she explains why and shares her concerns.
- The ability to provide realistic estimates. This includes time, money, and effort.

The project leader gets results. When choosing a project leader, consider the experience and the skills the person has already demonstrated. Strong leadership attributes bring results. The demands of the project will not alone improve the skills of the manager who lacks leadership attributes. These skills can be learned if the candidate has the willingness and a strong potential to learn them. They will be learned more quickly if the learning process is supervised by an experienced coach.

In a nutshell

Communication: Collaborative leaders have a talent for different communication styles. They can persuade as well as command, be reflective as well as decisive.

Collaboration: In collaborative projects, how you lead is as important as what you lead. The ability to be flexible, make decisions based on the project vision and to explain why is key.

Project Management: Use different leadership styles depending on the need rather than relying on a one-size-fits-all style of leadership. Styles include the ability to persuade, command, explain the vision, be democratic, set the pace, build consensus, and empathize.

EXERCISE

This table lists challenges faced by leaders in collaborative projects. Which leader might be best suited in each situation?

1. A *command-and-control person* who would take charge, make decisions, and offer clear directives?

2. A *diplomat* who would engage the team and boost morale and productivity?

3. A *coach* who would keep her cool, look for opportunities, and mitigate risks?

4. A *visionary* who can steer to the end result and not be phased by bumps along the way?

5. A *democratic leader* who will value the expertise of team members and ensure everyone has input toward the solutions?

6. A *pacesetter* who will lead the way and draw out the best from his experienced team members?

Activities or challenges leaders face	Type of leadership best suited
Managing team members from different departments	
Challenging assumptions of a team member	
Introducing the project to the team	
Communicating the vision to the team	
Solving problems in a creative way	
Gaining consensus from team members	
Running effective meetings	
Delegating and giving direction	
Meeting deadlines that are in danger of being missed	
Correcting poor performance of a team member	
Motivating team members	
Listening to team members and following their recommendation	
Boosting morale	

Exercise answer

Activities or challenges leaders face	Type of leadership best suited
Managing team members from different departments	Democratic leader
Challenging assumptions of a team member	Coach
Introducing the project to the team	Visionary
Communicating the vision to the team	Visionary
Solving problems in a creative way	Coach
Gaining consensus from team members	Democratic leader
Running effective meetings	All
Delegating and giving direction	Coach
Meeting deadlines that are in danger of being missed	Pacesetter
Correcting poor performance of a team member	Command-and-control
Motivating team members	Pacesetter
Listening to team members and following their recommendation	Democratic leader
Boosting morale	Diplomat

Try this group activity

Balloon Game: This is a fun game to try in a group of six to eight people. It brings out the leadership styles of the participants and provides a base for discussion.

The activity leader has a bag of about 10 inflated balloons. The participants stand together in an open, roomy space. There is only one instruction: *Keep the balloons in the air.* The leader then takes the balloons out of the bag one at a time, batting each into the air. The game continues until the balloons have all dropped to the floor or the group gives up in frustration.

As the participants try to keep the balloons in the air, watch their actions. For example:

- ▸ Who is taking charge and giving directions?
- ▸ Who is cheerleading and encouraging the participants?
- ▸ Who is leaping and diving to get to as many as possible?
- ▸ Who is holding back and watching?
- ▸ Who is trying to organize and plan?

Discuss these different styles with the group: Which ones were helpful and when?

RECOMMENDED READING

Bower, Joseph L., and Clark G. Gilbert. "How Managers' Everyday Decisions Create or Destroy Your Company's Strategy." *Harvard Business Review,* Feb 2007.

Goleman, Daniel. *Emotional Intelligence: Why It Can Matter More Than IQ.* New York: Bantam Books, 1995.

Goleman, Daniel. 12Manage: The Executive Fast Track. Leadership Styles. http://www.12manage.com/methods_goleman_leadership_styles.html.

Goleman, Daniel, Richard E. Boyatzis, and Annie McKee. *Primal Leadership: Realizing the Power of Emotional Intelligence.* Boston: Harvard Business School Press, 2002.

Leader to Leader Institute. Thought Leaders Gateway, http://www.pfdf.org/knowledgecenter/leaders.aspx. (An excellent general online resource on leadership.)

Warner, Charles. Chapter 6: Leadership, in *Media Sales Management.* http://mediaselling.us/media_sales.html.

10

Choose Your Team

"I'd like to be sure my team members are committed to the project," says the Project Manager. "It will be new, challenging work that will bring about change— and the emotions that go along with change. Which is more important to look for: skill or experience?"

"A positive attitude," answers the Facilitator. "And a collaborative supervisor."

Select for talent

A successful collaborative project is the result of a diverse group of people dedicating their time, individual skills, strengths, and interests to accomplish a shared goal. Reaching the goal requires commitment, expertise, and a high standard of performance from each team member. The most important requirement is commitment to achieving the goal—a *positive attitude*. Team members with a positive attitude tend to

listen with an open mind;

reach agreement (consensus);

commit to the goal of the project and want to see the project completed successfully;

share ideas and have the discipline to share in the workload;

present a positive, team-centered attitude, including the ability to trust and be comfortable with change;

set goals and work hard to achieve them; and

learn quickly.

Individual expertise is also essential. Consider whether or not the person will bring expertise to the project, or will develop it in the course of the project. If he will develop it, the ability to learn quickly is a must and the time to learn should be scheduled into the project. For a Web redesign, expertise would include

technical expertise for programming, security, access rights;

design expertise for functionality, brand identity, advertising;

customer experience expertise for e-commerce, self-help, policies, etc.;

editing expertise for content organization, search results, product display, etc.; and

program planner expertise for education presentations and contributor recognition.

A high standard of performance is also a key requirement. This is evidenced by

a record of meeting deadlines and commitments,

the ability to work well with others,

realistic estimating skills, and

accountability for results.

What if your project team has already been assigned? You may feel you have no choice about who is on your team, and you must try to make the best of those assigned. In this case, take the time to review the talents of these individuals and their match to your project. If there is not a match with attitude, it is advisable to request that the person be replaced. Skills can be learned, performance can be improved, but attitude is very difficult to change, and dealing with a poor attitude will drain your energy and the energies of your team members. A project brings new activities and expectations; guard it from falling prey to old habits of criticism and judgment.

How do you determine attitude? Ask this one question of a potential team member: What goal(s) did you set for yourself in the last year and what progress have you made in achieving it? If you hear, "It wasn't worth it," "I didn't have time," "I tried to set a goal but was blocked from reaching it (by someone else)," "What difference does it make?" etc., you are hearing *negative* responses. If you hear "I set a goal," "I made a schedule (plan)," "I worked hard and learned new things," "I asked for help," "I made small improvements and I'm proud of them," etc., you are hearing a *positive* attitude. This is the attitude you need for teamwork to be successful.

Gaining release time: Manage for collaboration

You have determined your dream team. You are halfway there. The other half is gaining release time from their supervisors. Gaining release time for team members to work on your project is of itself a collaborative approach and starts before a member is invited to the team. It is helpful that the sponsor and supervisor support full cooperation with the redesign project. But is cooperation enough? How will you handle conflicting priorities for time as the project progresses and deadlines compete? Will cooperation fade as those deadlines approach? Most likely.

Cooperation does not require commitment to a shared goal. Two parties can share staff, data, and facilities, but keep their own distinct goals. When supervisors cooperate but have not created a shared goal, conflicts arise as their own individual interests and priorities challenge the agreement to cooperate. Cooperation gives way to competition, accommodation, compromise, and avoidance. The result can be disappointing for the supervisor, team leader, and team members.

To make the request for release time a collaborative approach, begin with the project sponsor. Ask the sponsor to communicate the goals and organizational support for the project to managers and supervisors. Help the supervisors to understand how their staff members will play a fundamental part in the project's success and, ultimately, the organization's success. You now have a common frame of reference with the supervisor when you make the request for release time. It is helpful to:

- ▶ Meet with the supervisor well before the team member is needed. Be realistic about what you expect the team assignments to be and the amount of time you need released for the project work.

- ▶ Explain what new skills the team member will learn and how these will benefit his department in the long run.

- ▶ Give the supervisor background information about the project and the team. Keep him informed on a regular basis about what is going on with the project and with his staff member. If there are any changes, commit to informing the supervisor immediately, allowing him to work with you to continue achieving his department goals.

- ▶ Include the supervisor in celebrating the milestones along the way with the team as they move forward.

- ▶ Explore whether or not the project work will actually become the team member's regular work—work that, due to his expertise, will be assigned to him even if he is not on the team.

- ▶ Help the supervisor explore options to achieve his department goals. How can his goals for department work be accomplished without the team member's 100 percent contribution to his assignments? Make the staff sharing a win-win process.

- ▶ What if there are conflicting deadlines? Conflicting priorities? If you are truly collaborating and committed to supporting each other's needs to achieve the common goal, how the conflict is worked out will be a win-win. Otherwise, you are faced with deciding in advance who will make the call. Stick by the decision graciously. When the next conflict arises, again, put the goal first and work for a win-win.

Who initiates the discussion with the team member when she is invited to join the team? The supervisor initiates the discussion. Who does the team member turn to if there are conflicts with being on the team? The team member turns first to the team leader and then to the supervisor.

The following example details a plan to keep the supervisor informed about the team's activities, particularly those that impact the team member he supervises.

Communication plan between team leader and supervisor

Topic (What to communicate)	Occasion (When to communicate)	Method (How to communicate)
Status of the project	Monthly, typically. Can be more often, depending on what each agrees is needed to feel informed.	Monthly status report as e-mail attachment
Change in the plan's schedule or request for additional release time	As soon as it is determined there will be a change	Face-to-face meeting
Invitation to team celebration of achievement	When a milestone is reached	E-mail
Performance concern	If staff member misses x number of team meetings	Face-to-face meeting
Request for extra training for staff member	Usually before the project starts or as soon as it is known	Face-to-face meeting
Special achievement by team member	As soon after it occurs as possible	E-mail

In a nutshell ▸ ▸ ▸

Communication: When selecting your team, look for members who communicate a positive attitude. A negative attitude is difficult to overcome and will diminish your effectiveness. During the project, include supervisors as well as team members in communication plans.

Collaboration: A collaborative relationship with supervisors as well as team members is the best foundation for conflict resolution as the project progresses. If you rely on cooperation, conflicting priorities and competing deadlines will challenge the agreement to cooperate, giving way to competition, compromise, accommodation, or avoidance.

Project Management: Be open and realistic with team members and supervisors about time estimates for project work. Talk directly to team members, or others who also have expertise, to get time estimates for the work. If expertise is to be learned on the project, allow sufficient time in the plan for training and for the team member to progress to the level of expertise needed.

EXERCISE

What goal(s) have you set for yourself in the past year? What progress have you made in achieving it?

TIME-SAVER

Handout: Characteristics of a Good Team Member

Characteristics of a Good Team Member

Friendly, pleasant, and well liked

Listens to and accepts the views of others

Supports teammates and builds morale

Communicates clearly

Attends all meetings and is on time

Gives credit to and praises others' contributions

Willing to work to achieve consensus

Bases decisions on objective data

Does his/her fair share of the work

Engages in all discussions

RECOMMENDED READING

Buckingham, Marcus, and Curt Coffman. *First, Break All the Rules: What the World's Greatest Managers Do Differently.* New York: Simon & Schuster, 1999.

Buckingham, Marcus, and Curt Coffman. *Now, Discover Your Strengths.* New York: Simon & Schuster, 2001.

Gordon, Jon. *The Energy Bus.* New Jersey: John Wiley & Sons, 2007

SECTION II: Initiating

11

Recognize the Stages of Team Development

"This is great," says the Project Manager. "I have the agenda for my first meeting. I'll line up the sponsor and get the business case together. I'm ready to go."

"Not so fast," says the Facilitator. "For your first few meetings, focus on relationship building. Give your team members a chance to get to know each other and to understand how they will work together as a team. I know a great icebreaker to start you off."

The 80/20 rule: Developing trust

The conversation we started is a familiar one. Here is how it continues.

"Thanks, but no thanks," says the Project Manager. "We have worked here for years. My team members know each other pretty well. And they know their stuff. This project needs to get going. We can't waste time playing games. They're not going to sit through a round of 'What's your favorite vacation spot?' "

"They may know each other, I'll give you that," says the Facilitator. "Have they worked as a team before? Have they worked with you as a team leader? Have they been part of a collaborative initiative? They are bringing their talents to your team. They are also bringing their own interests and needs. Do they trust that their interests and needs will be met through the team's work? An icebreaker, if done well, opens channels of communication and invites team members to share what they have in common—this is foundational to trust."

When a team is forming, the general rule is to spend 80 percent of the time on *relationship building* and 20 percent on the task. As the team develops *trust*, that ratio will move to 50:50. A high-performing team spends 20 percent of its time building relationships and 80 percent on tasks.

Stages of team development

How long it takes to develop trust depends on the dynamics of the group, the skill and experience of the leader, and the nature of the work to be done. Teams pass through five stages as they develop trust and become productive. These are the stages and the leadership style that is most helpful to use at each stage:

Forming: In this stage, team members move from individual to member status. They are nervous and polite—often hesitant to participate because they are uncertain of their place or role on the team. You may hear complaints about the organizational environment and intellectualizing about what the team tasks are and how to gather information. Work productivity can be minimal. The leadership style most helpful to use at this stage is *visionary/introducer*. Prepare well for meetings. Introduce goals and purpose; help members get to know each other; understand the charge (mission) of the team; establish the ground rules.

Storming: This stage is true to its name. Team members are likely to express animosity or apathy as they struggle for control. There is reluctance to let go of self-interests and trust the team. Other characteristic behaviors include infighting, tension, polarization of group members, and concern over excessive work. Some teams are unable to develop the trust that moves them past the storming stage and disband as a result. The leadership style most helpful to use at this stage is *teacher/diplomat.* Openly acknowledge the conflict; examine your own response to conflict; reinforce positive conflict resolution (collaboration). Do not become authoritarian, but rather revisit the goals, rules; focus on process (how will we accomplish our goals?).

Norming: In this stage, team members accept the team, including their roles, and develop the ability to make decisions and resolve conflict. They are better able to express their emotions constructively, and they will have more time and energy to focus on their purpose. Work productivity increases. The team may also experience groupthink. The leadership style most helpful to use at this stage is *coach.* Support the work of the team; provide feedback; focus on tasks (what do we need to do?); develop leadership in team members.

Performing: The performing team accomplishes a great deal of work. The team solves problems quickly and effectively. Loyalty, interdependence, and respect for individual differences are characteristics of members at this stage. The leadership style most helpful to use at this stage is *delegator/pacesetter/observer.* Allow team members to work; prepare for setbacks if there is a change (someone leaves or is added to the team).

Adjourning: When the team finishes its work it will celebrate and disband. This phase can be marked by grief or mourning, as the members struggle with letting go of the team. The leadership style most helpful at this stage is *democratic.* Give members recognition for their achievements and contribution to the organization. Help team members express their feelings and move on to the next project or achievement.

Each stage of development is important to the productivity and problem-solving ability of the team. Supporting the team as it forms—that is, building relationships through acknowledging the process and giving team members time to adjust and space to discuss the issues, as well as occasionally encouraging the discussion rather than charging full steam ahead—will provide a foundation for weathering the storming stage that follows. The trust that is developed as conflicts are worked out through establishing norms—the expectations for team behavior—process and participation, will support high productivity.

Focus first on relationships as the team forms. Help the team members get to know each other through common experiences. Several activities promote team formation:

- ▶ Icebreakers are a way for the project leader to focus the attention of the team on getting to know each other and begin to break down barriers to communication.

- ▶ Answering basic questions about the purpose of the team, why each member is on the team, what is expected of them, and who will support them will help define their status and build trust.

- ▶ Securing the needs of the team members. The team leader should be aware of Abraham Maslow's well-known hierarchy of an individual's needs. (See Recommended Reading at the end of this lesson.) Progressively securing the basic needs of an individual leads to high productivity. According to Maslow, the most basic need is for physical safety. This must be met before there can be progress in meeting psychological security—the next, higher-level need. The other needs follow in order: shared responsibility, respect, and the chance to exercise initiative. Meeting each need moves the team member to the next level.

- ▶ Establishing the rules of conduct for team meetings guides team members as they learn to work together as a team. These rules become important tools for communication, decision making, and problem-solving processes. Here is a good relationship-building exercise for a first team meeting: Give your team a copy of the following Rules of Conduct. Now ask the members to prioritize the items and list them in order of importance. Team members resist taking the time to do this, but when it is done they value and appreciate the result of the discussion.

Rules of Conduct for Meetings

Share ownership of the team's mission

Start and end the meeting on time

Listen objectively

Respect teammates and their views

Criticize only ideas, not people

Question and contribute

Share responsibility

Attend all meetings

In a nutshell ▷ ▷ ▷

Communication: Focus 80 percent on relationship building as a team forms to break down barriers that prevent productive communication, problem solving, and decision making. Icebreakers and discussing the Rules of Conduct for Meetings are very helpful activities that build communication among team members.

Collaboration: The basis of collaboration is trust. As trust develops, individuals will disclose their needs and goals, gain comfort with interdependence, seek win-win solutions to conflict, be comfortable with change, and hold each other accountable for results. Relationship building is foundational to developing this trust and is especially important to help the team weather the storming phase of the collaborative team development.

Project Management: It is tempting to skip the relationship-building activities when time constraints push the manager to create and implement the plan that will result in project delivery. For high productivity and a greater likelihood of success for your project, spend time on the front end to build team skills. These skills will be invaluable to your team when your deadlines approach, when problems need to be solved, and when work needs to progress quickly.

EXERCISE

Here are possible topics to discuss at a first team meeting for a Web design project. Indicate which topics will result in building your team relationships and which might jump to the task at hand. Which topics would you include in your first meeting? What order would you give them on the agenda?

- ▸ Introduction of team members
- ▸ Why we are here: Overview of the project description
- ▸ How teams work: Rules of conduct
- ▸ Outline of the project plan
- ▸ Elements of the Web design business plan
- ▸ Agreement on meeting dates and times

Exercise answer

Relation-building activities and order on the agenda

1. Introduction of team members

2. Why we are here: Overview of the project description (This is a brief introduction of the project and how the team members will relate to it.)

3. How teams work: Rules of conduct

4. Agreement on meeting dates and times (this can be brief and lead to next steps.)

Presenting an outline of the project plan or discussing the elements of the Web design business plan is jumping to the task.

TIME-SAVER

Handout: Suggested Icebreakers

Suggested Icebreakers

Note that a success factor in using icebreakers well is to debrief them properly. Consider the purpose and any learning goals in this varied listing of icebreakers. Many have learning goals as simple as "getting to know you."

1. Pick a partner, find out three or four things about each other and introduce each other to the team.

2. Tell about the first job you got where you got a regular paycheck and had to report to work every day.

3. Bingo: Develop a grid of statements that are true about yourself and gather signatures from people who share that characteristic (only one person is allowed to sign in a box per sheet). Sample statements: "I like prunes." "I've been on television." "I know a famous person personally."

4. Five of Anything. Ask team members to share their five favorite movies of all time, or their five favorite novels, or their five least-liked films, and so forth. The topic can be five of anything—most liked or disliked. For the complete version of this icebreaker, see http://humanresources.about.com/od/icebreakers/a/icebreaker_five.htm.

5. Ask each person to share their expectations for what they would like to get out of being on the team. Write the answers on a flipchart.

6. Talk about your favorite [candy, food, game, music, etc.] when you were a child.
   - What *kind* of a car are you and why?
   - What *part* of a car are you and why?
   - Name a food or a fruit that describes you.
   - Name an animal that describes you and why.

7. In a small group of four or five people: Name one thing you all have in common.

8. What would it be like if you had an ideal world (or an ideal day)?

9. Ask each person to write down his or her first (instant) response to the following questions (asked in order with time for them to write the response after each one). What do you think of first when you are asked to name:

- A color?
- A flower?
- A piece of furniture?

After the responses are written down, read the most typical response and ask how many had the same response. How many said:

- Color: blue, then red
- Flower: daisy, then rose
- Furniture: sofa or couch, then chair

Discussion that follows centers on how alike we really are.

Handout: Rules of Conduct for Meetings

Rules of Conduct for Meetings

Share ownership of the team's mission

Start and end the meeting on time

Listen objectively

Respect teammates and their views

Criticize only ideas, not people

Question and contribute

Share responsibility

Attend all meetings

RECOMMENDED READING

Dent, Stephen M. "Comfort with Change." Chap. 10 in *Partnering Intelligence: Creating Value for Your Business by Building Strong Alliances.* Palo Alto, Calif.: Davies-Black Publishing, 1999.

Maslow, Abraham. *Motivation and Personality.* New York: Harper, 1954. (Maslow's Hierarchy of Needs has been applied in many business contexts, and numerous references to it can be found on the Internet.)

Tuckman, Bruce. "Developmental Sequence in Small Groups." *Psychological Bulletin,* Vol 63, No 6, pp 394–99.

12

Develop the Shared Vision

> *"I think I understand the business case," says the Project Manager. "I'm having trouble explaining the Web First concept, though. It seems so far off in the future and so different from how we work today. If it were a thing, I could draw a picture of it. But how do you draw a picture of an idea?"*

> *"A picture is just what you need," responds the Facilitator. "A word picture. What change will the idea of Web First make when it is implemented? How will it make the users and workers feel? What will people be doing? What goal will we have reached? Describe this as if it were done and happening now."*

What is a shared vision?

The redesign team is charged with using Web technology to provide faster service, better search results, effective products, and a clear brand identity for customers. The requirements for the redesign project are specified in the *business case*. Collaborative projects work from a *shared vision*. What is the difference between a business case and the vision?

The business case describes the need for the change and helps determine feasibility. The vision paints the picture of what the end result or outcome looks like as if it were already finished. The vision can take longer to realize and may change over time. It may include elements that cannot be implemented with the immediate project. In this case later elements are identified and incorporated in successive versions of the project. Each version delivers a working part of the project until the entire project is completed. This is referred to as agile project management.

The business case as described in Lesson 7 details the business need and goals for the project. It lays out the skeleton of what is needed. The vision adds flesh. It paints a picture of how your organization will look after it has realized its goals.

By painting a picture of your end result, your team is better able to make a coordinated plan to get there. Without a shared vision, the Web redesign team members and stakeholders might be tempted to fix the immediate problems and not consider how the solution fits with the long-term goals. They might form separate work groups and meet together only to share information on their individual progress as they improve their separate areas.

Without a shared vision, project members will only cooperate; they will continue to work from the standpoint of their individual interests. With a shared vision, project members will collaborate: they will work together to achieve the shared goals of the project.

To write a clear vision, here are some guidelines:

- ▶ Draw a word picture in the present tense.
- ▶ Describe the best possible outcome.
- ▶ Describe it as if it were already done. Make it as real as if it were happening today.
- ▶ Create an emotional connection that persuades. Describe how the users will feel.

Creating the shared vision

To gain a shared vision, take these steps:

1. Invite the sponsor to introduce her vision for the project.

2. Identify the expectations and assumptions in the vision. Encourage the team members to ask questions.

3. Establish a common vocabulary. Do the words in the vision mean the same thing to everyone?

4. Discuss the role each team member has in fulfilling the expectations.

5. Ask each team member to write a brief vision of what his or her expectations are. What do they see as the outcome of their work on the project? What individual goals do they want to achieve?

6. Discuss these visions and find the common goals. Where goals conflict, work together to create a common goal.

7. Finish with one shared vision that aligns with the sponsor's vision.

Here is an example of how to follow the steps that lead your team to a shared vision:

1. The sponsor provides the vision

The sponsor has provided this brief vision for the Web redesign project.

> The Web site is at the core of ICLE's values and operations. Web First is the basis for product development and production as well as for how the Web site functions for customers. When product developers, IT, customer service, marketing and design receive an assignment for any new project or initiative, they ask themselves: how will this product be researched, written, developed, designed, supported, and advertised using Web tools. How do I know customers need it? How will it function on the Web site? How will customers find it quickly? How can I make it easy to use? How will customers recognize instantly that it is an ICLE product?

Creating quality content is the top priority for ICLE's product developers, programmers, designers, and customer service staff. They meet in subject area groups (such as probate and estate planning, family law, etc.) to plan and implement their projects. Thinking Web First, they use the Web to get customer feedback and analyze what the customer wants. Research and processes stem from how the Web works and are translated into products that are delivered in the way the customer chooses: print on demand, online Webinar, how-to kit, etc. All content is organized and tagged to key to the search engine dictionary to return instant, relevant results.

The customer turns on his computer and is greeted with the ICLE Web site on his desktop. He recognizes it instantly. Case updates, seminar schedules, news, and transaction guidelines are one click away. He sees customer service has sent a reminder about the seminar he will attend tomorrow. He keys his search question into the search box and the relevant case, forms, statutes, and a how-to kit appear instantly. "This is so easy," he says to himself. "*Everything is right here*. It saves me so much time."

2. Identify the expectations and assumptions

Team members identify the following assumptions and expectations from the sponsor's vision. They are encouraged to ask questions to clarify the expectations and assumptions.

With each new project, the developers use a Web First research and development approach.

Content creators work with IT, design, and customer service to ensure that the product and the process are Web First and use the latest technology.

The priority is on creating quality content. Technology is used to deliver it in the best possible way.

Search engine results are fast and relevant.

Customer service expects the customer to look for service updates on the Web site.

Customers find the site instantly recognizable.

Customers find the site amazingly easy to use.

3. Establish a shared vocabulary

For each member to visualize the end result, it is important that they have the same picture or idea of its components. Even familiar words such as "fast" or "quality" need to be clearly defined in the context of the vision. Asking members to voice their definition of a term can help the group clarify exactly what was intended and how it will be explained when decisions are called for throughout the project. For example, "fast" to one user may be within 10 seconds; "fast" to another user may be "1 second or instant."

4. Discuss the role each team member has in fulfilling the expectations

▶ *Customer Service:* communication with and to the customer

▶ *Marketing:* instant recognition of the organization and ease of use of the site

▶ *IT:* latest Web technology; efficient maintenance and upgrade

▶ *Content developers:* relevant search results, the latest information, products that solve customer problems

▶ *Editing:* cost-effective production methods and processes that deliver quality content

5. Ask each team member to write his or her vision. How will the Web redesign meet their needs? What are their goals?

Customer Service: When the redesign is finished, customers never need to call for service. They know everything they have purchased, how to use it, what is on sale, what their credit status is. We know what their problems are, what products they use, and what they want to have.

Marketing: When the redesign is finished, our identity appears on every page. Customers always know they are on our site. Functions are familiar and don't change just because there is new technology. Customers are not asked to learn new tricks to get what they need.

IT: When the redesign is finished, the site uses advanced Web technology. We switch easily to new technology whenever a new product or application is developed.

Content: We use the Web technology to find new content as well as to develop products. We know what products and information customers want and how they want to get them because we have asked them. Training and demos are built into the products. Search results are instant and relevant because we have tagged the content in advance to be searchable and because we have the latest search technology.

Editing: When we produce the content we actually use the Web interface. We see what the customer sees.

6. Find the common goals and deal with conflicting goals

Common goals in the brief visions:

> ▶ To get customer feedback from surveys and other communication methods for service and product development
>
> ▶ To use Web technology that is the latest and fastest
>
> ▶ To think Web First throughout the organization

Conflicting goals:

> ▶ IT will switch to the latest technology when it becomes available.
>
> ▶ Design calls for *not* switching to new technology so customer is not confused.

What will resolve the conflicting goals?

Discuss the conflict. Work to provide a solution that serves both the need to advance to new technology and the need to maintain customer loyalty by keeping the site familiar and easy to use. A new goal might be to switch to the latest technology, but do it on a beta site that allows sufficient customer testing and can be installed in the new site in more gradual phases.

7. *Finish with one shared vision that aligns with the sponsor's vision*

Note the new paragraph set in italic. It resolves the conflicting goals between IT and Design by introducing the agile project approach, a way to meet both needs.

> The Web site is at the core of ICLE's values and operations. Web First is the basis for product development and production as well as for how the Web site functions for customers. When product developers, IT, customer service, marketing, and design receive an assignment for any new project or initiative, they ask themselves: how will this product be researched, written, developed, designed, supported, and advertised using Web tools? How do I know customers need it? How will it function on the Web site? How will customers find it quickly? How can I make it easy to use? How will customers recognize instantly that it is an ICLE product?
>
> Creating quality content is the top priority for ICLE's product developers, programmers, designers, and customer service staff. They meet in subject area groups (such as probate and estate planning, family law, etc.) to plan and implement their projects. Thinking Web First, they use the Web to get customer feedback and analyze what the customer wants. Research and processes stem from how the Web works and are translated into products that are delivered in the way the customer chooses: print on demand, online Webinar, how-to kit, etc. All content is organized and tagged to key to the search engine dictionary to return instant, relevant results.
>
> *Web redesign is planned using agile development methods. The overall goals are established. Individual projects align with the overall goal. Priority is assigned to the projects and they are designed and implemented as versions. Each version rolls out when its objective is met, it has been tested on a beta site, and customer support is fully prepared. Staff are pleased with how manageable the versions are to implement and celebrate their successes. Calls to customer service decrease 30 percent.*

The customer turns on his computer and is greeted with the ICLE Web site on his desktop. He recognizes it instantly. Case updates, seminar schedules, news, and transaction guidelines are one click away. He sees customer service has sent a reminder about the seminar he will attend tomorrow. He keys his search question into the search box and the relevant case, forms, statutes, and a how-to kit appear instantly. "This is so easy," he says to himself. "*Everything is right here*. It saves me so much time."

It is important to recognize that the vision can be lofty. It can take several years to reach. As time passes, don't be surprised if the vision changes to meet new customer needs. During the planning stage you will identify the most important steps you can take now to help you realize the current vision.

In a nutshell ▶ ▶ ▶

Communication: Develop the ability to describe your goals in a vision statement that details a present state—one that is, not will be. This helps others see what you are seeing.

Collaboration: To collaborate, individuals develop a common vision that meets the goals of the group. It lifts the group beyond information sharing to commitment to achieving the goal.

Project Management: A clear vision will do the most to eliminate the rework that often is the result of assumptions, self-interest, and "fuzzy" vision. Take the time up front to develop the common vision, question assumptions, and gain agreement.

EXERCISE

Set a business or personal goal for yourself. Write a brief vision statement of what you have achieved when you reach your goal. Include how you feel. Write in the present tense, as if it has already happened.

13

Agree on Key Elements
and Guiding Principles

"Business case, vision, key elements, guiding principles—they're all high-level views of the project outcome," says the Project Manager. "Do we need so many different lofty views? The team is anxious to come down to earth and get something done."

"The key elements are the stars," says the Facilitator. "Shoot for them. It's the guiding principles that bring you down to earth. When you're called on to make tough decisions throughout the project, you'll make them on solid ground."

Keeping your eye on the goal

With the business case and shared vision completed, you have reached a major point of agreement essential to collaborative project work. You have agreed on the end result of your project. The next step is setting the framework to get there.

To establish a framework for your project you must understand two items. First, you must understand your project's *key elements*. The key elements are the deliverables described in your business case and the vision that will bring about strategic advancements. For example, one strategic change in the Web site redesign project was to carry a very consistent page design and functionality across our site. This strategic change would both reinforce our brand and standardize our Web site programming to make support and maintenance easier. Creating a list of your project's key elements helps to focus your team discussions and planning efforts on the most important areas of your project.

Second, you must understand your organization's *guiding principles*. Guiding principles tie your project to the mission and vision of your organization. They are the broad standards you will point to when working with the team to make tough decisions throughout your project. For example, we used the guiding principle "the strategic benefit of any product will outweigh the cost of development, training, and support" throughout our Web site redesign project. By keeping this principle in mind, we balanced design elements against the time needed to create them and limited functions based on the time needed to support them. For example, our pages cannot require manual formatting on an ongoing basis. The design must be limited to what we can automate.

By agreeing to base your decisions on the organization's guiding principles, your team will elevate decision making over self-interests or strong opinions and begin to focus on the mission of the organization. Your guiding principles keep you grounded.

Develop the key elements and guiding principles with your team and gain *consensus* for them. Getting agreement at the front end of the project both allows the team to anticipate issues that may come up during the project and prepares the team to deal with them. This is especially helpful when your project brings change to the organization. It also helps direct the focus during problem solving to achieve a solution that supports the goals of the project. Having the guiding principles identified and approved in advance allows for better decision making and smoother implementation of the project. This is keeping your eye on the goal.

Creating key elements and guiding principles

Some people find the discussion about key elements and guiding principles to be challenging. It is often difficult for people to distinguish between the two. If you find your conversation getting murky, try using the following formula.

"We are going to [key elements] in a way that [guiding principles] so that we can achieve our vision."

For example, **"We are going to . . .**

▶ develop a Web site that is available 24/7

▶ update our content weekly

▶ use technology that can be supported by two full-time staff positions

▶ allow content to be displayed by product line and subject area

▶ have page load times of one second or less

▶ develop and apply a standard format that reflects our identity and that is easily maintainable

in a way that . . .

▶ establishes our Web site as the cornerstone of our business (Web First) and meets business objectives

▶ allows personalization based on customer need

▶ meets customers expectations for accuracy and speed

▶ is maintainable and advances our strategic direction

so that we can achieve our vision."

The team may be reluctant to take the time for this important step before planning begins. During the process you may experience storming by team members as they struggle to gain control and confront self-interests. This is an important opportunity to give your team the tools to help them work together, solve the problem, and develop trust. Here are some practical tips to aid this process.

In general

▸ Keep it simple. Focus on the *key* elements and a *few* guiding principles that are foundational to your strategic intent. For example: Web First, customer testing, speed, cost effectiveness, modular content, and ongoing customer feedback.

▸ Review the consensus process *before* you begin. Remind the team of the rules of conduct at meetings and follow them. This is especially important if signs of team "storming" surface. (Storming can include behaviors such as animosity or apathy, reluctance to let go of self-interests, infighting, tension, polarization of group members, and concern over excessive work. See Lesson 16.)

▸ Once you complete your lists of key elements and guiding principles, write them on a flipchart and post them on a wall during your meetings. You will refer to them often during your project to guide discussions and manage scope.

▸ Like all major deliverables of the project, it is important to get input and support from the project sponsor and other project stakeholders for the key elements and guiding principles documents.

Key elements

▸ Use the vision and business case to pull out your key elements. Create a list of key elements from the project vision for the team to review. Hand them out in advance of the meeting and also make a flipchart of them so there will be a shared focus at the meeting.

▸ Direct the initial discussion toward suggestions on how to make the key elements clear and complete. Were any left out? Do we agree on what the terms mean? Ask for consensus on the final list of key elements.

▸ Instruct the team that all ideas will be noted and encourage all members to participate. Analyze, combine, and filter the ideas at a later meeting.

▸ Discuss conflicting elements. Help team members collaborate to find ways to achieve both goals despite apparent conflicts.

Guiding principles

▸ If you don't have an organization-wide list of guiding principles, use past projects, your organization's vision or mission statement or conversations with your organization's leaders to identify guiding principles relevant to your project. As the strategic direction of your organization changes, so might its guiding principles. By including organization leaders in this discussion, you can be sure your guiding principles are up-to-date.

▸ It is acceptable to include guiding principles that are specific to your project provided they do not conflict with the organization's guiding principles and your team agrees to follow them when making decisions.

▸ If you are having trouble starting the conversation on guiding principles, ask your team what rules they would use to choose between two options that provide similar results. For example: The team has the choice of two vendors. One is local, but more expensive. The other vendor is more cost effective, but not a local business. Describe a guiding principle that would give the team direction for making their choice. Consider that your company values supporting their community, including local businesses.

▸ Strive for a few fundamental principles that will be adhered to and directly relate to your project. Ask for consensus on these. More can be added at a later time as the project unfolds.

▸ Discuss why these guiding principles are relevant to your project and measure your key elements against them. Be sure your key elements do not conflict with your guiding principles. For example: the key element of providing 24/7 personalized phone support would conflict with the guiding principle that customer support will be self-serve and Web-based.

The importance of working styles in the process

The discussions to uncover the guiding principles provide a valuable communication bridge between procedural learners and navigators (see

Lesson 2) who typically approach projects from very different perspectives. The *procedural* learner naturally focuses on the steps needed to make the project work (what do I need to do?), while the *navigational* learner naturally focuses on the big picture of why the change is being made (how does this work?). To avoid talking past each other throughout the project, each type of learner needs to understand the other's perspective and appreciate the strengths that each brings to the project.

For example, consider these different perspectives if the sponsor says "Web First will be the new standard for all content production processes. All of our content will be developed to first be available on the Web."

The navigator will leave the meeting thinking, "I can see how this works. More people will log in on our site more often to look for new content. Of all our content, the course materials will probably be the most difficult to produce because they are the least uniform, but let's do it. We'll figure it out as we go." The navigator is focusing on the big picture without considering the details of the work.

The procedural listener who hears the same concept may leave the meeting thinking, "What will I have to do to make course materials Web First? When there is an error, I might not see it soon enough and I will have to pull the materials off the Web site to fix it. That will cause rework. If I personalize the intake process to avoid the glitch, it will slow the process down. This doesn't sound efficient, but if that's what we need to do I'll add some extra steps. I need to get the rules in place now so we minimize the rework from glitches." The procedural person is focusing on the detail, deciding how the work will get done.

At this point, both are anxious to get started and feel they are ready to dig into the project work. One has committed and will figure out how to do it along the way. The other is hesitant, but sees a way to accomplish her goal of no errors. Both are unlikely to realize the tough calls they will need to make during project implementation. For example, to gain efficiency, will they be asked to lower quality standards? Each will have a different conclusion based on his or her perception. "To gain speed we will have to accept some glitches." Or, "Our standard of quality is our brand; we will take time to fix all glitches."

The guiding principles discussions provide the bridge to bring both perspectives together to be able to develop a principle that furthers the project goals, is agreed to up front, and fosters understanding. It is important that the discussions not be rushed. It takes extra time at the front end of the project, but it saves a great deal of time and frustration during implementation.

The procedural learner, who most naturally listens for "what do you want me to do," must gain a better understanding of why the change is important. She must understand the big picture and strategic implications of the vision. The navigator, who most naturally listens for "how does this fit into the big picture," must gain an appreciation for the order and structure needed to carry out the vision and transition the change to the organization's regular work plan.

In a nutshell ▷ ▷ ▷

Communication: The discussions to define the key elements and guiding principles open channels for difficult conversations as team members and stakeholders confront their individual interests and assumptions. Storming may surface. Pay attention to the different working styles on your team. Listen to all views.

Collaboration: Shared agreement on key elements and guiding principles supports collaboration. When strategic decision points surface later in the project, you may find you have already worked through the conflict and just need to be reminded of the agreement. Expectations are clarified and trust develops.

Project Management: Use the guiding principles and key elements as the foundational pieces of the project. They are your guideposts for what is most important to accomplish and to keep the project aligned with your organization's mission and vision. Measure your plan against them.

EXERCISE

"[T]here is nothing more difficult to plan, more doubtful of success, nor more dangerous to manage than the creation of a new system. For the initiator has the enmity of all who would profit by the preservation of the old system and merely lukewarm defenders in those who would gain by the new one."

~Machiavelli, *The Prince*, 1513.

Explain how establishing key elements and guiding principles for your project would make your project easier to plan, more certain to succeed, and safer to manage.

Exercise answer

Key elements and guiding principles define the major pieces of the project (as well as what will *not* be delivered), enabling the team to make more realistic time and cost estimates for the project. Defining a set of key elements and guiding principles provides the clarity that is needed to efficiently create the plan and establish the ground rules for making decisions so the plan can be adjusted at any time.

The key elements of a project keep team members focused on specific, defined goals. Guiding principles provide an objective framework for resolving conflict, solving problems, and making decisions throughout the project. This important step reinforces collaboration and increases the likelihood that both the team's goals as well as the organization's strategic goals will be met.

Clearing up expectations and assumptions, creating a shared vocabulary, and gaining consensus on the key elements and guiding principles at the front end of the project foster acceptance from the stakeholders. Keeping a chart of the principles on the meeting room wall is a quick reference for making good decisions throughout the process.

TIME-SAVER

Handout: Standard Guiding Principles for an Organization

Standard Guiding Principles

The following guiding principles may apply across all projects in your organization.

1. Requests for additions or changes to the project scope will first be evaluated on their strategic merit.

2. Processes as well as purchases will be cost-beneficial.

3. We will provide only what we can support.

4. Development will set a priority on staff and customer self-service.

5. Customer expectations will be determined by what our customers tell us, not what we tell each other.

14

Raise a Red Flag If Important Information Is Missing

"The sponsor just asked me how the project is coming along," says the Project Manager. "I'm ready to go, but I feel as if there are too many unmade decisions. I don't want to miss the deadline, but I'm really not comfortable starting with so many unknowns. I don't feel like I can give my team good direction. Why can't the sponsor just spell out what she wants?"

"Step back a minute," suggests the Facilitator. "Your sponsor might be feeling a similar uncertainty. Are you asking for exact specifications as if this were a routine project? It sounds to me like she can only give you ideas because she's breaking new ground and needs your help to first develop a concept of the product. You need to ask some more questions."

Approach "new" projects from a different perspective

When you are asked to begin a project plan but have the funny feeling that you do not have all the information you need, stop and consider whether or not this project is similar to one you have done before or if it is new for your organization.

A project that is similar to one your organization has done before often has clear direction and sufficient detail. It is generally easy to get started. Your organization may already have the experience and understanding to proceed with the project. Your confidence level is high because you know with some degree of certainty what you will encounter along the way. If you feel you are missing information, you often can check documentation from past projects and talk to coworkers to fill in any gaps.

A project that breaks new ground in your organization, however, is often started with many assumptions and unknowns. For example, if you are developing a new product for your Web site, you may not know how it should look or function. You may lack the experience to know what you will encounter as you work through the project.

It is important to remember that the project isn't new only for you. This is a new endeavor for your organization, including your sponsor. Although you might be hearing a directive to begin work to create the product, you might need to slow down and fill in some missing pieces first.

Understand what information is gathered during each phase of a project

Each piece of information you gather during the project management process adds detail and clarifies the piece before it. In the end, you have all the information you need to build and maintain the product or service. It is rare that a complete set of information is handed off at any one point in the process. Most of the time, a fair amount of back and forth is needed to move from one level to the next. It is the *collaboration and consensus building* during these discussions that move you from an idea for a project to its completion.

During the beginning of the project—or initiation phase, you are gathering the high-level view of the project, strategic objectives, requirements, and measures. The information that is generally provided during the initiation phase is developed in these documents:

- business case
- vision
- key elements
- guiding principles
- requirements and measures

By the time you reach the planning stage of the project, you should have a good understanding of what the project is and any expectations, measurements, and requirements that go along with it. During the planning stage, you focus on deciding the best way to approach, execute, and deliver the project. The documents derived from the planning process will be

- scope statement
- work breakdown structure (WBS)
- task analysis

If you believe you are missing critical information before you can plan and execute a project, such as what functions it will have and what you might encounter as you move through the project, chances are there is still some work needed in the initiation phase. Your sponsor might want to be involved in completing the initiation phase or is leaving it up to you to complete. In any case, it is dangerous to proceed to planning and execution without gathering all of the information.

Be clear on the objectives and expectations of the current project

If you find you are missing information from the initiation stage and after talking to the sponsor you realize the information just doesn't exist, *reframe your current project* so that the goal and objectives focus on answering the key questions needed to move out of the initiation phase.

Remember, you can't effectively plan for the completion of a project without the information from the initiation phase. In this case, your best bet is to change your focus from creating the end product to providing the information needed to define it.

Providing options can be helpful and tricky

The trick to answering the questions needed to move you out of the initiation phase is remembering to answer *only* those questions.

For example, there is no doubt that finding or creating samples that reflect the overall objectives of a product are often helpful in breaking through mental blocks. Make sure when you are asked for a sample that you understand specifically what stakeholders are trying to decide. Make sure your samples focus on answering those questions. Be aware of the pull to start developing the project, designing as you go. This can be a very frustrating and costly approach to product development as you will find yourself reworking the product throughout the project as key elements and requirements change. For now, focus your samples on answering only the remaining questions needed to move you out of the initiation phase. Save the detailed development for later in the project when you have all of the needed information.

The process for answering remaining questions might be the following:

▶ to provide sketches of options, find online samples (or something close), survey customers, or find standards that answer the biggest unknowns

- to have further dialogue with the sponsor to refine the options or provide new ones that would result in a concept that may be used for market research
- to define and answer the next set of key questions
- to refine the business case or vision based on feedback from the samples or customer surveys
- to complete a go/no-go evaluation to decide if the project is worth continuing

Whether you are providing information to the project's sponsor or providing information to your team, it's important to take the time to answer the questions needed to complete the vision, the key elements, and the guiding principles before proceeding. Starting to plan and execute a project without a clear sense of direction is a recipe for rework, extra cost, and a poor end result. Be sure your sponsor knows what questions need to be answered and check in frequently as you work through them. This will make sure that your project, when complete, meets the stakeholders' expectations. Document the information and decisions as they unfold.

Where are the handoffs in the project management process?

A handoff implies that a set of instructions, responsibilities, or timelines is passing from one person to another. As a football would be handed off from the quarterback to a running back, a stakeholder might hand off a set of specifications to the project manager to do what it takes to deliver it, or to reach the goal. A handoff implies that the instructions are complete and the project manager can proceed with the next step in the process, whether it is planning, execution, or delivery.

Some projects seem so familiar that handoffs are expected. The business case would be handed off by the sponsor to the project manager. A clear scope statement and project plan would follow. There is little need to return to the sponsor to clarify unknowns.

Most projects that will produce strategic change, however, are not so familiar. The project manager is carving out the path to be able to deliver the project. This process does not travel from handoff to handoff. It is a back-and-forth process, uncovering new information at each step and often returning to prior steps to revise and adjust. For example, new information uncovered while defining the scope of the project may alter the vision. Generating options to get a sense of what the product may look like could challenge assumptions and alter the scope. The project manager is flexible and welcomes this back-and-forth dialogue. It ensures that what is delivered meets the goals of the stakeholders.

In a nutshell ▶ ▶ ▶

Communication: As the project moves from one stage to another, communication between the project manager and sponsor is critical to identify and resolve missing information. As a project manager, you may find you have to first help the sponsor gather information and see options before she can provide the detail you need to plan the approach and execution of the project.

Collaboration: The boundaries of the initiation and planning processes are not clean-cut. The information gathered during these phases builds on itself until you have a complete and detailed description of the project. It is collaboration among the project manager, sponsor, stakeholders, and team members that make this progression possible.

Project Management: As a project manager, it is your responsibility to get the information you need to successfully complete your project. If you feel something is missing, think carefully about what it is and how to best find it. Raise a red flag to your sponsor and work with her and team members until you feel you have the information needed to proceed.

EXERCISE

What signs may indicate that your project is missing critical information and that you should raise a red flag to the sponsor?

Exercise answer

Signs might include

- ▶ Questions for specific information are answered by "I don't know," or "that isn't figured out yet."
- ▶ You cannot describe the goals to your designers and programmers.
- ▶ You cannot estimate how long it will take to build the product.
- ▶ You are unsure how to proceed.
- ▶ Stakeholders have differing opinions about what it should look like.

SECTION III

▼

▼

Planning

It takes as much energy to wish as it does to plan.

~Eleanor Roosevelt

Lessons

15

Understand the Planning Process

"Write the Web redesign project plan," the Project Manager notes in her planner. It should take about a month or two of work, she figures, allowing for some planning meetings and time in between to pull it together. "The plan will be done in a couple of months," she messages to the Facilitator.

"The plan will be done when you deliver the project," comes the reply. "It's not a report that you turn in, it's the road map you keep with you until you get where you're going. And just like following a road map, you might need to make adjustments to your route as you run into new construction or encounter bumps along the road."

Who writes the plan?

The project manager sketches out the major elements of the plan from understanding the business case and the vision. This draft plan is presented to the project planning team, who provides its expertise to work out the detailed plan. Throughout the project, this plan is both a guide and a work in progress for the team.

What forms the basis of the plan?

A project has a start and an end, it produces a unique output, and it is progressively elaborated. These principles form the basis for planning. The documents needed for planning are the business case, the vision, the key elements, and the guiding principles:

- ▸ The *business case* (see Lesson 7) tells you why the project is important to your organization and ensures the hundreds of decisions you make throughout your project move you closer to your organization's purpose.

- ▸ The *vision* (see Lesson 12) shows with broad strokes the end result: what the stakeholders want and what they considered to be a priority when they wrote it. Understand that the vision may change as the project progresses, new technology becomes available, or business needs change.

- ▸ The *key elements* and the *guiding principles* (see Lesson 13) are guideposts for accomplishing the project. Measure your plan against them.

If you don't have these important guides, get them before planning. They provide critical information that will make or break your project plan.

What the project plan is not

- ▸ Perfect and unchanging.
- ▸ The method to deliver *ongoing* work. A project, by definition, must have a beginning and an end. It cannot be ongoing.

Why plan?

The plan is your realistic approach to your project. If the business case tells you why and the vision, key elements, and guiding principles begin to tell you what and how, the plan fills in the rest. Use the plan to clarify what will be accomplished and decide

> how it will be accomplished
>
> who will do the work
>
> where the work will be done
>
> when the work will be done

Treat your plan as a living thing. As you learn more about what you are building, you will want to and should revise how the work will be done, who will do it, and when. This is a normal part of managing any project. *Expect it to happen.*

What are the major elements of the plan?

- ▶ Scope (what you will do; what you promise to deliver)
- ▶ Approach (how you will do it?; also called a Work Breakdown Structure (WBS))

    schedule of tasks and activities (who will do it and when)

    estimates (time and cost estimates)

    quality standards and measures (how you will know you have succeeded—i.e., met expectations)

- ▶ Communication (who needs to know what and when?)
- ▶ Risks and opportunities (what could go wrong and what you will do about it)
- ▶ Resources (what human and nonhuman resources are required)
- ▶ Transition (guidance for how the new project outcome will be added to the organization's regular work plan)

As you work with your team on the elements of the plan, evaluate whether or not you learn anything that should prevent the project from continuing. Is it feasible to deliver the project? Has anything changed? This process is called a go/no-go evaluation.

Expect the plan to change as you work through the project

Every project is unique. You may have worked on projects that are similar, but you have not faced this exact challenge. You are bound to hit some unknowns along the way, and every unknown has the potential to affect your plan. Adjusting to new information and adjusting to unknowns is a normal part of managing projects. Having to adjust the plan is not a sign of failure or poor planning. It would be irresponsible for a project manager to not adjust the plan when presented with new information. The challenge for project managers is to anticipate the changes and minimize their effects. As you create your plan, you can put practices in place that will help identify changes early and manage them with minimal effect.

Some common questions

Why not hold off on your plan until you have all the information you need?

That day will never come. Even if you make an exhaustive spec list and think you have everything set, it is highly likely something will happen along the way—the business need changes, your resources change, or technology changes. You can't control every aspect of a project or the people you are working with. *Accept that there will be changes.* Your job is to create a plan that anticipates and manages changes, not necessarily prevents them.

Why bother making a plan if you know your plan is going to change?

In most cases, your plan is going to change when you begin digging into the details of the project or hit an unknown. In short, you are planning for what you know and changing your plans to handle the unknowns. By failing to plan, you are leaving your project to chance. You are not controlling aspects of the project that you easily could. As time management author Alan Lakein said, "Planning is bringing the future into the present so that you can do something about it now."

Is there a standard form or template for creating a project plan?

Yes. The planning document template is included in the Time-Savers section of this Lesson. This template was developed to provide a simple guide to plan the project and to report the status of the project as it is implemented. We will use it throughout the Planning Section as we detail each important element of a plan.

Teamwork during the planning stage

Your team will move from forming to the storming stage of development as relationships become more comfortable and team members openly question assumptions, opinions, and decisions. The team leader can expect some struggles as members are asked to give up personal preferences and instead focus on meeting shared goals. The storming may surface as disruptive behavior, apathy, antagonism, power struggles, and the like. The next Lesson gives the leader and team members guidance on working through the storming process and seeing it for what it is, the development of trust.

In a nutshell ▸ ▸ ▸

Communication: Expect changes to the plan as more information becomes known or as business needs change. Use collaborative communication skills to make sure that everyone is informed and understands the goals of any change.

Collaboration: Any change in plans or operations can bring about conflict and setbacks in collaborative team building. Allow time to adjust to changes and be certain that goals are established and agreed to.

Project Management: A project has a beginning and an end, it produces a unique output, and it is progressively elaborated. These principles are the basis for planning. The documents needed for planning are the business case, the vision, the key elements, and the guiding principles of the project. These will be anchors to decision making when the inevitable changes to the project occur.

EXERCISE

Identify the basic sections of a plan in the following template. Which documents—business case, vision, key elements, guiding principles—will provide the answers you need to complete each section?

Scope

Approach

Schedule of tasks and activities

Estimates

Quality standards

Communication

Risks and opportunities

Exercise answers

Scope: business case, vision, key elements, guiding principles

Approach: vision, guiding principles

Schedule: business case and prioritization of key elements of vision

Estimates: business case, key elements

Quality standards: vision, guiding principles

Communication: key elements, business case

Risks and opportunities: business case, vision

TIME-SAVER

Template: Project Plan

Project Plan	
Project:	**Initiation Date:**
Project Lead:	**Budget:**
Sponsor:	**Planned Completion Date:**

Project team

Scope

Be sure you understand the scope as described in the business case and vision. Add anything that is missing. What are the requirements?

Introductory paragraph

Summarize the project in a short paragraph that captures the essence of the business case, vision, and key elements documents.

Requirements list

Provide a prioritized list of the project's requirements, including a description of how success for each requirement will be measured. If the project is lengthy or complex, consider completing the project as a series of versions.

Project boundaries

If necessary, state what is not included in the project.

Planning Team

Who do you need to help you plan the project? This is not necessarily your final team.

Person	Department

Approach

Work Breakdown Structure (WBS): How do you break down the project into phases?

After each phase, evaluate whether or not it is still okay to proceed or if the project should end.

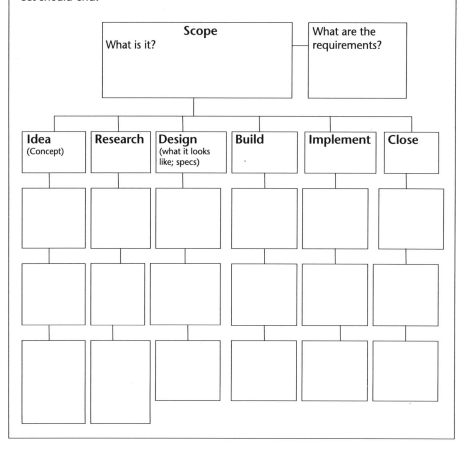

(Deliverables by Phases) The interim milestones	Resource	Est/Act. Cost	Est/Act. Date
Idea (Business Case) What is your concept?			
Research Requirements? Are there best practices to be researched? Do you need to make a model? By when?			
Design What are all the different pieces? What are the specs? Do you need to make a prototype? By when?			
Build Make the product itself. By when? Make a prototype? Do you need a testing plan? By when? When is testing? Quality check.			
Execute Putting it into place. By when? Do you need training plans? Do you need documentation?			
Closure Evaluation. What are lessons learned?			

Project Team and Other Resources

Human and physical resources Staff/roles, budget, technology needs	Est. Cost/ Act.	Est. Date available/ Act. Date

Schedule and Cost

Now that you know who is doing the work and when they are available, (re)estimate the time and/or cost in the Approach interim milestones.

Quality Measures

What are the quality standards and measures?

Standard	How and when will measure

Risk Assessment

Risk and Trigger that would alert you to the risk	Mitigating strategy

Communication Plan

Who needs to know what, when?

What	Who	When

16

Recognize Team Storming

"I don't know what is wrong," the Project Manager laments. "I have a great team. They were working well together. We're through the hardest part of the initiation phase. I was looking forward to moving ahead quickly with the planning and implementation. Now our meetings feel more like hockey games—with power plays, rudeness, and bickering. I feel more like a referee than a project manager."

"Don't worry," says the Facilitator. "Your team is storming. It's temporary."

Storming signals a new stage of growth for the team

The stage of team development called "storming" is true to its name. There are clashes over who has control, uncertainty about what will happen next, destructive elements that challenge the progress and unity of the team, and strikes on the team leader. Just as a thunderstorm refreshes the earth and lightning adds nutrients to the soil, the process of team storming actually promotes the growth of trust. Even though you may feel like running for cover, take the lead, but avoid exercising authoritative control. Here are some tips for handling the storming stage of team development:

Understand what is happening. Storming is a natural progression of team growth. As the team develops relationships and starts to feel comfortable with the project work, members are challenged to give up their self-interests and accept the goals of the team. The politeness that characterized the forming stage gives way as these challenges create conflict and members resort to their primary conflict resolution style: avoidance, accommodation, competition, or compromise.

Be up front about the behaviors. When you see apathy, domination, arguing, loss of interest in attending meetings or being on time, unwillingness to take assignments, cliques and divisive behavior, hostility, lack of productivity, discouragement—especially about "this team stuff"—discuss it openly with the team. Advise the members that they are storming and that this is a natural progression in team development that leads to trust. Rather than be discouraged by it, help them to use collaborative tools to work through it.

Develop the win-win style of collaborative conflict resolution. Encourage argumentative members to listen to the goals of others. Encourage withdrawn members to voice their concerns and goals. Practice gaining consensus as often as possible on simple issues. Gaining a series of agreements on small issues can lift the mood and create momentum.

Establish control. Remind and reinforce team rules and processes. The fact that you have gained consensus in these areas early in your teamwork is a great boost to you now—they provide a point of agreement that will center the team. This establishes control for the benefit of all the team members as they work out their differences and learn to resolve conflict using the win-win style of conflict resolution. (See Lesson 3.)

Encourage the team to share any concerns they have about the project or teamwork. Help team members realize how their concerns can lead to better collaboration. For example, help team members collaborate to work through

- decisions they do not agree with (developing trust)
- changes the project will bring to the organization or to their present jobs and workload (responding positively to change)
- fear of the unknown (letting go of the past and looking forward)
- uncertainty that each person involved on the project is giving the same commitment (holding others—and themselves—accountable)
- concern that their voices will not be heard and their needs not met (resolving conflict about expressing their needs and helping others to express their needs)
- fear that they will be criticized (welcoming feedback and offering constructive criticism)

Resist the temptation to take authoritative control. Let the team work through this stage with your support. They must use the skills that result in trust by practicing them. Get advice from an experienced team facilitator if needed. Remember to lead your team through storming by modeling the behavior you would like to see from them.

After a team works through the storming stage, it becomes a productive work group that is able to make decisions and solve problems quickly and efficiently. A change in the team dynamics may bring back storming. If, for example, the leader or a team member is replaced, or if the organization's strategic priorities are realigned, the team will need to reform and work out control issues. An experienced team will work through this fairly quickly, and the second storming stage should not be as disruptive as the first.

Organizational implications

If your organization is undergoing system-wide changes as it restructures, re-engineers, downsizes, or expands, you will see your staff generally storming as they struggle to make the shift to meet new expectations, learn new processes, establish communication channels, adjust to a new vocabulary, and trust that they have a place in the new system. It is helpful to work with your managers as team leaders. Be sure they are trained and have the basic skills to deal with storming: They should recognize storming, be up-front about the behaviors, deal with conflict in a win-win manner, and establish control without becoming authoritarian. Remember that giving workers a clear connection between their success in their new responsibilities and the success of the organization establishes their purpose, gives meaning to the new work, and mitigates this struggle. (For more information on organizational change, see Lesson 1.)

In a nutshell ▶ ▶ ▶

Communication: Storming challenges communication because it can strip away politeness, respect, and other rules of conduct. It is important to enforce these rules of conduct and encourage open discussion about what is bringing about the storming process.

Collaboration: Storming is a normal and important step in building trust, a key attribute in successful collaboration. Guide the team through storming and do not try to sidestep it or become authoritative. This will delay the ability of the team members to give up their self-interests and develop the win-win orientation needed for trust.

Project Management: Storming develops comfort with change, the ability to deal with the unknown, make trade-offs, and the interdependency skills necessary in collaborative decision making throughout the project work. Projects may fail or be poorly executed if teams are unable to progress through the storming stage.

EXERCISE

What do you advise the team leader to do in these situations?

1. Team members have developed initial relationships, are working well together, and express their pride in how well everything is going.

   a. Feel relieved that things are going so well that storming is not going to happen to this team.

   b. Prepare the team for the storming stage and warn them how awful it will be when it happens.

   c. Be prepared for signs of storming and be ready to handle them.

2. A team member skips team meetings or shows up late and complains that "this team stuff is too boring and nothing is getting done."

   a. Ignore him and praise the members who do attend and come on time.

   b. Assure this member and the team that his feelings are common and a normal part of the team-building process. Reinforce the team rule that meetings be attended by all and will start on time.

   c. Speak to him outside the meeting and try to gain his co-operation by allowing him to skip meetings if he feels they will not be worthwhile to him.

3. One team member has become very argumentative and controlling. You notice that others are unwilling to speak up at the meetings and tend to go along with his demands.

   a. Tell the controlling member if his behavior does not improve he will be replaced on the team. Reinforce this by going to his supervisor.

   b. Speak for the team members who are unwilling to talk to make certain that their goals are presented at meetings.

   c. Go around the table and require that each person provide input while others listen.

4. The team members feel it is unnecessary to thoroughly discuss or gain consensus on rules of conduct. They do not want them posted on the wall during meetings.

   a. Encourage members by explaining that although teams are often reluctant to discuss the rules of conduct, they are later happy they did. Provide a meaningful exercise, such as asking them which rule they think is the most important, that engages the team to think about what all the rules mean.

   b. Skip it. They are right: Professionals are beyond having to agree to rules of conduct.

   c. Simply take consensus without discussing the rules. Everyone knows what they mean and will approve them quickly.

5. The team has moved beyond storming and is working very productively. A team member has left the organization and will be replaced by a new member.

   a. Do nothing. The team is so experienced there is no need to be concerned. The team members will help train and support the new member.

   b. Give the team a quick refresher on the stages of team development and remind them that they will reform and storm and that this experience will help them, as well as the new member, get up to speed.

   c. Assign a team member to take the new member under her wing and try to avoid the need to reform and storm.

Exercise answers

1. *c.* Storming is a normal and important part of the team-building process. It is helpful to both expect it and be prepared for it. If you put into the minds of your team that it is an awful process, you may set them up to resist it rather than learn from it.

2. *b.* When members exhibit storming behavior, it helps the team to discuss it openly as a normal part of the process and work it out as a team. He is probably not the only one feeling this way, so to ignore it or pacify the behavior will not help the team move forward.

3. *c.* Going around the table will allow the silent member the opportunity to speak without being interrupted and signal to the dominant member that she needs to listen. It is most helpful to the team members to develop their ability to communicate their goals. This will not happen if the leader does it for them or provides an unrealistic atmosphere where they will never be challenged.

4. *a.* Getting agreement on these rules is an important building block to team development. When they are discussed in an open manner, assumptions are questioned, vocabulary is defined, and team members get to know one another and what is important to each member. There is a strong temptation to take this consensus quickly to "get it over with." Take the time to make it an exercise that encourages open discussion and brings out what members feel is important.

5. *b.* Expect and prepare the team for the storming process. It should be less intense than the first storming phase. Trying to avoid the storming process will delay the time and effort it takes to establish trust.

17

Encourage Communication

"Everyone seems stressed-out and nobody is getting along. I think we need a break," the Project Manager confides to the Facilitator. "I'll do a draft plan this week. No meetings! You get a vacation."

"Your team is storming," replies the Facilitator. "Consider these meetings the most important you will have. Not only do your planning experts need to communicate with you, they need to communicate with each other. Remember, storming leads to trust, the foundation of collaboration. It's time to master your meeting skills."

The work of the planning team is done in meetings

An efficient and effective plan requires efficient and effective planning meetings in which participants come prepared, express their ideas openly, and come to agreements that are shared and will be followed. Team members question assumptions, voice their priorities, participate in decisions, share quality standards, and begin to understand others' processes. The result is a realistic plan and the foundation of trust to deal with any changes that arise.

This is a good time to go back to the basics and review the guidelines for successful meetings:

- ▸ Create purposeful agendas with realistic time limits.
- ▸ Provide handouts in advance so there is plenty of time to study them.
- ▸ Start and end meetings on time.
- ▸ Stick to the agenda.
- ▸ Use flipchart scribing to focus the discussion.
- ▸ Be sure that all voices are heard and all ideas represented.
- ▸ Record decisions, action items, and meaningful discussions.
- ▸ Follow the rules of conduct and consensus.
- ▸ Follow guiding principles of the project agreed to in advance.
- ▸ Evaluate the meeting and improve the next one.

Consistently following these meeting management basics creates an atmosphere of trust that supports the planning team and allows the project manager to make full use of the team members' expertise. Expectations are positive because the agenda is realistic and is followed. Meetings are productive because informed decisions can be made. Continuity is maintained because important discussion and decisions are recorded. Discussion is focused because there is a mechanism (flipchart) to draw attention to what is meaningful. Individuals talk because they know they will be heard.

Meeting roles

Team members also contribute to the success of the meeting by performing important meeting roles. The first role is that of team member, which is held by all on the team. The other roles are more specialized and are assigned by the leader before each meeting. They give team members the opportunity to support the meeting leader and master meeting skills.

Team Member: Commits to the team by attending meetings and doing the work assigned. Supports the team leader and the other team members by having a consistently positive attitude and adhering to team rules. Participates in discussions by listening as well as speaking. Makes constructive comments and is able to move toward consensus. Focuses on the agenda to help the team stay on track and reach the goals of the meeting.

Recorder: Takes the meeting notes. (See the meeting notes template in Lesson 5.) The notes are an important record of the meeting and include attendance, meeting purpose, any consensus or decisions made, action items assigned to team members, and important discussion items. The notes are to be distributed within 48 hours after the meeting. Team members should review the meeting minutes to be sure decisions were accurately reflected.

Scribe: Makes legible/clear notations on the flipchart if used at the meeting. It is advisable that the scribe have good penmanship skills.

Gatekeeper: Makes sure the meeting stays on time and sticks to its agenda. It is advisable that the person performing this important role have training in how to do it effectively. The gatekeeper warns the leader when time is running out for any agenda topic under discussion. He advises the leader when a discussion has gotten off topic. The gatekeeper must be willing to politely interrupt and move the discussion toward its planned purpose. The gatekeeper also signals to the team when the meeting time is over and strongly advocates that the meeting end.

Team leader: Creates the atmosphere of trust by ensuring that all voices are heard—all team members are encouraged to participate, the discussions are meaningful, and results stick beyond the meeting. Experts tend to have strong views, and the skilled meeting leader will blend these views into a realistic plan. Use the following tips to spur meeting discussions.

Tips on how to deal with issues that may surface during planning meetings

Storming behavior. Review Lesson 16 on storming and accept that it is a natural part of team maturation. The suggestion to avoid or cancel meetings or to become autocratic in running them is tempting to the inexperienced meeting manager. Avoid this temptation by using meetings to master the basics of relationship building and blend the knowledge and skills of the planners to form a realistic plan.

Lack of full participation by all the team members. Some members may be forceful in their opinions and speak often and with authority. Others may hold back or yield to pressure. Others may question the value of their suggestions. The team leader invites and supports a rich, open discussion.

The effect of new information on decisions already made. Team members may feel discouraged if what was already agreed to needs to change because of new information or because the clarification of an assumption causes delay or reworking of the plan. Use these opportunities to praise the team members for uncovering a misconception or for being open to new ideas, especially if the new idea will pay good returns as the project unfolds.

Tips for encouraging communication

Use the following tips to encourage understanding, clear up assumptions, build consensus, move off an issue to the next one, and encourage listening. The project manager's goal as meeting leader is to provide the atmosphere that allows the planning experts to hear each other.

Ask questions that will draw out feelings, opinions, and ideas.

> What do you think about our recent user testing?
>
> You mentioned revising our plan. Why do you feel we should?
>
> Are there other options to solve our problem with testing?

Encourage rephrasing between team members to create a common understanding.

> Are you saying we should find another approach to this project?
>
> Let me see if I understand your position. Are you saying that cross-selling should be our top priority?
>
> This is what I heard. Tell me if I'm correct.

Encourage quiet team members to participate by asking for feedback.

> Tom, can you think of anything that might help us solve this?
>
> Tina, you are the expert in this area, what do you think?
>
> Rick, from your perspective, is there anything we are forgetting?

Ask for a summarization of ideas to encourage communication.

> We came up with a lot of great ideas today. Can someone summarize them before we move on to our next agenda item?
>
> I lost track of the decision we made on this issue. Can someone summarize it for me?
>
> Tina, you do not seem satisfied with this decision. Will you summarize your concerns?

Ask for clarification and examples.

> I didn't understand that last comment. What would happen if a customer forgot his password?
>
> The examples you gave concern our online books. Do they also apply to audio and video?

Test for consensus when it seems like you have agreement.

> It seems like we agree on this issue. Let's go around and get consensus.
>
> Does everyone agree that our search results are the top priority?

Ask for suggestions on actions that would move the project forward.

> How do you think we should organize this phase of the project?
>
> What are some ways we can make our customers aware of these changes?

Explore alternative approaches.

> What are some other ways to solve this usability problem?

> How can we get around this timing problem?

Suggest a procedure that will focus attention and encourage participation.

> Let's put these ideas on a flipchart so we can review them later.

> Let's go around the table and get everyone's thoughts on this issue.

> Let's focus first on the top priority issues. They're highlighted in red.

Confront your feelings as well as those of team members.

> I feel frustrated. I don't think we have all of the information to discuss this today and cannot make a good decision.

> Gary, it seems like you feel dissatisfied with our decision. Is that right?

Question assumptions and limitations that team members are imposing.

> The concern you just raised assumes we have a set number of resources. If we hired additional help, would your opinion change?

> Is there a better way to approach this problem?

Provide a new perspective on a discussion.

> How do you see this working three years from now?

> If you were a customer, how would you react to this news?

Focus on action. Make choices that will move the project forward.

> We have a list of viable alternatives. We need to choose one and move forward.

> We are down to the wire. We need to determine if the request for this feature is a showstopper or if we can accept it.

The work of the planning team is largely done in the meetings. It is important that the members share ideas and expertise so that the plan will be realistic, assumptions can be questioned, and trust developed.

In a nutshell ▶ ▶ ▶

Communication: Planning meetings are rich opportunities to master the basics of meeting management. Provide the atmosphere of sharing: expressing views as well as listening to others. The use of good questions by the meeting leader is a skill to master.

Collaboration: Developing trust is the foundation of collaboration. The controlled process of good meeting management fosters trust by ensuring that all participate, information is shared, and good listening happens.

Project Management: At the planning stage, project management is meeting management. Avoid the temptation to write the plan without input from experts or by talking one-on-one to the experts and assembling their input. Experts need a collaborative atmosphere to talk to each other.

EXERCISE

How might you stimulate discussion in these situations?

Team member behavior	Possible ways to handle
A team member has not said anything during the meeting.	
A team member has dominated the meeting discussion and frequently interrupts.	
A team member has raised a question that has pulled the meeting off topic.	
Team leader notices that someone is uncomfortable with a decision.	
Team members have brought up issues that are important, but off topic.	
A team member is engaged in a side conversation.	
Team member is late to meetings.	
Discussion has come to a standstill. A decision must be made and no new ideas have been raised.	

Exercise answer

Team member behavior	Possible ways to handle
A team member has not said anything during the meeting.	Call on the team member directly: "Jane, what do you think?" Or, go around the table and ask for input from each member.
A team member has dominated the meeting discussion and frequently interrupts.	Ask the group: "What do others think?"
A team member has raised a question that has pulled the meeting off topic.	Gatekeeper should interrupt and remind the group of the agenda item and that this discussion is off topic.
Team leader notices that someone is uncomfortable with a decision.	Encourage the person to express their feelings: "You seem uncomfortable with this decision. Can you explain what it is you disagree with?"
Team members have brought up issues that are important, but off topic.	Ask the scribe to record them on the parking lot flipchart so they are recognized, but do not throw off the meeting.
A team member is engaged in a side conversation.	Stop the discussion and ask the person if it would help to clarify the previous point that was made.
Team member is late to meetings.	Start the meeting on time. Do not catch the person up on the discussion. If the person continues to be late to meetings, speak to him outside the meeting, referencing the meeting rules that all have agreed to.
Discussion has come to a standstill. A decision must be made and no new ideas have been raised.	Focus on action. "We need to make a decision. We have discussed the issue thoroughly and it is time to make a choice."

TIME-SAVERS

Handout: Characteristics of a Good Team Member

Characteristics of a Good Team Member

Friendly, pleasant, and well liked

Listens to and accepts the views of others

Supports teammates and builds morale

Communicates clearly

Attends all meetings and is on time

Gives credit to and praises others' contributions

Willing to work to achieve consensus

Bases decisions on objective data

Does his/her fair share of the work

The Role of the Team Leader

Establishes the purpose of the meeting
and prepares the agenda.

Leads the meeting, keeping to the topics and
time limits on the agenda.

Keeps the group focused on the purpose of the meeting.

Seeks participation from all team members.
Encourages discussion.

Assigns recorder, scribe, and gatekeeper roles.

Builds relationships while accomplishing agenda items.

Shares experience and knowledge.
Asks for facts, opinions, and suggestions from the team.

Reaches consensus on important decisions.

Assigns tasks and action items, giving deadlines.

Handles administrative tasks.

Has the team evaluate the meeting during the last five minutes.
What went well? What could be improved next time?

18

Trust Your Planning Team

"Here's the rough draft of the plan I wrote for the Sponsor," says the Project Manager. "It includes every key element of the vision. Any feedback for me before I review it with the Sponsor and get into the details with the planning team?"

"This is okay for a rough plan," says the Facilitator, "but to be confident that the project is feasible you need to know what your experts agree to—what they say is realistic."

The planning team—who they are and what they bring to the table

The project manager is charged with producing a project plan that is effective, efficient, and feasible. This plan is largely worked out with a planning team and includes agreements on approach, estimates, process, resource use, and quality standards.

The planning team has an important role in creating the plan. They are experts who advise the project manager on the details of the plan elements. The planning goal is to have a realistic approach to delivering the project.

The planning team should consist of stakeholders with a vested interest in the project's outcome, decision makers with authority to support the work, and advisers with relevant experience and knowledge.

Planning team roles	What they bring to the team
Stakeholders who will be affected by the outcome of the project, including experts who represent the major interests of various departments (for example: design, technology, content, creation and production, customer experience, etc.)	They understand the key elements of the vision and goals of the project and how the organization will measure project results. They understand the requirements that define what is to be delivered.
Decision makers, including managers, supervisors, and others who assign priorities and resources	They have the authority to make time and resources available to complete the project and will shape the communication plan.
Advisers with first-hand experience and expertise to implement the project plan and advise on the risks and opportunities of the project	They include staff members who actually do the work. They know, for example, how long a task will take or what a supply will cost and recommend how best tasks can be achieved. They can give advice on whether or not outsourcing will be needed to meet a crucial technology deadline or if a bulk purchase made ahead of schedule will avoid a costly price increase later in the year.

What guidance the planning team provides

The planning team is a source of valuable information for the project plan. Count on them to provide insight and expertise on many issues. For example,

- ▶ whether or not the requirements are realistic for the time frame being considered
- ▶ what other approaches are available
- ▶ what options exist for outsourcing of some or all of the work
- ▶ whether or not there are actually enough resources available to do the project in the necessary time frame
- ▶ what space, equipment, technology, documentation, training, or other needs must be taken into account
- ▶ who needs to be kept informed about the project's progress and issues, how, and when
- ▶ what quality standards must be used and how they will be measured
- ▶ if there are additional risks or opportunities not identified in the business case as well as strategies for dealing with them
- ▶ what determines the priorities of the project's features, and the version in which each can be rolled out
- ▶ what else, if anything, needs to be considered (i.e., has anything been overlooked in the project concept?)

Plan elements	What is determined
Scope (see Lesson 19)	Includes a short summary capturing the essence of the business case, vision, and key elements document; a prioritized requirements list with measures for success; and a statement, if necessary, of what is *not* included in the project.
Initial approach (see Lesson 20)	Should the project be out-sourced? Or developed in-house?
Structure of the project (WBS) (see Lesson 20)	How the project will be completed, i.e., the methodology of steps or process that will be followed. The standard methodology for project work proceeds through six stages: Idea (business case and vision), Research, Design, Build, Implement, and Close.
Project tasks (see Lesson 21)	What work or steps need to be taken within each stage of the project? These are the interim deliverables, and completion of these measures the progress of the project.
Resources required (see Lesson 23)	Estimates of the staff time and other resources required. Are there space, equipment, technology, documentation, training, or other requirements?
Time and cost estimates (see Lessons 24, 25)	Realistic estimates of time and cost best come from the experts who do the tasks on a regular basis. Listen to them.
Quality standards (see Lesson 26)	Standards for quality and how it will be measured.
Communication needs (see Lesson 27)	Who needs to know what information, which method of communication (e-mail, face-to-face meeting, report, etc.) is needed, and when it needs to be received.
Risks and opportunities (see Lesson 28)	Additional risks or opportunities not identified in the business case; strategies to mitigate the risks and take advantage of opportunities.
Priority of project features so that the project can be delivered or rolled out in versions	If a project is complex (scope is large or may require advanced technology), the deadline for completion is short, or the cost needs to be spread over time, delivering versions is an efficient option. Each version delivers a subset of the features required for the entire project and is handled as a project in its own right. Whatever is learned from producing one version is applied to the next as the processes become more efficient and productive.

See the sample project plan template provided at the end of this lesson.

Things to anticipate and avoid

Storming. The storming behavior that signals this progressive step of team building will surface. In fact, it may already be evident. Follow the steps outlined in Lesson 16 to work through the storming period and build trust.

Great ideas/new options. Record these as they arise and weigh them strategically against the goals of the vision.

Conflicts in priority and process. The planning phase will uncover more clearly what the stakeholders really want. Priorities and processes that were agreed to may be challenged as terms and assumptions are clarified, new information emerges, and estimates (what the work will cost and the time it will take) are realized. This is the time to focus on shared goals so that collaboration rather than competition prevails.

Discussion and debate. This can be a sign of progress and also of bewilderment as past decisions are questioned. This is the time you are grateful that guiding principles have been established. Keep them posted on the wall and refer to them to anchor your discussions.

Many possible approaches. The team will need to agree on one and move on, which is sometimes difficult. The consensus-building skills the team has practiced in routine activities provide the foundation to reach agreement more effectively and move on. Also, realize that if the agreed-upon approach proves unfeasible, the plan can and will be changed.

An overly complex plan. Keep it simple; minimize overhead. Don't lose sight of the forest for the trees. Focus on the goals and the major milestones or steps toward reaching those goals. The detailed steps will be worked out by those doing the project work.

The struggle between ideal planning and accurate planning. How realistic are the time estimates? The cost estimates? The resource estimates? Stakeholders not "in the trenches" may base decisions on their assumptions of how long something "should" take or how much something "should" cost. Others may "pad" or add extra time and cost beyond realistic estimates to cover unknowns. Encourage realistic estimating with the understanding that as more information is known, the plan can change. This is not encouraging scope creep (the accumulation of unscheduled changes that overtaxes the resources of the project); it is the normal process of uncovering facts. The more open and honest the discussion, the more realistic the plan.

Planning with self-imposed limitations. Realize all your options. Question assumptions and encourage open dialogue to ensure that all voices are heard and new ideas, technology, approaches, etc., are strategically considered.

Scope, cost, schedule, or quality changes. Manage these together. Adjusting the plan for one generally affects the others. See Lesson 19 on scope.

The value of the guiding principles document

Conflicting goals will show themselves in the planning process as priorities and time constraints are identified and assumptions are questioned. The guiding principles document will be a valuable reference. You will want to have it posted on the meeting room wall as a quick check on what was agreed to and how you will resolve issues and concerns.

Once the detailed plan is finished and approved, the planning team's work has ended and the project leader assembles an implementation team to carry out the plan.

In a nutshell

Communication: Both the planning and meeting processes use valuable tools for communicating results. The project plan document, the agenda, meeting flipcharts, and the meeting notes are designed to convey information in a specific and meaningful way. Master their use for successful planning.

Collaboration: The planning team determines the realistic approach to deliver the project: the outcome of the shared vision. Priorities and contribution of effort become more clear. The guiding principles document aids the collaborative effort; it is a quick reference for what the team has already agreed it will use to guide decisions.

Project Management: A planning team develops the project plan and the work is done largely within meetings. Meeting management skills as well as project planning skills are key to successful planning.

EXERCISES

1. Create a guiding principle for how you will approach suggestions for changes to a project.

2. Using the meeting agenda form, create an agenda for a first planning meeting. Assume there are 8 participants and 3 are new to the project and the team.

   Who are the participants?

   What is the purpose?

   What are the agenda items and time limits?

Exercise answers

1. Requests for additions or changes to the project will first be evaluated on their strategic merit.

2. Participants: The planning team of stakeholders, decision makers, and advisers assigned to the project.

   Purpose: To introduce the planning team members

                  Overview of the planning process

   Agenda with time limits

   1. Introductions and icebreaker (15 min)

   2. Goals of the planning team: how we will work (15 min)

   3. Consensus on the Rules of Conduct (25 min)

   4. Wrap and agenda items for next meeting (5 min)

TIME-SAVERS

Template: Project Plan

Project Plan	
Project:	**Initiation Date:**
Project Lead:	**Budget:**
Sponsor:	**Planned Completion Date:**

Project team

Scope

Be sure you understand the scope as described in the business case and vision. Add anything that is missing. What are the requirements?

Introductory paragraph

Summarize the project in a short paragraph that captures the essence of the business case, vision, and key elements documents.

Requirements list

Provide a prioritized list of the project's requirements, including a description of how success for each requirement will be measured. If the project is lengthy or complex, consider completing the project as a series of versions.

Project boundaries

If necessary, state what is not included in the project.

Planning team

Who do you need to help you plan the project? This is not necessarily your final team.

Person	Department

Approach

Work Breakdown Structure (WBS): How do you break down the project into phases?

After each phase, evaluate whether or not it is still okay to proceed or if the project should end.

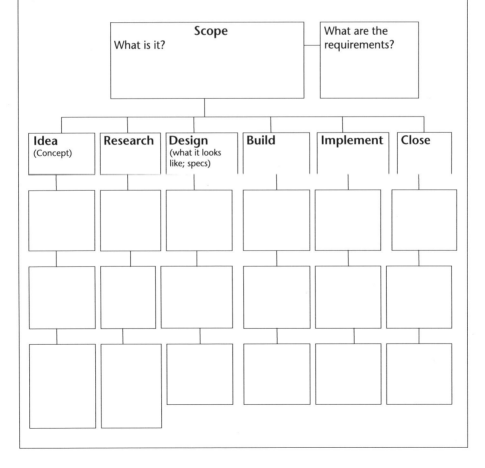

(Deliverables by phases) The interim milestones	Resource	Est/Act. Cost	Est/Act. Date
Idea (Business case) What is your concept?			
Research Requirements? Are there best practices to be researched? Do you need to make a model? By when?			
Design What are all the different pieces? What are the specs? Do you need to make a prototype? By when?			
Build Make the product itself. By when? Make prototype? Do you need a testing plan? By when? When is testing? Quality check.			
Implement Putting it into place. By when? Do you need training plans? Do you need documentation?			
Closure Evaluation. What are lessons learned?			

Project team and other resources

Human and physical resources Staff/roles, budget, technology needs	Est. Cost/ Act.	Est. Date available/ Act. Date

Schedule and cost

Now that you know who is doing the work, and when they are available, (re)estimate the time and/or cost in the Approach interim milestones.

Quality measures

What are the quality standards and measures?

Standard	How and when will measure

Risk assessment

Risk and Trigger that would alert you to the risk	Mitigating strategy

Communication plan

Who needs to know what, when?

What	Who	When

Template: Meeting Agenda

Agenda	
Project Name:	**Meeting Date:**
Project Manager:	**Meeting Time:**
Meeting Leader:	**Meeting Location:**
Recorder:	**Timekeeper:**

Meeting participants

Meeting purposes

•

Decisions needing consensus

•

Agenda (with time limits)

1.

Attachments

•

Meeting Guidelines

• *Start and end on time.*
• *Encourage participation.* "Talkers" should try listening more and "listeners" should speak up.
• *Welcome bad news* as an opportunity to do risk management and problem solving. Do not be afraid to identify what is going wrong.
• *Encourage brainstorming.*
• *Use good meeting manners.* Do not make personal put-downs. Do not interrupt the speaker.
• *Use good listening skills.* Try to understand the entirety of what is being said, not just what you want to hear. Ask questions if you don't understand. Do not pre-judge on the basis of past history.
• *Use good speaking skills.* When communicating an idea, use common language so the listeners understand. Give people time to communicate an answer to your questions. Try to be succinct.
• *Reward input.* Celebrate contributions.
• *Keep the meeting focused.*

ICLE thanks Marianne Clauw for permission to reprint this agenda template.

Standard Guiding Principles

The following guiding principles may apply across all projects in your organization.

1. Requests for additions or changes to the project scope will first be evaluated on their strategic merit.

2. Processes as well as purchases will be cost beneficial.

3. We will provide only what we can support.

4. Development will set a priority on staff and customer self-service.

5. Customer expectations will be determined by what our customers tell us, not what we tell each other.

19

Define the Project's Scope

"I know scope is what I promise to deliver" says the Project Manager. "What can I do to keep my promise?"

"Scope describes the requirements the project needs to fulfill," replies the Facilitator. "The project is shaped by the balance between what you are required to deliver, its quality, how much time you are allotted, and how much you can spend. As long as you keep that balance, you will keep your promise."

Scope statement

The project plan document begins with a scope statement. The scope is written by the project manager and is based on the requirements set forth in the business case, elaborated in the vision statement, and summarized in the key elements list. The scope statement identifies the items the team promises to deliver, such as features, functions, training plans, and documentation, and the priority of each. It includes the quality, cost, and time measurements that will be used to gauge the success of your project. It also specifically states what the project does *not* include.

Although scope statements vary by project or organization, it's helpful to break the scope statement for your project into three sections: an introductory paragraph, a requirements list (with measurements, priorities, and version), and boundaries.

Introductory paragraph

The introductory paragraph summarizes your project. It is a reminder of the big picture and captures the essence of the business case and key elements. For example, the scope statement's introductory paragraph for a Web redesign project could be the following:

> The project will deliver an up-to-date Web site as well as the in-house processes and technology required for departments to think Web First when they are developing their products and policies.

Requirements list

The requirements list describes the project's deliverables. For example, the initial requirements list for the Web redesign could be:

- ▶ Underlying structure is the latest technology and easy to upgrade.
- ▶ Customer accesses for himself what he wants and the way he wants to view it.
- ▶ Log-in speed is less than a second.
- ▶ Content is tagged with key numbers, is accurate, and is up-to-date.
- ▶ Marketing is personalized and cross-sale advertising is available on the site.
- ▶ Customers recognize our organizational brand instantly.
- ▶ Functions are easy to navigate and require minimal training to use.
- ▶ Search results appear quickly and are relevant.
- ▶ Courses are offered online for credit.
- ▶ The Web site provides subsites for subject areas.
- ▶ Customer service is self-serve.

▸ Web site is structured so that we can create customized subscriptions to electronic content for particular customer groups.

The requirements list, along with key measures, will be used to gauge whether or not the project is completed. It will be referred to when the sponsor signs off on the project during the closing process.

Assigning priority and key measurements

The project manager works with the project sponsor and project team to decide the priority of the requirements. Base the priorities on what will move the project closest to its eventual goals and what is *foundational* for the project, factoring in the logical, efficient progression of the work and the organization's budget, available resources, operational needs, etc.

Key measurements are also defined to help the project manager and team understand the specific goals they are trying to meet.

Here is the prioritized list of requirements with measurements for the Web redesign project.

1. Content is tagged with key numbers. A process keeps the information accurate and up-to-date. *Measurement:* Every piece of content is classified with a key number.

2. Functions are easy to navigate and require minimal training to use. *Measurement:* User testing indicates users are very satisfied with the usability of our site.

3. Underlying structure is the latest technology and easy to upgrade. *Measurement:* All pages are converted to asp.net and the Web site can be upgraded on a three-month cycle.

4. Searches are fast and relevant. *Measurement:* Search results appear in less than one second for users on a high-speed internet connection.

5. Log-in speed is fast. *Measurement:* Log-in speed is less than one second for users with a high-speed internet connection.

6. Courses are offered online for credit. *Measurement:* Credit codes are added to webcasts and information is tracked so users can download certificates of completion.

7. Web site provides subsites for subject areas. *Measurement:* All content is displayed and sorted by key number.

8. Customer service is self-serve. *Measurement:* The percentage of telephone calls compared to online use for common transactions decreases.

9. Customer recognizes our organization's brand instantly. *Measurement:* User testing indicates users instantly recognize our products and Web site.

10. Marketing is personalized and cross-sale advertising is available on the site. *Measurement:* 15 percent of sales on our site are initiated by clicking on a customized ad.

11. Customized subscriptions. *Measurement:* None available. We have not finalized plans for this area.

12. Customer accesses for himself what he wants and the way he wants to view it. *Measurement:* None available. We have not finalized plans for this area.

Planning and releasing the project in versions

The project plan provides a realistic approach to delivering the project on time and on budget. If the entire scope of the project is too complex or costly to deliver in the time required, consider creating and releasing the end result in versions, or planned successive stages. Each version delivers project features managed and implemented as a separate project.

The Web Redesign Project Versions table on page 184 shows the Web redesign project with the priority of the features and how they are grouped. Because this project was so complex, we decided to release the core (top priority) features first. Notice that the items in the Core Version have more detail than the items scheduled for the future. Be aware that, as each version is completed, the remaining list will be reviewed again for priority and new developments. Features for future versions can be rearranged based on business and customer needs.

Web Redesign Project Versions	
Version	**Requirements/features to be delivered. Explanation for priority assigned are in italic**
Core version (complete first)	Content is tagged with key numbers. A process keeps the information accurate and up-to-date. *Measurement:* Every piece of content is classified with a key number. *This should be done immediately so that it does not delay any programming for site development. The key numbers serve as a foundation for several pieces of later development.* Functions are easy to navigate and require minimal training to use. *Measurement:* User testing indicates the users who are testing are very satisfied with the usability of our site. *This is required throughout all development on the project and will drive the technology research and decisions.* Underlying structure is the latest technology and easy to upgrade. *Measurement:* All pages are converted to .net, site can be upgraded on a 3-month cycle. *The site needs to be programmed into the latest programming language to facilitate any changes or new development.* Searches are fast and relevant. *Measurement:* Search results appear in less than one second for users on a high speed connection. *This will combine the latest technology and the content tagging. It is a high customer priority.* Log-in speed is fast. *Measurement:* Log in speed is less than one second for users with a high speed connection. *This makes use of the latest technology and is a high customer priority.* Courses are offered online for Continuing Education (CE) credit. *Measurement:* Credit codes are added to webcasts and information is tracked so users can download certificates of completion. *This responds to high customer demand and organizational need.* Web site provides sub sites for subject areas. *Measurement:* All content is displayed and sorted by key number. *These structures pull from the key number system.*

Future versions	Customer service is self-serve. *Measurement:* Online sales increase 10%. Invoices paid online increase 20%. Calls for mail tracking and address changes decrease 20%.
	Next logical progression for use of technology and meeting customer and organization's needs.
	Begin implementation of goal that customer recognizes ICLE brand instantly.
	New design aspects of site come to play so customer has not been shocked by a changing look as well as changing functionality.
	Fully implement customer recognizes ICLE brand instantly.
	Working now with redesigned and redeveloped site.
	Customized subscriptions. *Measurement:* None available. We have not finalized plans for this area.
	Moving into new, innovative features.
	Customer accesses for himself what he wants and the way he wants to view it. *Measurement:* None available. We have not finalized plans for this area.
	Moving into new, innovative features.

Boundaries

It is also helpful to say what is *not* in the scope of the project, outside the boundary of the project. For example, the Web redesign will not include the development of our e-newsletter or our studio seminar products. These will be developed by separate teams.

Sample scope statement

A plan document with a sample scope statement is provided in the Time-Savers section of this lesson.

Balance of scope, time, cost

Scope, time and cost are commonly referred to as the triple constraint for your project. Just as your requirements list is prioritized, the project sponsor should tell you the priority of the constraints. Which is the top priority?

▸ Scope? We must offer certain features or we will lose customers.

▸ Cost? We have a limited or fixed budget.

▸ Time? We will have it on display at the October conference.

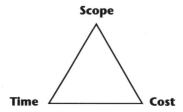

The priorities will govern the balance of the constraints. When a change is made to one of the constraints, you must consider making adjustments to the other two. For example, if the scope of the project changes, then the project's schedule (time) and cost must adjust to keep the balance. If it is a priority to offer rich features to the customer, then consider that the time and cost of the project will need to increase. If the constraints are not kept in balance, your project is at risk to be delayed or have cost overruns.

Although people often limit their discussions to scope, cost, and time they are not the only variables in a project that might be affected when a change is made. For example, quality and risk are two areas of your project that can also be affected by change. As you begin planning and executing your project, be sure you consider all of the areas that might be affected by change and be sure to consider them whenever your plan is adjusted. Time (schedule), cost (resources), quality, and risk are handled in Lessons 24–26 and 28.

In a nutshell

Communication: Scope defines what the project manager promises to deliver. It is easier to deliver on that promise if you understand what each deliverable requires. Make sure you identify and agree on priorities and measurements for each deliverable so that you, your team, and your sponsor know when you have met your goals.

Collaboration: Establishing a realistic requirements list that clearly indicates priorities, measurements for success, and versions will help establish trust between you, your stakeholders, and your team. Evaluate the deliverables on their strategic merit. Challenge your team and the stakeholders to clearly define each deliverable and confirm that each furthers the goals of the project.

Project Management: Scope, cost, and time must be in balance to complete your project successfully. If the scope of your project changes, the cost and time must also adjust. Scope, cost, and time are the most common constraints to consider. However, many project managers also factor in quality and risk.

EXERCISE

Imagine you are planning to repaint the interior of your house. Your house is two stories. The first floor contains the kitchen, dining room, and bath. The second floor contains the master bedroom, office, and guest room. Draft a scope statement for this project.

Exercise answer

Your scope statement for a painting project might include the following:

Scope statement

Introductory paragraph

Summarize the project in a short paragraph that captures the essence of the business case, vision, and key elements documents.

The interior of the house will be painted before the upcoming holidays. The rooms scheduled for painting include the first floor—kitchen, dining room, bath—and the second floor—office, master bedroom, guest room. The goal is to introduce a coordinated color palette to the house, which is currently painted white.

Requirements list

Provide a prioritized list of the project's requirements, including a description of how success for each requirement will be measured. If the project is lengthy or complex, consider completing the project as a series of versions.

Version 1

Hire designer to help select color palette.
Measurements: Design cost must be below $250. The palette must factor in all of the rooms to be painted.

Paint first floor—kitchen, dining room, and bath.
Measurements: There should be no visible paint runs or other mistakes. Painting must be completed by August 1 to work around house guests arriving.

Version 2

Paint second floor—office, master bedroom and guest room.
Measurements: There should be no visible paint runs or other mistakes. Painting must be completed by December 1 to be ready for the holidays.

Project boundaries

If necessary, state what is not included in the project.

This project does not include repainting the upstairs bath or refurnishing any of the rooms.

TIME-SAVER

Sample: Scope Statement

Scope Statement

Project Plan	
Project:	Initiation Date:
Project Lead:	Budget:
Sponsor:	Planned Completion Date:

Project team

Scope

Be sure you understand the scope as described in the business case and vision. Add anything that is missing. What are the requirements?

Introductory paragraph

Summarize the project in a short paragraph that captures the essence of the business case, vision, and key elements documents.

The Web redesign project will deliver an up-to-date Web site as well as the in-house processes and technology required for departments to think Web First when they are developing their products and policies.

Requirements list

Provide a prioritized list of the project's requirements, including a description of how success for each requirement will be measured. If the project is lengthy or complex, consider completing the project as a series of versions.

Version 1

Content is tagged with key numbers. A process keeps the information accurate and up-to-date. *Measurement:* Every piece of content is classified with a key number.

> This should be done immediately so that it does not delay any programming for site development. The key numbers serve as a foundation for several pieces of later development.

Functions are easy to navigate and require minimal training to use. *Measurement:* User testing indicates users are very satisfied with the usability of our site.

> This is required throughout all development on the project and will drive the technology research and decisions.

Underlying structure is the latest technology and easy to upgrade. *Measurement:* All pages are converted to asp.net, site and can be upgraded on a 3-month cycle.

> The site needs to be programmed into the latest programming language to facilitate any changes or new development.

Searches are fast and relevant. *Measurement:* Search results appear in less than one second for users on a high speed connection.

> This will combine the latest technology and the content tagging. It is a high customer priority.

Log-in speed is fast. *Measurement:* Log-in speed is less than one second for users with a high speed connection.

> This makes use of the latest technology and is a high customer priority.

Courses are offered online for CE credit. *Measurement:* Credit codes are added to Webcasts and information is tracked so users can download certificates of completion.

> This has high customer demand and organizational need.

Web site provides sub sites for subject areas. *Measurement:* All content is displayed and sorted by key number.

> These structures pull from the key number system.

Version 2

Customer service is self-serve. *Measurement:* Online sales increase 10%. Invoices paid online increase 20%. Calls for mail tracking and address changes decrease 20%.

> This is the next logical progression for use of technology and meeting customer and organization's needs.

Begin implementation of goal that customer recognizes ICLE brand instantly. New design aspects of site come into play so customer has not been shocked by a changed look as well as changed functionality.

Version 3

Fully implement customer recognizes ICLE brand instantly.

> We are working now with redesigned and redeveloped site.

Version 4

Customized subscriptions. *Measurement:* None available. We have not finalized plans for this area.

> We are moving into new, innovative features.

> **Version 5**
>
> Customer accesses for himself what he wants and how he wants to view it.
> *Measurement:* None available. We have not finalized plans for this area.
>
> >   Moving into new, innovative features.
>
> **Project boundaries**
>
> If necessary, state what is not included in the project.
> The Web redesign will not include the development of our Top Tips video
> segments or our studio seminar products. These will be developed by separate
> teams.

RECOMMENDED READING

Brenner, Rick. "How to Say 'No': A Tutorial for Project Managers."
   Chaco Canyon Consulting, http://www.chacocanyon.com/essays/
   sayingno.shtml.

20

Decide How to Approach Your Project

"What's a good approach for a project that deals with complexity and conflicting priorities?" asks the Project Manager. "If our plan is a road map, it feels like I've got to schedule Niagara Falls and the Grand Canyon in the same trip. How do I manage that?"

"Niagara Falls and the Grand Canyon?" the Facilitator asks. "Let's break it down. You might do some research to find travel alternatives, design a cost effective trip, and build in some sightseeing along the way. Or, go to Niagara Falls this year, Grand Canyon next year. You can benefit from the planning for your first trip to make the second trip even more fun."

Taking a closer look

As you approach something, you get closer to it. You see the components in more detail. The scope has described what you will deliver. In the approach, you describe how you will research, build, and implement the project. This includes breaking down the work into a sequence of steps that can be carried out by the team and controlled by the project manager.

> *"The secret of getting ahead is getting started. The secret of getting started is breaking your complex overwhelming tasks into small manageable tasks, and then starting on the first one."*
>
> ~attributed to Mark Twain.

Creating a work breakdown structure (WBS)

After you and your team understand the project's big picture, you are ready to begin mapping out the approach you will take to complete it. Breaking down the project to identify all the deliverables for your project is the best way to do this. The resulting diagram of this breakdown is called a work breakdown structure—or WBS. Just as an organizational chart is a hierarchical representation of a company, a WBS is a hierarchical representation of a project. It is not a list, but a graphical representation.

Your WBS will be used as a basis for setting your schedule and tracking your project. (See Lessons 21–24). Creating the WBS is a team exercise. The feedback and discussion that are generated as you work through the tasks of your project are invaluable. Don't try to do it alone. Creating a WBS does not have to be complex. No software is required. Keep it simple and try this exercise using sticky notes on a wall. Follow the pattern in the Keep it simple—try sticky notes diagram that follows.

Keep it simple—try sticky notes

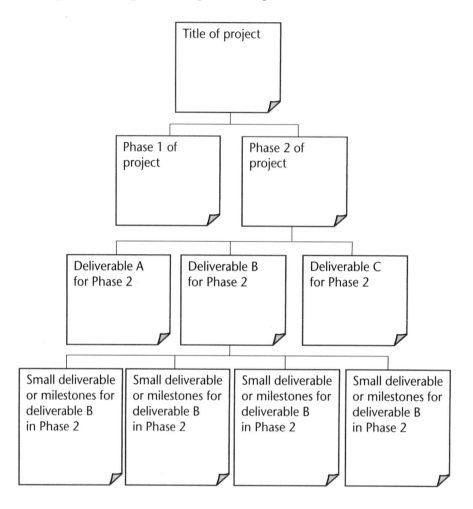

In the next sections, we will use "summer vacation" as a simple project that will walk you through building a WBS.

Step 1: To begin your WBS, write the title of your project on a sticky note and put it on the wall.

Step 2: Decide on the highest level outcomes you want to use to track your project and write those areas on sticky notes. A typical WBS uses the standard project lifecycle outcomes (idea, research, design, build, implement, and close) as the highest level. Others use the main deliverables of a project. In either case, 100 percent of the work required to complete your project should fall under one of these main headings. Decide on this level before moving on to lower levels.

The following describes a typical project life cycle that is often used as the highest level of our WBS and includes questions to ask to help determine what work may be involved in each of these major areas.

▶ Idea

Do you understand the business case and vision? Can you describe the concept and the business value to the organization?

▶ Research

What do the requirements entail? Are there best practices to be researched? Do you need to make a model? By when?

▶ Design

What are all the different pieces? What are the features and functions? What are the specifications? Do you need to make a prototype? By when?

▶ Build

How and when you will make the product itself, or the prototype? Do you need a testing plan? By when? When is the testing to be done? What is planned for quality checking?

▶ Implement

How and when you will put the product in place? Do you need training plans? Do you need documentation?

▶ Close

Evaluate the product and the process. What are the lessons learned? What will go into the next version?

Although there are some typical approaches for projects, take a minute to think about what will work well for you and your team. Here are some questions to consider as you begin to determine your approach.

▸ Think about your project constraints (scope, cost, time, quality, risk). Which are flexible? Which are not?

▸ Think about your team. Will training be needed? Is outsourcing an option?

▸ Does your project have many unknowns that should be thought about separately?

As you choose an approach, think about the issues that are critical to your project. Choose an approach that helps focus attention to those areas.

The following diagram shows the project phases for our summer vacation project.

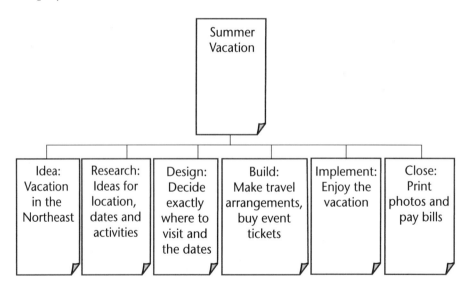

Step 3: Break down the project phases into smaller deliverables and milestones (significant steps accomplished). Phrase your deliverables and milestones as nouns. They are parts of the project you are delivering to show progress—they are not activities. Each level should be more detailed than the level above it. Ideally, you want to end at a level that is specific enough for you to gauge project progress. A good rule of thumb

is that the deliverables in your WBS should take no less than one day and no more than two weeks to create. Talk to your team to decide what level of specificity is best for you. As you work on lower levels of your WBS, consider the following:

▸ Are there interim deliverables to be reviewed by customer representatives, the project sponsor, or others to make sure that the project team builds the right product?

▸ Are there deliverables outside the product itself, for example, staff training guides or new hardware requirements?

▸ Are any deliverables required to maintain the product once it's up and running, e.g., usage and error reports?

▸ Where will user testing and other quality checking occur?

▸ Are there big unknowns that need research?

▸ Are there milestones you want to include to help you monitor the project?

The lowest level of your WBS is called a *work package*.

A sample WBS that shows the *design phase* of planning a summer vacation might look like:

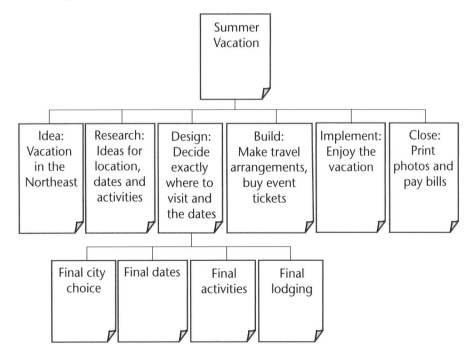

Working with the planning team

Do not underestimate the value of including your team in creating the WBS. Planning is a hands-on approach. Meetings are alive with activity, suggestions, and "I didn't know that" realizations as information is shared and confirmed. Meetings can also include times when disbelief, anger, power struggles, and fear threaten the collaboration effort. Here are some practical tips that support productive planning meetings.

1. It is okay for the project manager to sketch a possible approach to use as a draft model. This should not be detailed and would not include any estimates of time, cost, or resources. It would simply be a place to focus the group's attention and invite dialogue.

   For example, the project manager might recommend the top levels of the WBS to begin the discussion.

2. Post the *guiding principles* on the wall. Weigh approaches and decisions against them. This will save time and lessen the stress of managing strong opinions.

   For example, a guiding principle for the Web redesign is Web First—or developing content and products with the Web site as the main product. Other products can spin off the Web. Does the approach result in functions and processes that are developed using Web technologies and online components? An approach that includes creating print products and then posting them to the Web site, although comfortable and efficient at this time, would be ruled out, not by the project manager, but by the guiding principle.

3. Be certain that the business case, vision, and guiding principles are up-to-date. By the time a project is ready for planning, the business case may have been revised or the organization's needs may have changed. This would require an update to the vision, key elements, and guiding principles. The project manager must be alert to changes in general and be part of a communication loop that is kept informed of changes.

For example, passage of a new law or a downturn in the economy may result in the change of business relationships, budget, or organizational structure. There would be a corresponding change in the vision, which may affect how the project is approached. Perhaps it was scheduled to be outsourced on a quick time frame. A change in funding may require the work to be done in-house in a longer time frame and provide less functionality. The core of the vision, Web First, however, would remain in tact.

4. Provide hands-on experiences that help the team break down the work and use their expertise.

   For example, brainstorm the major deliverables. For the Web redesign, these might include: programs that are rewritten in a new programming language, a new design for the navigation for the site, the application of key numbers to all content. Ask the meeting's scribe to record them on sticky notes. Apply each sticky note deliverable to the applicable phase.

5. Keep administrative work for the team to a minimum. The project manager should translate the decisions and output of the team into the project plan document and give it to the team for review before the next meeting.

   For example, take the information from the sticky note exercise and enter it into the project plan document.

Here is an example of a sticky note exercise to create a Web redesign WBS. It shows only the *Build* phase.

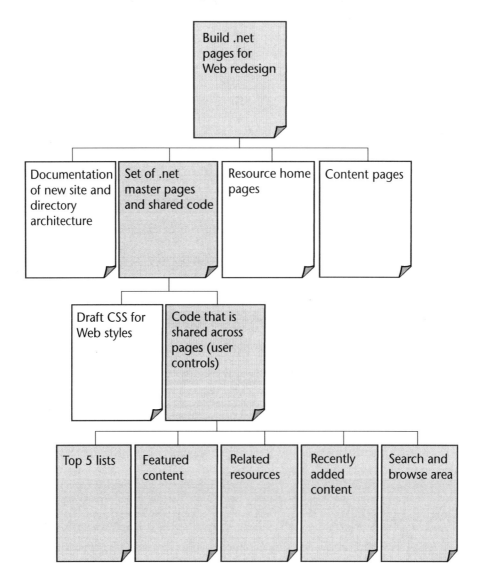

In a nutshell

Communication: Encourage listening skills as much as participation skills in building the project approach. Clarify, rephrase, summarize, and focus the discussions. Expect to hear and to process new information as the project and deliverables are clarified.

Collaboration: The shared vision and goal becomes an anchor in the planning discussions. The guiding principles document enables the team and project manager to stay focused on the goal and encourages innovation in reaching it.

Project Management: Releasing working versions of a project until all the requirements are met is very effective for complex projects that build on new technologies and may require a longer time to complete. Remember to consider the level of detail needed to manage your project as you create the WBS. Avoid micromanaging, but provide enough detail to maintain control of the project.

EXERCISE

Continue defining the approach for the summer vacation project. Identify the deliverables you need while making travel arrangements for your vacation. (This is the *Build* phase of your project.) Remember that deliverables and milestones are things (nouns), not activities.

Exercise answer

The *Build* phase for your trip might include these items.

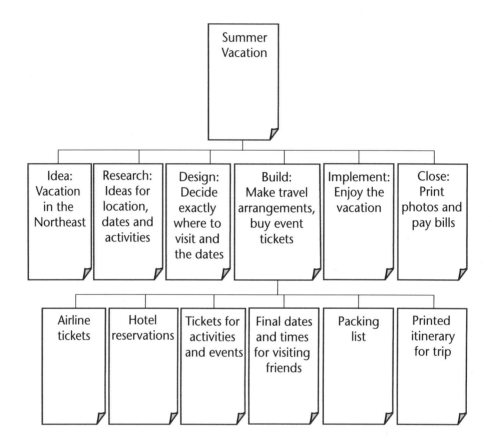

21

Create an Activity List and Estimate Time

> *"My lead programmer gave me his time estimates
> for the tech activities. He said it will take only half
> as long as I estimated to create the Web pages,"
> the Project Manager says. "How do I know whose
> estimate to trust?"*

> *"How did he come up with the estimate?" asks the
> Facilitator. "Ask him to show you the list of steps he
> used to make the estimate. If he doesn't have one, work
> with him to create it. Then you can estimate time."*

What is an activity list?

During Lesson 20, you created a work breakdown structure (WBS) that
identified all the deliverables required to complete your project and any
major milestones you added to help you manage the project. The lowest
level in the WBS is called a work package.

The next step is to create an activity list. The activity list contains the
list of steps—or activities—needed to complete each work package. For

example, a work package for the summer vacation project we started in the last lesson is to "Choose city to visit." In this simple example, this work package might include the following activities:

- create a list of airfares for top three cities
- create a list of attractions for top three cities
- create a list of transportation options and costs for top three cities
- create a list of average lodging costs for top three cities
- contact relatives and friends in cities to check their availability
- compare the lists and choose the city you will visit

Goals of the activity list

The goals of the activity list during project planning are to

- help you identify gaps in your WBS
- accurately estimate the time and resources required for your project
- give you the information needed to create a network diagram as described in Lesson 22
- give the team members the list of activities needed to complete their work
- reduce fear and reluctance about a project by beginning to define the unknown

Later in the project—during project execution—the activity list will be used by subgroup leaders and team members who are responsible for completing the work. They can use this information as a checklist to work through the project and alert you to problems that might affect the schedule. The activity list will be updated throughout the project in response to changes.

The level of detail you and your team choose to provide in your activity list is up to you. Consider the complexity of the project, the experience of the team, and your experience as a project manager as you decide on the level of detail that is most appropriate. A more complex project or less experienced team or manager may need a more detailed activity list.

In general, the smaller the task, the more easily and accurately it can be estimated for time and resource needs. Smaller tasks also make it easier to track when a project is falling off schedule. Be careful— unfortunately, the smaller the task listed, the greater the temptation to micromanage.

For example, note the WBS for the *Design* phase of our summer vacation project and its related activity list.

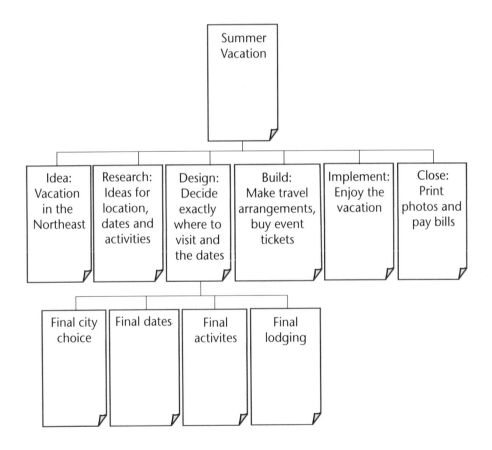

Summer Vacation: Design Phase		
Activity	**Time**	**Resource**
Final city choice		
Create list of airfares for top three cities		
Create list of attractions for top three cities		
Create list of transportation options and costs for top three cities		
Create list of average lodging costs for top three cities		
Contact relatives/friends in cities to check availability		
Compare the lists and choose the city you will visit		
Final dates		
Check schedule		
Check event schedule in chosen city		
Check availability of friends and relatives		
Check travel/hotel costs (less during certain times?)		
Select dates		
Final activities		
Check calendar for city (festivals, special events)		
Check local attractions (museums, parks)		
Review guide books		
Check local entertainment (theaters, music)		
Check schedule for local sports teams		
Review list and choose top activities		
Final lodging		
Check hotel rates and locations		
Check bed and breakfast rates and locations		
Check for campground rates and locations		
Compare locations, rates, and amenities		
Review factors and choose lodging		

Team building

Working with team members to create an activity list is also an opportunity to continue building strong team relationships and establish trust. As you work with team members to identify the activities needed to complete each work package, you can help define the expectations and requirements for the project. If you are not an expert in the area, it is an opportunity for you, as the project manager, to understand what it takes to complete the activities in each work package. In addition, it helps the subgroup leader or team member accept responsibility and feel ownership of the work package. Each is confident that he has the information needed to complete the work package, and you have the information you need to trust that each will do a good job.

Estimating time

Estimating time and cost on projects will fall into one of three categories.

Analogous estimating: Analogous estimating is based on experience and past projects. Estimating time in this way is generally quick and not based on much detail. This type of estimating is often asked for at the beginning of a project—during project initiation—when stakeholders are just looking for a rough estimate. If you are creating an analogous estimate, expect low accuracy (+/– 50 percent).

Parametric estimating: Parametric estimating takes a closer look at data from many projects to predict the time and cost of similar projects. It works very well if the projects are exactly the same or if differences between projects are clearly understood. Parametric estimating works best for projects that you have done many times and for which you have a large amount of data to calculate averages. The quality of these estimates depends largely on the quality of data.

Bottom-up estimating: Bottom-up estimating can be the most accurate type of estimating. These estimates are created from the activities on your activity list. This type of estimating can be time-consuming but very effective in projects where maintaining time and cost is critical. This type of estimating starts in the planning stage, but it continues through the project to keep track of the time and money needed to complete it.

In this lesson we suggest bottom-up estimating as a way to create a good plan. The time it will take to complete the estimate depends on the level of detail you include in your activity list. Remember to find the right balance for your project and organization. Make your activity list detailed enough to provide adequate information for your team to reasonably estimate time, and more important, understand the project well enough to complete it successfully.

Final dates	Est. time	Resource
Check schedule	1–2 hr	Bob
Check event schedule in chosen city	2–3 hr	Bob
Check availability of friends and relatives	2–3 hr	Bob
Check travel and hotel costs (less during certain times?)	4–6 hr	Bob
Select dates	1–3 hr	Bob

Communicating time estimates

Estimating project time, just like talking about the activity list, is a great way to increase the communication between team members and develop trust among them. The discussion is often geared toward solving problems and finding approaches that take advantage of the team's experience and minimize time. It's an effective way to identify potential thorny issues and find the right resources for activities. See Lesson 23 for more information on assigning resources to your project.

There are two pieces of information that are important to communicate when talking to your team about estimates.

1. Discuss the level of accuracy you expect from your estimates. You can explain this by talking about the type of estimating you

did and what information you based your estimates on. Keep in mind that more general estimating, such as analogous and parametric, results in less certainty about your estimates. Providing this information helps everyone understand the level of accuracy included in the plan and sets an expectation for what changes might occur. The more general the estimate, the more likely the project plan will change.

2. Provide a range of hours you think it will take to complete the activity. The chances of predicting an exact number of hours are slim. Understanding the range is critical to building enough flexibility into your plan.

For example, in developing a list of top-used resources to display on a Web site, an *analogous estimate* might be stated as "I know roughly what this project includes and know that we have done similar work in the past. I'm about 60 percent confident it will take between 20 and 30 hours to build."

A *bottom-up estimate* might be stated as "I reviewed the requirements and mapped out the steps to complete it. There are no unknowns and most of the work is very similar to work I've done several times before. I am 80 percent confident that this work will take between 25 and 28 hours to complete."

In a nutshell ▷   ▷   ▷

Communication: Working with your team to create the activity list helps your team understand the work and requirements for each work package. While discussing the activity list you will often identify deliverables that are missing from the WBS. Adding this missing information increases your chances for a successful project.

Collaboration: Working with your team to create the activity list and estimate time can be a great way to strengthen the relationship, trust, and understanding among team members. It gives team members the information they need to complete the work package successfully. It gives the team the opportunity to work together to find the best approach to the project. It gives you the reassurance and understanding you need to let team members take responsibility for the activities while you focus on managing the project at a higher level.

Project Management: During planning, creating an activity list is the best way to accurately estimate time and resources required for the project. The activity list breaks each work package into activities that can be accurately estimated. While executing the project, team members use the activity list as a checklist to complete the work package. The activity list is updated as the project changes.

EXERCISE

Create an activity list for the *Build* phase of the summer vacation project. Include time estimates for each activity. Consider what level of detail you would need to include to estimate time accurately. The WBS for the *Build* phase is listed here.

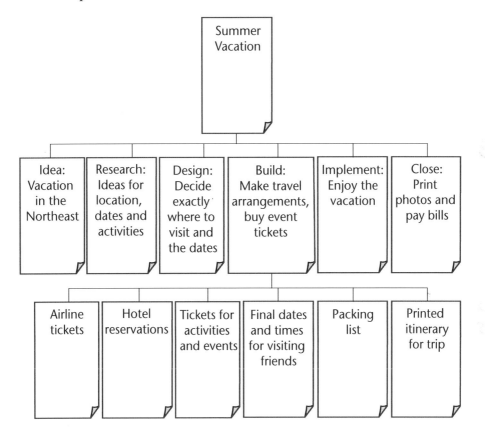

Exercise answer

A very detailed activity list for the *Build* phase of the summer vacation project might include the following:

Summer Vacation: Build Phase		
Activity	**Time**	**Resource**
Airline tickets		
Get airline miles card number	<1 hr	
Choose flights that match schedule and allow you to use miles	<1 hr	
Complete the purchase of tickets	<1 hr	
Hotel reservations		
Log on to hotel site or online reservation service	<1 hr	
Choose hotel and dates	1–2 hr	
Choose type of room and number of people	<1 hr	
Complete registration process	<1 hr	
Tickets for activities and events		
Choose dates for events and number of people	1–2 hr	
Choose seats for events	<1 hr	
Complete the purchase of tickets	<1 hr	
Print tickets	<1 hr	
Final dates and times for visiting friends		
Call friends to confirm availability	<1 hr	
Call friends to confirm dates	<1 hr	
Packing list		
Review trip itinerary	1–2 hr	
Write down items you can't forget to pack	<1 hr	
Printed itinerary for trip		
Gather flight, hotel, event info into one document	1–2 hr	
Print itinerary	<1 hr	

TIME-SAVERS

Sample Project Activity List

Build .net Pages for Web Redesign		
Activity	**Time**	**Resource**
Documentation of new site and directory structure		
. . .		
Set of .net master pages and shared code		
Draft CSS for Web styles		
. . .		
Code that is shared across pages		
Work package: Top 5 list		
Activities		
Document tech approach and testing requirements		
Database queries complete		
Page formatting complete and styles applied		
Developer testing and revisions complete		
External testing and revisions complete		
Work package: Featured content		
Activities		
Document tech approach and testing requirements		
Database queries complete		
Page formatting complete and styles applied		
Developer testing and revisions complete		
External testing and revisions complete		
Work package: Related resources		
Activities		
Document tech approach and testing requirements		
Database queries complete		

Page formatting complete and styles applied		
Developer testing and revisions complete		
External testing and revisions complete		
Work package: List of recently added content		
Activities		
Document tech approach and testing requirements		
Database queries complete		
Page formatting complete and styles applied		
Developer testing and revisions complete		
External testing and revisions complete		
Work Package: Search and browse area		
Activities		
Document tech approach and testing requirements		
Database queries complete		
Metadata reviewed and correct		
Search indexes reviewed and correct		
Page formatting complete and styles applied		
Developer testing and revisions complete		
Resource home pages		
. . .		
Content pages		
. . .		

Sample Project Time Estimates

A section of the preceding activity list with time and resources estimated for a project might look like this:

Build .net Pages for Web Redesign		
Activity	**Time**	**Resource**
Work package: Top 5 list	**30–40 hrs (total)**	
Activities		
Document tech approach and testing requirements	2–4 hrs	Bill
Database queries complete	8–10 hrs	Bill
Page formatting complete and styles applied	4–6 hrs	Bill
Developer testing and revisions complete	8–10 hrs	Kate
External testing and revisions complete	8–10 hrs	Kate

22

Create the Network Diagram and Critical Path

The Facilitator walks into the Project Manager's office and sees the sticky notes of the work breakdown all over the walls and a flipchart of the activities in the corner. The Project Manager looks up. "The sponsor is asking when the project will be done. I am uncertain at this point. Any good ideas?"

"I can help you determine the longest amount of time it will take," says the Facilitator. "The first step is to turn your activities and time estimates into a flowchart."

Make a flowchart—the network diagram

After you know what activities are included in your project (the activity list) and how long they will take (the time estimates), you can decide the order in which to do them and determine when they will be done. Making a map, or flowchart, of this order will give you a diagram of the steps you will take to complete the project. You will also see the relationships between each activity. These relationships are important to know; they affect where you will focus your attention as you monitor the progress of the project. If an activity cannot start before another activity is finished, it needs to be tracked. If you need to get your project done more quickly, the diagram will show the chain reaction you could set up by revising any of the activities or the order in which they get done.

There are several approaches to and reasons for choosing a particular order (the logical sequence) of activities. You might sequence activities out of necessity—that is, you can't start one until another is completed (mandatory dependencies). Other activities may be sequenced in a particular way because you prefer that order over others (preferred dependencies). Finally, you may sequence activities in a particular order because of external factors. For example, you might have to wait for a vendor to be available for a project (external dependencies).

A diagram that shows the order of activities in a project is called a network diagram. To create a network diagram, follow these steps.

1. Start with your activity list, described in Lesson 21. Remember that as you work through the planning process, you add more detail to the work involved to complete it. You may identify activities you missed earlier. Your activities should be at a level that can accurately be estimated for time. This level may vary by project and by team.

2. Determine the dependency for each activity. Map out which activity must be finished before the next one can start (finish-to-start) and which activities can run in parallel (at the same time) with others. Arrange all the activities in a sequence. Be aware that there are several different types of dependencies, but the finish-to-start dependency is the most common. (See the Project Activity Dependency Chart in the Time-Saver section for more explanation.)

3. Draw a flowchart that links the activities according to their sequence. Several software packages are available that can help

you create flowcharts, or you can use sticky notes on a wall. Your diagram doesn't need to be high-tech to be effective. The result will be a diagram that provides a quick view of your project. You can use and update it throughout the project.

4. Add the time estimates from your activity list to your flowchart.

The critical path

The critical path is the path through the network diagram that takes the longest time to complete. That means delays along this path will most likely extend your deadline and possibly affect other areas of the project. Because completing the activities along the critical path on time and according to specification is so important to meeting the deadline for the project, it is most important to monitor the activities along this path.

It may not be possible to monitor all of the activities closely in a complex project, so identifying the critical path activities gives the project manager a focus on the activities that matter.

If overtime or additional resources are needed, they are often assigned to critical-path activities. Special effort should be taken to protect the time allotted for the resources in the critical path.

If time must be cut from the project (this is called schedule compression), you will most likely be cutting time from the critical path. Your options may include assigning experts who can complete the work more quickly, removing some of your preferred dependencies and completing activities in parallel rather than consecutively, and delaying some of your non–critical-path activities to put more resources on the critical path. Be aware that compressing time can also be accomplished by decreasing the scope of the project or increasing the budget for the project (e.g., by adding resources). Compressing the schedule may also result in quality compromises. Be sure you are considering *all* factors of your project when schedule compression occurs.

Good communication channels are essential for activities on the critical path. Any possible delays or problems should be brought to the project manager's attention immediately so the team can work on ways to mitigate the potential issue. Communicating during the handoff from one activity to another is also important so team members know where the project stands and what work is ready for them.

To create a critical path:

1. Use your estimates to assign the time needed to complete each activity. Use the same unit of measure, for example, days or weeks.

2. Identify the path through the diagram that takes the longest time to complete. This is the critical path. All of the activities along this path must be completed on time, or the project deadline will be missed.

An abbreviated sample network diagram with the critical path highlighted is shown here. Note the activities that can be happening at the same time (parallel), such as building the site search and building the Top-5 lists. Then note what cannot be started until the activity before it has been finished. You cannot do testing until the pages for both the site search and the Top-5 lists have been completed. Note also that you need more time to do the site search pages (24 hours) than to do the Top-5 pages (17 hours). That is why the site search pages are on the critical path.

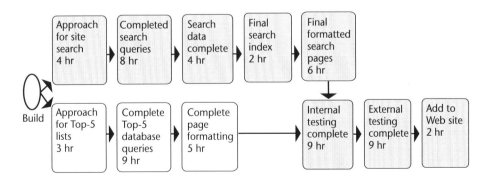

In a nutshell ▶ ▶ ▶

Communication: The network diagram shows the dependencies of activities in the project. It is important for those working in different departments to see these dependencies and understand their role in another's work. Communication warning of any delay is crucial.

Collaboration: The critical path highlights the collaborative nature of the project as dependencies are identified. The focus is the overall goal of the project and how it will be achieved. This helps those focused on individual tasks to see the importance of their work in meeting the overall goal. It also identifies the need to be accountable for achieving their work.

Project Management: The project manager focuses on the critical path throughout the project not only in receiving reports of the work progress but by observing and talking to the individuals doing the work. If there is a problem with an activity on the critical path, the sooner it is made known, the greater the chance to minimize the risk of delaying the project.

EXERCISE

What would be the effect of adding an activity to the critical path? How might a project manager add an activity and still meet the project deadline?

Exercise answer

Adding any activity to the critical path will increase the time it takes to complete the project. To add an activity to the critical path and still meet the project deadline, the project manager should consider available options and pick the best one.

1. The activity can be done in parallel with (at the same time as) a critical path item rather than in sequence.

2. The activity can be added if another activity on the critical path can be done in less time than estimated or moved out of the critical path.

3. Resources may be added to speed up other activities on the critical path. This would increase cost.

4. Quality may be reduced, decreasing time by cutting corners or eliminating steps such as testing or proofreading.

5. Resources may be swapped so that expert resources can more quickly complete items on the critical path. Items not on the critical path can be completed more slowly.

6. An activity not on the critical path may be delayed and that resource shifted to the new critical path item.

TIME-SAVER

Handout: Project Activity Dependency Chart

Project Activity Dependency Chart

As you begin creating your network diagram, be sure to note the dependencies between activities. Choose from the following:

Dependency	Definition
Finish-to-start	You must finish one activity before the next can be started.
Start-to-start	You must start one activity before the next can be started.
Start-to-finish	You must start one activity before another can be finished.
Finish-to-finish	You must finish one activity before the other can be finished.

Also account for any lead or lag time that should be built into your work flow. Lead time is how much time needs to pass before an activity can start. Lag time refers to how much time you have to wait before one activity is considered complete and the next one can start.

23

Work with Resource Estimates

"Trouble on the line," says the Project Manager to the Facilitator. "I have a couple of iffy resources on my critical path. One is an outside vendor for programming work—I don't have the contract nailed down. The other is the Web designer. She might be on extended vacation when the concept pages are due. Any advice on how I can estimate for these uncertainties—and still deliver on time?"

The Facilitator thinks a minute. "Resource estimates are about the right people doing the right thing at the right time. If those are uncertain, consider a contingency or another option."

Reviewing resource estimates

Resources can be personnel, equipment, money, or anything else that you need to have at a certain time in a certain place to complete the tasks on the activity list. Resources required for critical path activities must be available when they are needed and must complete the tasks as estimated or the project will risk delays or failure.

Resource estimates may have been determined by experienced team members who are actually assigned to do the work. These are usually the most reliable estimates. Or they may have been a "best guess" estimate done by someone who might know about the work but does not understand all that is required to complete it. Regardless of who is doing the estimating, we are not good at predicting the future. There are always uncertainties. It's just life.

Resource estimates are reviewed and tracked throughout the project to confirm that

> ▸ the right people
>
> ▸ are doing the right things
>
> ▸ at the right time.

The right people

The right people include staff and vendors who are skilled and experienced at doing the work. They have a track record of meeting deadlines to quality standards on similar projects. This is especially important for activities along your critical path, as delays and mistakes in these areas can easily throw the project off target. To refine estimates, your resources may find the following information useful.

> ▸ A clear description, expectations, and measurements for the work involved, should be found in the project scope. If these are not addressed in enough detail, add additional documentation during this process.
>
> ▸ The authority the resources will have and what they will be accountable for. They should know the approval process—when and from whom they must seek approvals. For example, as the project manager, you might choose to include some deliverables and reporting requirements that, while not mandated by the project sponsor, are necessary for you to monitor to keep the project on track.

- ▸ What is specified for the quality standards and testing requirements. For example, is the project manager requesting top-notch quality, or just good enough? Is user testing part of this requirement? Are additional resources needed for that?
- ▸ It is a good idea to ask your resources to review the business case, requirements, guiding principles, scope document, etc., so they have a full understanding of the details. It is not uncommon for one part of a project to impact another. The more insight you can give your team members into the breadth and width of your project, the better.

Ideally, you will have access to the best resources in your organization. Realistically, you will be working with the best resources *available at that time*. This is fine as long as your estimates reflect staffs' skill levels. For example, consider whether or not they work at a senior level—they are experts—or at a junior level—they have less experience or need training. Senior-level staff will have higher pay rates than the junior level. Junior-level staff may require more time to complete the task or need extra time to get training. Junior-level staff may need more frequent follow-up from the project manager to keep the project work on track. Take all of this into account when adjusting your time estimates for resources.

If you are working with vendors, remember that they require clear, complete specifications to accurately estimate time and cost. This information will also be spelled out in the contract, so be sure your specifications are as complete as possible. Do not assume a detail is too small and do not assume the vendor will infer your basic requirements. Although your requirements might be "common sense" in your organization, they are not necessarily common sense for others.

Doing the right things

The right things are activities that use the resource's expertise and skill, add value to the project without increasing the scope, and move the project toward reaching its goal.

People who are asked to give estimates need the ability to offer recommendations, based on their experience and knowledge, if they see a problem with the work breakdown structure or the project plan. For example, they might identify preparation work that must be done before the task is turned over to them.

The project manager may need to estimate that two resources are needed to complete a task. There may be a senior-level person assigned to the task, but he may assume that a junior-level person will support him. Be sure to include this when estimating. If a senior-level person is overbooked, the assistance of a junior-level resource may allow the senior-level resource to commit to the project.

Carefully check that outside vendors and internal resources are doing only work that will advance your project. Resist the temptation to fold in unrelated or extra tasks simply because a resource is an expert at doing them. Adding these unnecessary activities will only increase your timeline and costs.

At the right time

The right time means your resource will work on an activity when it will add value to the project, when it is ready to be started with an acceptable (preferably low) risk of rework and when it supports the critical path.

Once you estimate the time needed for a project and set the schedule, it can be challenging to maintain it. You can mitigate changes to your schedule by following these tips:

Clear the time you need from your resources with their supervisors. Be formal and put it in writing so there is a shared reference. Help each supervisor understand the place of his staff person's work on the project: what she is dependent on receiving and who depends on her work being finished.

Translate the hours estimated to calendar days. For example, the task may take only 10 hours of work to complete but your resource is only available 2 hours a day for your project. This increases your schedule from about 1.5 workdays to 5 workdays (2 hours of work each day).

Factor staff vacations into due dates and assignments. For example, if a senior-level person is taking a long vacation when her part of the work is needed, you might choose to delay that date or assign a junior-level person to complete the task. You may have to consider factoring in extra time for the junior-level person to complete the work to quality standards.

If training is required, or a new work process will be used, *allow extra time* (and cost if the training fees will be charged to the project).

If you are hiring a vendor, allow time for the bidding process, if necessary. This includes writing and sending the Request for Proposal, gathering and evaluating the bids, and hiring the vendor. Also allow extra time for formal meetings to accommodate the approval process.

Allow loops (time for tasks to go back and forth or be redone) during the approval and testing processes. These may result in requests for corrections and changes as what is wanted becomes more clear.

Allow transition time between activities.

Purchase material resources in advance, especially to take advantage of sales, low prices, or saving by making a bulk purchase. Be sure that you have storage space and that the materials will be available when you are ready for them.

What about unknowns?

Unknowns are the unplanned events or costs that enter into the project. For example, the project manager is notified that a software program the project designer planned to use is no longer being supported by the manufacturer and will be discontinued. There will be extra time and cost to research, purchase, and learn new software. Finding this out at the planning stage is very helpful. The plan and critical path will be adjusted. Finding this out *after* the project has started is more problematic. There are fewer opportunities to shift tasks or resources because they may already be committed.

To allow for unknowns, the project manager adds a contingency, a percentage of time and cost to the project. A contingency sets aside a certain amount of time and money in case the project falls off schedule. The amount of time and money set aside depends on the scope and complexity of the project. For example, you and your team believe you can complete the project by January 1, but you have not promised to make the product available to customers until March 1. You have built in a two-month contingency.

Allowing for contingency is different than padding your project. Good project managers *do not* pad. Padding is adding time to individual activities. Padding distorts your time estimates and makes your schedule less reliable because you are more likely to finish some activities earlier than scheduled and others later than scheduled. This makes it extremely difficult for your resources to reliably predict when the work will be coming to them. For example, if you believe your resource can create a database in 8 hours, but you decide to pad this estimate and give him 24 hours just to be safe, you may end up with the person ready to hand off the database, but the person receiving it is still working on another project. Project managers often focus on avoiding being late with work, but sometimes being early is just as disruptive.

Contingencies reflect adding time or cost to cover risks. Providing a contingency is the preferred method for planning for unknowns. Padding often reflects poor estimating.

In a nutshell

Communication: Getting realistic and reliable estimates from resources requires good communication skills: Be clear about what is needed and the standards expected, ask questions to understand details of the work, interview vendors and review bids, weigh what resources estimate against past records, and check availability with supervisors.

Collaboration: Reaching a shared goal (e.g., a schedule your team can believe in) rests on interdependence and the willingness to be accountable. Resources committed to a shared goal are not just cooperating. They should understand their place in and contribution to the larger goal. As issues and conflicts surface, seek a win-win solution that will fulfill the shared goal.

Project Management: Estimating resources has an impact on the critical path of the project. Make sure you are assigning the correct resources to your critical path and that your resources agree that the time estimates are realistic. Convert hours into actual calendar days and add a contingency to mitigate the risks from unplanned events or costs. Do not pad your estimates.

EXERCISE

Match the best process to gain reliable estimates and commitment of time from the resources listed.

Resource	Process to gain reliable estimates
Vendor: Your organization requires you to select the lowest bidder who may require more time to complete the work.	Interview supervisor and ask if a junior-level resource can assist.
Senior-level resource who has worked on similar projects.	Require a signed contract with not-to-exceed-cost and time estimate.
Senior-level resource who has not worked on similar projects.	Review records from past projects, including time sheets, logs, invoices.
Junior-level resource who has worked on similar projects.	Interview supervisor, explain details of the work and ask if there will be training requirements.
Junior-level resource who has not worked on similar projects.	Give specs in writing, go over the details of the tasks, and ask how he will approach the work.
Supervisor.	Include time for extra monitoring of work and more corrections.
Senior-level resource who is known to be a perfectionist.	Seek bids from 3 vendors. Require references.
Vendor: Vendor proposes working on a time and materials basis to estimate a lower cost.	Interview in person.
Senior-level resource who is very efficient, but overbooked.	Break down the tasks into smaller chunks with shorter turnaround time and more frequent handoffs.

Exercise answer

Resource	Process to gain reliable estimates
Vendor: Your organization requires you to select the lowest bidder who may require more time to complete the work.	Seek bids from 3 vendors. Require references.
Senior-level resource who has worked on similar projects.	Review records from past projects, including time sheets, logs, invoices.
Senior-level resource who has not worked on similar projects.	Give specs in writing, go over the details of the tasks, and ask how he will approach the work.
Junior-level resource who has worked on similar projects.	Interview supervisor, explain details of the work and ask whether there will be training requirements.
Junior-level resource who has not worked on similar projects.	Include time for extra monitoring of work and more corrections.
Supervisor.	Interview in person.
Vendor: Vendor proposes working on a time and materials basis to estimate a lower cost.	Require a signed contract with not-to-exceed-cost and time estimate.
Senior-level resource who is known to be a perfectionist.	Break down the tasks into smaller chunks with shorter turnaround time and more frequent handoffs.
Senior-level resource who is very efficient, but overbooked.	Interview supervisor and ask if a junior-level resource can assist.

24

Create a Schedule

The Project Manager shows a draft of the schedule to the Facilitator. Pages and pages of tasks numbering into the thousands fill a three-ring binder. "I tried to think of everything," she says. "I just hope I can keep this project on schedule."

"If you make the job of project manager 'keeper of the to-do list' for every task," cautions the Facilitator, "you will become a micromanager. The job of project manager is to be a problem solver. To be effective, keep your eye on the major milestones and their key activities."

Project schedule

In the past several lessons we talked about the information you need to create your plan and estimate time. It is often confusing for project managers to decide the right level of detail to include in these reports. If there is not enough detail, you do not have the information you need to spot when the project is heading off track or to identify potential problems. If there is too much detail, you become a micromanager and your team members risk losing their sense of accountability for the project. Tracking your project in too much detail can also bog down your team meetings in reviewing checklists that most find boring and confusing. Most important, spending too much time on the details diverts your attention from solving problems and mitigating risks—the primary job of the project manager.

So how do you find the right balance? Like many other areas of project management, you need to consider the needs for your project and the needs of the team members. Consider whether you have subgroups completing tasks or just a few individuals completing the work. Is your team comprised of experts, or are some people learning as they go? These variables should factor into how much detail you choose to put in your project plan.

In general, as the project manager you should try to focus on problem solving and tracking deliverable and milestone dates. The specific details of how the work is getting done shouldn't be of great interest to you as long as the work is meeting deadlines; meeting functional, quality, and cost specifications; and is completed in a way that conforms with your organization's ethics and general guidelines. A rule of thumb is for the project manager to track activities that require *a week or longer* to complete. This gives the project manager a higher level view to coordinate cross-department activities and the flexibility to make trade-offs if necessary to keep the project on schedule.

The project schedule template is a tool that focuses your attention at the deliverable/milestone level. It shows how long the deliverable will take to do and who is assigned. The schedule is the result of gathering data and commitments from those who will be doing the work. This information can be gathered while completing the WBS and activity list and while estimating time. It does not list every activity needed to complete the project. The leaders of the subgroups or individual activities are accountable for scheduling and accomplishing the lower levels of detail.

The original schedule will serve as your project baseline (see Lesson 36) while you execute the project. You will use the baseline to gauge your project progress and identify when changes need to be made to keep the project on track.

To create a schedule the project manager needs:

1. The start and end dates for the project.

2. The start and end dates for the version you are working on, if you are using agile project management.

3. The start and end dates for the interim deliverables for the project (or version). These are called the *major milestones.*

4. A list of the significant tasks needed to complete the major milestones.

5. What must be completed before each task can be started. This is called the *dependency.*

6. The time it takes to do each task (in calendar days). This is called the *duration.*

7. The person assigned to the task and when she is available.

8. The task that follows. This is called the *successor.*

These items can be plotted on an Excel spreadsheet or entered into a project scheduler. (See the Sample Gantt Chart in the Time-Saver section of this lesson.) If there is a change in these items, it will ripple through the project. Note that if activities along the critical path are impacted, the project deadline will be affected.

Here are some factors that impact schedule and may be overlooked by the project manager making the schedule:

▸ The work schedule being used by collaborative partners. Other organizations may not follow the same processes or quality levels as your organization. Establish good communication channels and the understanding of processes early in the relationship. Establish one accountable point of contact who has authority to approve decisions and can assist in problem solving.

▸ Vacations and other planned or unplanned times when work does not happen.

- Unrealistic or optimistic estimates. It is very common to under- or overestimate work.

- Competitive estimates from vendors who may be overbooked or understaffed.

- The timing of contracts that need to be signed.

- The scheduling of testers, especially if they are volunteers or customers.

- The availability of material resources that are designated in the requirements list such as software program upgrades that bring the functionality you need.

Additional tips to consider when scheduling

- If a task is too large, add weekly milestones so you can track the progress.

- Assign each task to an individual, rather than to a team or a group. You want to establish who is accountable for the work. Be sure the individual knows what the requirements and expectations are for the task. He may manage a task group.

- Have the people who will do the work commit to the due date. If they have estimated the time themselves, they are more likely to commit.

- Assign calendar days rather than hours. A person working on several projects who can commit only 30 percent of his time to your project will spend only 2.6 hours per day. If the estimate is 40 hours of work, the duration will be 16 calendar days.

- Be aware of *float time* in the activity list. This is the extra time activities on the critical path provide if they are finished early. This essential time may be used to shorten the project or to mitigate an overage of time in another activity.

Problem solving

If there is pressure from stakeholders to finish the project more quickly than the schedule indicates, the project manager must be able to problem solve and make tradeoffs that will allow her to deliver the project with an agreed timetable. Remember the triple constraint discussed in Lesson 19. If the schedule is adjusted, you must adjust cost or scope. You should also consider the effect your changes will have on risk and quality.

In a nutshell ▶ ▶ ▶

Communication: New terms are added to the team's vocabulary: *dependency, duration, float, calendar time.* Help your team understand these terms and feel comfortable using them.

Collaboration: The processes and understanding of the tasks that need to be done may differ from department to department and organization to organization. The more reliable estimate for duration and effort will come from the person who will do the work. Get that estimate from cross-functional or cross-department workers.

Project Management: Scheduling activities at a minute level that reduces the schedule to a detailed to-do list invites micromanagement. This should be avoided. The project manager needs to be an effective problem solver. Manage at the level of major milestones.

EXERCISE

Here are the tasks, duration, and resources that make up the activity of preparing a dinner. Fill out the chart to create a schedule for completing this activity on time.

Task	Dependency	Duration	Resource	Start/End date

Tasks and duration:

The dinner will be held Saturday at 6 pm

Set the table Saturday—30 min

Shop for ingredients Friday—2 hours

Prepare lasagna Friday—3 hours

Bake lasagna Saturday—1 hour

Toss salad Saturday—30 min

Resources:

Sandy, junior level, available Saturday afternoon

Fred, senior level (has never made lasagna), available Saturday morning

Cindy, senior level (accomplished chef), available Friday and Saturday

Bill, junior level, available Friday, if baseball practice is cancelled

Exercise answer

Task	Dependency	Duration	Resource	Start/End date
1. Shop for ingredients		2 hrs	Cindy	Friday 9:00–11:00 am
2. Prepare lasagna	1	3 hrs	Cindy	Friday 6:00–9:00 pm
3. Set table		.5 hr	Fred	Saturday 11:00–11:30 am
4. Bake lasagna	2	1 hr	Cindy	Saturday 5:00–6:00 pm
5. Toss salad	1	.5 hr	Sandy	Saturday 4:00–4:30 pm
6. Dinner	3, 4, 5	3 hrs		Saturday 6:00–9:00 pm

TIME-SAVER

Sample: Gantt Chart

Gantt Chart

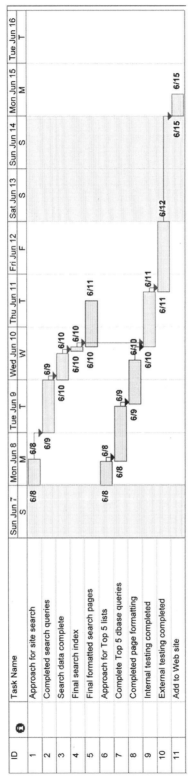

ID	①	Task Name	Sun Jun 7 S	Mon Jun 8 M	Tue Jun 9 T	Wed Jun 10 W	Thu Jun 11 T	Fri Jun 12 F	Sat Jun 13 S	Sun Jun 14 S	Mon Jun 15 M	Tue Jun 16 T
1		Approach for site search	6/8	6/8								
2		Completed search queries		6/9	6/9							
3		Search data complete			6/10	6/9						
4		Final search index				6/10	6/10					
5		Final formatted search pages				6/10	6/11 6/10					
6		Approach for Top 5 lists		6/8	6/8							
7		Complete Top 5 dbase queries			6/9	6/9						
8		Completed page formatting				6/10 6/10						
9		Internal testing completed				6/10	6/11 6/11					
10		External testing completed						6/12		6/15		
11		Add to Web site									6/15	

© 2010 Change Leadership Network, University of Michigan, Institute of Continuing Legal Education

25

Understand Budgeting

The Project Manager is sharpening her pencil. "What's the best way to approach this budget?" she wonders out loud. "Take the total that is allotted and divide it up—tell my resources this is what you have to spend, go make it happen? Get estimates of what each resource needs to do the tasks and add them all up? Make my best guess based on other projects like this one?"

"It's not really a guessing game," the Facilitator responds, "but it is a balance. Dividing the budget allotment is overly optimistic. Adding each individual estimate—with the corresponding padding that is sure to be included—may result in sticker shock. Historical data may be incomplete. But if you balance them all together, add a risk factor, and monitor what is happening, you should be okay."

Budget balance

Cost is an important factor in deciding whether or not the project will be feasible. If cost estimates are realistic, stakeholders can reasonably assess the value of the project outcome against their interests. Is it worth the cost? If the project is worthy, is there a way to fund it? For example, if the cost estimate is more than the allotted funds, they can reevaluate priorities or adjust scope. If the cost estimate is low, they can add features or ask whether the project can be delivered in a shorter time.

If cost estimates are *unrealistic,* stakeholders might reject the project entirely or they may have to face uncomfortable decisions as actual expenses are incurred. For example, if the expenses are over budget, stakeholders may be asked to lower quality standards or forego features to bring costs in line with available funds.

When making a budget, *strive for balance.* It is not possible to accurately estimate all the costs of each task or activity. In addition, we are not able to predict the future. There will be unforeseen events, items we did not consider, or other factors that must be taken into account. The budget, like the plan, must be accurate enough to allow an assessment of feasibility and flexible enough to adjust to unknowns.

Budgeting is the estimate of costs and contingencies, balanced by constraints.

- ▶ *Costs* include labor and materials. Labor is calculated in hours multiplied by a pay rate. Materials are estimated by their purchase cost or usage cost.
- ▶ *Contingencies* are percentages that are added to compensate for unknowns, such as labor shortages, delays, price increases, etc.
- ▶ *Constraints* are restrictions that may be imposed by the funding sources or by the resources. For example, the sponsor of the project may specify that no more than 200 hours of senior staff time may be allotted for routine programming work. More than that would make the project unfeasible for the organization to fund.

Costs

Your estimates will be as good as your list of requirements. Be clear about what the project requires. Have your sources be as clear about what work they will be doing.

If your project will be wholly outsourced, the costs will be included in the contract. If there are additional costs for staff time, such as the project manager's time for monitoring the project, those should be added. If you make changes to the project after the contract is signed, you will pay additional charges. Be sure you are aware of what those will be and allow a contingency in your budget to cover them. A rule of thumb is 20 percent. Also consider whether you will incur research costs to determine the vendor, start-up costs (testing, etc., after implementation), or whether you will need to purchase software, hardware, or training, and include these costs as well.

If your project will require staff resources as well as materials, estimate the work packages included in the work breakdown structure. (See Lesson 20.) This will give you enough detail to understand the effort that is required, but not so much detail that you get mired at the task level and become inflexible. Consider the experience level of the worker as you estimate hours and rate.

Use spreadsheet software such as Excel to estimate the effort. For example:

Work package	Resource	Effort	Rate	Materials cost	Total
Write dot net programming code for my account area					
	1 senior programmer	40 hours at 100%	$60/ hr		$2,400
	2 junior programmers	100 hours at 50%	$30/ hr		$3,000
	Training to learn code			$600	$600
	Server with operating system for testing code			$15,000	$15,000
Total Work Package					$21,000

Contingencies

Project estimates include a contingency, an amount that gives the project manager a cushion to allow for unexpected costs, which are certain to occur. A typical contingency is 20 percent and could be as high as 30 percent. In the work package example, the contingency would be an additional $4,200. This may be used if an additional programmer is needed to finish the programming code by the deadline. Perhaps the estimate did not allow for the time the training would take before programming could begin, and, to complete the programming on time an additional programmer must be assigned to the task.

It is not advisable to use contingencies to "squeeze in" additional features to the project. These add-ons should be evaluated on their merit, scheduled, and budgeted accordingly.

Constraints

Constraints restrict the amount of funds that may be used for an activity. Constraints assign value to intended work and thus provide guidance from the stakeholders on where the value is held. In the example, the senior programming time for this work package had a constraint of less than 200 hours.

Constraints also guide the project manager in finding the most cost-effective approach to take to deliver the requirements. In the example, junior programmers have been assigned to the programming task to leverage the senior programmer's experience and to use less costly time for routine coding work.

Your budget is your baseline

Once your budget has been approved, it becomes your baseline to measure actual costs. Your budget is one of the key measures that tell you if your project is on track. Record your costs as they are incurred and monitor them against the original estimate. If adjustments to the budget need to be made, it is best to find that out as early as possible.

Here is a form that is useful for planning your budget and tracking your costs. Notice that the costs column provides for estimates at the major work breakdown levels of Research, Design, Prototype, Build, and Deliver. A separate entry, Staff time, can also be subdivided by the major work breakdown categories and tracked as such.

Project management simple budget form

Costs	Constraints	Estimate	Actual-to-Date	Actual final	Variance (Final to estimate)
Research					
Design					
Prototype					
Build					
Deliver					
Staff time					
Contingency					
Total dollars					

General tips to consider when budgeting

Know what you have to work with. How much is being funded? How much do you as the project manager control? For example, $50,000 may be funded for the project but $10,000 of that is for customer training after the project is delivered and is not part of your plan. Your project has an actual funding base of $40,000.

Know your sources of information. The most reliable sources are those who have done this type of project work in the past and can document actual costs. If estimates are from sources who have not done this work before or have a history of underestimating, allow for this in your contingency. If estimates are from sources who have a history of overestimating, talk to them—or their supervisors—about the actual steps that will be taken and use your best judgment as to how they are arriving at their estimates. Is there unnecessary padding? If so, assure them the project will have a contingency so they do not need to pad the estimates.

Communicate clearly the constraints that funding sources have put on the project. Your resources should help you determine the impact of these constraints on features, timelines, etc.

Communicate clearly the quality standards that must be met. The approval process can also add hours to the costs, especially if approvals span departments or organizations.

Ask where the numbers or hours came from. Follow through with sources of information to get an understanding of how people are computing their figures.

Get an understanding of the significant (greatest) or essential costs. If these far exceed the budget allotment, you may need to reconsider the scope or determine whether the project is feasible at all.

Schedule the bidding for contracts if you are using outside vendors and allow enough time to meet your deadlines. Anticipate that you may need to rebid a contract if changes are made based on the returns of the first bids.

Consult your business office staff as well as your development experts in making your estimates. If outside contracts will be sought, they can advise you on the process and review contracts from a business perspective. Business office staff are also a source of past contracts, time sheets, and other documents that will help you assess the costs of this project against similar projects.

Consult your accounting staff for the accounting codes that will be assigned to your project. Get instruction on how your invoices and time records are to be marked so that your project is properly tracked in your organization's financial system.

Include related expenses. These include shipping, taxes, maintenance charges, software support charges, and others, where appropriate.

Watch for trends. Are programming costs consistently over their estimate? Or consistently under their estimate? Variances can accumulate and affect total costs.

Dealing with sticker shock

If your estimates are realistic and exceed the budget allotment for the project, you must be prepared to explain the source of the figures to your stakeholders, along with what options you are recommending. Options might include increasing the funding or finding more sources of funding, reducing the scope (features), adjusting the approach, or increasing the time allotted so smaller versions can be planned. You must also be prepared to accept that the project is simply not feasible to do at this time.

You must control your costs or they will control you

The budget process helps you *control* as well as estimate your costs. Control them by

 ▸ knowing what they are

 ▸ recording them and tracking them against your baseline as they are incurred

 ▸ monitoring them at the work package level so you have flexibility to adjust (watch for trends)

 ▸ involving your business office or legal staff (when appropriate) in creating contracts and dealings with vendors.

Cost overruns can lead to poor decisions such as skimping on quality, cutting corners that may affect customer satisfaction, cutting staff and putting more work on others, releasing the project before it has been tested, or putting off features that would have added value to the customer experience.

While it is better to complete your project under budget than over budget, a pattern of overestimating will not help your stakeholders or your organization manage their assets competently, especially if it leads to overstaffing.

The project manager's credibility is best established by competent budgeting and control.

In a nutshell ▶ ▶ ▶

Communication: The budgeting process involves gathering information from many sources and using many forms of communication. You may review a formal report from a supervisor estimating resource hours. You may prepare a formal RFP and review bids. You may consult with your business office or review historical documents. Be sure to follow through with face-to-face meetings so that each of you understands the basis for the estimate. "Where did the numbers or hours come from?" is one of the most important questions you can ask.

Collaboration: Different organizations or departments may have different budgeting methods or requirements for processes such as vendor review. Find this out in advance. Ask the leaders who provide estimates what formulas they use and how they assign resources. Determine up front what your review and approval process will be as well. Sharing information and interdependence are foundational to trust.

Project Management: Costs, constraints, and contingencies are balanced to provide the budget document. The budget provides not only guidance for assessing the feasibility of the project but also supplies the measures that help you control your costs and keep your project on track.

EXERCISE

What are the advantages and disadvantages of these budget processes?

1. Assigning a portion of the funding to the major work package leaders and asking them to tell you how they can meet the project requirements using these funds.

2. Getting estimates from the sources of the work activities and totaling them.

3. Basing estimates on similar project work done in the past.

Exercise answers

1. Assigning funds

   Advantages: Spurs innovation and gets buy-in.

   Disadvantages: More likely to be unrealistic or overoptimistic.

2. Totaling estimates from work packages

   Advantages: More realistic. Allows for problem solving and flexibility. Gets greater commitment from the resources.

   Disadvantages: May lead to sticker shock, if each activity is padded. May lead to micromanaging, if project manager delves into the details too much.

3. Using historical data

   Advantages: You see actual figures and trends.

   Disadvantages: May be incomplete or out-of-date. May not use current technology or approaches.

26

Determine Quality Standards and Measures

"Whose expectations do I use for the quality standards?" the Project Manager asks. "Stakeholders'? Customers'? Developers'? Sponsor's? Stakeholders expect top-of-the-line. Customers expect instant and easy to use. Developers expect easy to maintain and upgrade. Sponsor expects cost efficiency. Everyone expects delivery ASAP. What are the standards that will meet all these expectations?"

"Go back to the vision," answers the Facilitator. "This is your shared statement. You will find the basis for your quality standards there. Web First is a quality standard as well as your strategic goal. Quality expectations can also be determined by the market research that may have been done to develop a target market for the product in the business case."

The importance of quality standards

Quality standards define what will be accepted, or not accepted, in the final product. They answer whether or not the product is finished and if it meets the requirements as specified. They impact the budget, development, production processes, purchasing, approval process, testing, and user experience. Quality standards build trust because they clarify expectations up front and include the way they will be measured.

If quality standards are not specifically defined, they will impose themselves on the project:

> *as individual preferences.* Without specific guidelines, individuals will follow familiar routines. If the goal of Web First as a quality standard is not clear, new processes may not be established that require the development to be Web First.

> *as the organization's routine way of production or development.* In a collaborative project, different organizations may have different work cultures and different expectations. One organization may produce a product quickly and expect to make revisions. Another organization may strive for an error-free product and the need for correction will be viewed as poor quality control.

> *as requests from the stakeholders to make changes at the approval stage* because expectations are not met.

> *as cost overruns and delays* because work has to be redone to meet expectations.

> *as a scramble to meet customer expectations* based on testing results.

> *as ad-hoc product policy* quickly written to deal with customer complaints.

How to set quality standards

Quality is defined as the degree to which the project fulfills requirements. This can be determined by:

the requirements in the scope document. For example, the search results must appear on screen within one second.

budget constraints. For example, there are only enough funds to purchase a search engine that brings results within four seconds.

customer research. For example, 75 percent of customers surveyed expect search results to appear in three seconds and indicate most sites they visit deliver these results.

strategic interest of the stakeholders. For example, search results that appear in less than three seconds will give us a competitive advantage over sites that offer similar information to our customers.

strategic interest of developers. For example, all of our content must be searched to give customers the confidence that the search results are complete. We need to allow enough time for the search engine to return complete results.

When there seem to be conflicting expectations, it is important to use collaboration to set a shared quality standard that is agreed to and will be followed. Collaboration will resolve the conflict because the standard agreed to will meet the individuals' strategic goals. If the parties merely agree in order to be cooperative or to move ahead in the planning, conflict will resurface during project implementation. The shared quality standard should be:

- ▶ feasible
- ▶ practical
- ▶ measurable
- ▶ of obvious benefit or value
- ▶ affordable

Conflicting expectations can often be sources of innovation or positive changes. For example, a shared goal of quicker searches to provide a competitive advantage may spur developers to structure content in a way that can be searched more quickly with relevant results.

Conflicting expectations can also be the source of establishing priorities. For example, a shared goal of quicker searches can place a higher funding priority on a faster search engine.

Definitions, processes, and measures

Can you have *quality* if you do not have all the stated and unstated requirements defined in the project scope statement? No.

You need to know:

- ▸ what is acceptable quality
- ▸ what work you will do as part of your project to deliver acceptable quality
- ▸ how and when you will measure the quality to be sure it's acceptable

Tips

- ▸ For each requirement, specify the measure and how and when it will be measured.
- ▸ Quality should be considered whenever there is a change to the budget, scope, or schedule. (Did the change affect your quality?)
- ▸ Quality should be checked before an activity is considered complete.
- ▸ Remember: Prevention over inspection. Consider changing the process to guarantee quality rather than spending time inspecting for mistakes at the end. Quality should be planned in, not inspected in.

The project manager is ultimately responsible for the quality of a product or project, even though performing quality checks might be the responsibility of team members.

Example

Quality Standard	What is the measure, what is the work, how and when will it happen?
The search results will be relevant and appear within 3 seconds.	Measurement: Search results are relevant to the search terms, are not duplicative, and the most relevant appear at the top of the results. All results appear within 3 seconds. What work we will do, how, and when? Tag each level of content with a key number that the search engine will use to identify relevancy to a search term. Develop an editorial review process that includes copy editor and search engine developer who are familiar with key numbers. Use customers to test the search results and identify any problems.

In a nutshell ▶ ▶ ▶

Communication: It is important to use collaborative communication techniques in meetings to set quality standards. These techniques include consensus, listening, and win-win conflict resolution.

Collaboration: If the project vision is at all fuzzy, it is likely to surface as conflict in discussions to develop shared quality standards. Quality often defines an organization's identity or brand, and organizations working together who have differing quality standards need a shared understanding of the quality measures for their shared project. Be sure that the decisions made are driven by collaboration (win-win goal orientation) rather than cooperation (win-lose goal orientation).

Project Management: Quality standards define how you will measure whether or not the project requirements have been met. Clearly define quality standards and include the measure and the process of achieving it. If there are any changes to the plan, review the quality standards at the same time. If a change affects delivery time or budget, for example, there may be an adjustment to quality to allow for it.

EXERCISE

Which of the following requests or changes are likely to affect quality standards? How might the project manager handle the request?

1. Request by the sponsor to speed up the project delivery date by four months.

2. Request by the developer to add a round of testing before the search engine license is renewed. (Testing will aid the decision whether or not to keep the current search engine or switch to a more expensive, faster one. Purchasing a new search engine will delay the project six months.)

3. Request by the sponsor to add a new funding source to the project (A like-minded organization that has collaborated with the organization on several other projects.)

4. Change of leadership in the organization. (New project sponsor places high priority on cost cutting and customer self-service.)

Exercise answers

1. The project manager could reduce the time scheduled for testing or assign an additional, less-experienced worker to the project to reduce the time estimated to complete the project. This is a risk to quality and should be brought to the attention of the sponsor. The project manager may handle this risk by suggesting features that could be dropped now and introduced in a later version.

2. Testing and taking action on the result of the testing will add to the quality of the search results. Quality search results have high priority in the project. If testing will delay the project six months, the project manager may recommend lowering quality in an area with less priority to make up the time, or adding more workers to the project, increasing costs.

3. The collaborating organization may have a different quality standard than your organization. It will be important to clarify the quality standard for the project and make certain it is used and measured uniformly by other organizations. It may take extra time to work this out before the project implementation is begun.

4. Cost cutting can often be the source of lower quality standards. The project manager can recommend placing a priority on project features that lower cost by increasing high-quality customer self-serve that would not jeopardize customer loyalty. For example, lowering business office payment processing costs by introducing the ability for the customer to pay invoices online would accomplish this.

RECOMMENDED READING

Turbit, Neville. "Project Quality Planning." Project Perfect, http://www.projectperfect.com.au/downloads/Info/info_project_quality_planning.pdf.

27

Create a Communication Plan

The Project Manager is perplexed. "We use every communication device there is: e-mail, face-to-face meetings, phone, newsletters, reports, meeting notes, instant messaging, blogs, and Intranet postings. With all this communicating, why doesn't anyone know what is going on?"

The Facilitator just nods. "Do your project participants know where and when to expect information that is pertinent to them? And is it in a format that meets their needs? Ninety percent of project management is communicating. A good communication plan will help you sort it out and will keep everyone on the project in the loop and on-board."

What is the communication plan?

The *communication plan* describes how the project manager will let others in the organization or collaborative group know what the project plan is, where it stands, and what action they need to take.

When making the plan, identify:

What information is to be communicated. Consider what level of detail is needed so that the recipients clearly understand if their interests are being met and whether or not they need to take action.

How this information will be communicated. The method can be formal or informal, written or verbal, depending on what best meets the needs of the receiver.

Formal: reports (written), meetings or presentations (verbal)

Informal: e-mail (written), hallway or drop-in meeting (verbal)

Who are the recipients. Tailor the communication to meet their needs.

When and how often they need to know.

Why you are communicating.

Consider the needs and concerns of those affected by your project. What are their questions? What would make them feel successful? What might surprise them? Design your communication plan to anticipate and answer their questions. Anticipating their questions will help avoid surprises, which can undermine trust.

Sponsor: They are responsible for the strategic direction and the allocation of resources for the project and for the organization. Their concerns are setting the priorities for the organization, avoiding duplication and the proper management of resources and accountability issues. Sponsors are looking and listening for positive results, trends, risks, and opportunities. Their questions: Are we doing the right things? Has anything changed?

Stakeholders: They have a strategic interest in the outcome of the project. They are looking and listening for the status of the project and its outcomes. Their questions: Are my interests being met? Are there any changes?

Supervisors and mid-level managers: They are responsible for carrying out day-to-day operations efficiently and effectively and for the assignment and training of their staff. They are looking and listening for the status of the project and any decisions made that would affect the commitment of their staff or have impact on priorities they are setting for other work. Their questions: Are my staff successfully doing what they were committed to for this project? Is this a good use of time and resources? Are my staff overcommitted? Has anything changed?

Business Office/Accounting: They are responsible for financial oversight. They are looking and listening that proper procedures are followed for any purchases, including vendor selection and payment. Their questions: Are appropriate funds committed? Are the funds being properly used and accounted? Are there variances?

Team members: They are responsible for planning and executing activities of the project and managing their time. They are looking and listening for assignments and deadlines, next steps, the purpose for their work, and a sense of achievement. Their questions: What are my priorities? Am I meeting expectations? Is the work of the team successful? Has anything changed?

Keeping these questions in mind will help the project manager structure an effective communication plan that informs people at the right time and in the way they find most useful. It will help the project manager develop messages that include the information that answers their questions. It will also prompt the manager to go the extra mile to make sure that everyone who needs to know about changes in the plan is informed about the change. This allows everyone involved to revisit decisions, set new priorities, and determine what actions to take.

Sample basic communication plan for a typical project				
What	**Method**	**To whom**	**When**	**Why**
Business Case	Formal report and presentation	All stakeholders	Beginning of project	To start project with a shared understanding between the project manager and sponsor. To allow questions and answers. To get feedback on whether or not the project is possible.
Project Plan	Formal report	All stakeholders	Through-out project	To create a sufficient level of detail so that the project can produce the desired results. So that all involved will know the plan. To monitor throughout the project to avoid scope creep, missed deadlines, poor quality, potential risks and opportunities, etc.
Project activities, milestone schedule, and work (resource) assign-ments	WBS (Work Breakdown Structure with ac-tivities list) Formal report	Project manager and team	Team meetings	WBS: To identify major compo-nents of the project to be sure everything is being considered during planning and execution. Activities list: This is a detailed list of work that needs to hap-pen on the project. Used to track status of tasks and over-all progress, identify slippage in schedules, resource issues, and monitor problems, risks, opportunities.
Evaluation of changes	Change log and e-mail notification	Project manager, team, and sponsor, when appropriate	Through-out project	To track and evaluate each change against the project goals and constraints. To com-municate changes to everyone affected. To make sure the plan is revised to accommodate changes.

What	Method	To whom	When	Why
Sponsor review and approvals	Meetings. (Can be formal or informal, depending on the circumstance.)	Project manager and sponsor	At least monthly for formal review, and as necessary for informal updates and concerns.	To inform sponsor of the status and any issues or changes to the project. To seek sponsor approvals and to provide the opportunity for sponsor to ask questions. To confirm to the project manager that the project is meeting sponsor's expectations.
Agendas	Formal written. Attached in e-mail.	All called to a meeting	24 hours before meeting date, 48 hours if there is preparation needed. Should include any handouts.	To inform parties of the purpose of the meeting and give them time to prepare for it. A copy of the agenda can be sent to the sponsor, if appropriate.
Meeting minutes	Formal written. Posted on Intranet. Includes action items, decisions, next steps.	All who attended. Can also be sent to stakeholders and other functional managers, if there is resource sharing.	48 hours after meeting.	To record decisions (consensus), results of brainstorming, action items, and next steps for those in attendance and for those who cannot attend.
Status of project for sponsor	Formal written.	Sponsor	Agreed regular basis or when there are changes.	To inform sponsor in a way that can be kept as a reference. Should include any variances from scope, budget, resources, schedule, quality, with explanation.

What	Method	To whom	When	Why
Status of project for team	Meeting. (Includes master WBS and subgroups WBS.)	Team	Agreed meetings (weekly, bi-weekly, etc.)	To keep everyone in the loop on the big picture and if there are any issues that would affect others. To provide opportunity for discussion and to identify whether or not there needs to be problem solving.
Vendor bidding process results	Formal written. RFP with specs and bids.	Purchasing, business office, project manager	During research phase.	To select the best vendor.
Final project sign-off	Written list of require-ments, measures, and com-pletion status.	Sponsor, project manager, team	At the end of the project.	To document the requirements and measures for the project along with agreement that these requirements have been met or have been transferred to future versions. To confirm the completion of the project, which now moves from devel-opment to normal upkeep and maintenance.

Communication plan tips

Consider the recipients of the communication and their needs. This will aid in determining the best method of communication. Major stakeholders who want to know the status of the project and if it is on track will expect a formal report, perhaps quarterly. Team members who need to share details of ongoing activities and need assignments reviewed will want to meet weekly or bi-weekly. They need clear meeting agendas and any corresponding background information to review.

Consider the learning styles of the recipients. Written reports and documents will be more welcomed by the procedural workers. They will also benefit, however, from face-to-face meetings that show concern about their welfare, discuss the context of a decision, or why things are happening as they are. Face-to-face meetings will be more welcomed by the navigators. It will be beneficial to them if the meeting is followed up with written documentation, especially if priorities, processes, or deadlines have to be changed.

What should recipients do as a result of receiving the communication? Include the desired action in the communication. If consensus will be taken at the meeting, include this information in the meeting agenda as well as any materials team members need for review.

It is helpful to explain where the communication documents will be stored and how they can be accessed. Posting documents on a Web interface such as your organization's Intranet provides a convenient location for organizing and updating the communication plan as well as corresponding materials that can be linked to the plan.

Avoid information overload. Record needed information, but use a format that can be scanned easily by the reader. This includes use of bullets, short paragraphs, charts, etc.

Be consistent and punctual with communications. Send agendas 24 hours in advance. Send meeting minutes within 48 hours after the meeting. Send status reports regularly on their scheduled dates. Consider the impact of any changes in the plan or implementation on recipients. Deliver bad news immediately and face-to-face.

Don't expect the formal communication plan to cover all communi-cation needs. The project manager should develop the skill to know when to rely on formal communications and when an informal follow-up chat is needed. Remember that 51 percent of communi-cation is nonverbal. Perhaps a team member has issued a formal written status report that she will meet her assigned task deadlines. The project manager may informally drop in to check on things and find a different situation: a very stressed individual who is struggling with the work and actually falling behind.

Develop a communication plan and make it available to all project par-ticipants. This will keep participants involved, supportive of the project, satisfy their expectations for being kept in the loop, and knowing what actions they need to take. More important, *follow the plan.* Keep com-munications relevant, up-to-date, concise, orderly, and accessible.

In a nutshell ▶ ▶ ▶

Communication: Ninety percent of a project manager's job is communication. Be skilled at the different types of communication—formal, informal, verbal, written—and know best when to use them. Using different methods will give you a greater opportunity to connect with recipients who have different learning/working styles. (See Lesson 2.) Develop a good communication plan and follow it.

Collaboration: To keep cross-functional stakeholders and team participants on-board and in the loop requires that they know where the project stands and what is expected of them—what actions they need to take. A good communication plan will ensure that everyone receives essential information in an orderly, timely, and concise manner. This promotes trust.

Project Management: Relevant, timely, and clear communications are the heart of project management success. They provide information about what has happened and what needs to happen for the project to stay on track. Used expertly, they help the project manager guide the project and make good decisions.

EXERCISE

Here are typical items that tend to fall through the cracks or don't get communicated in the best method, or in a timely way, to the people who need to know.

  ‣ Changes to the original plan

  ‣ Vendor contract review or changes to the contract

  ‣ Interim milestones completed and other team successes

  ‣ Conflicts or overlapping with other projects

  ‣ Issues that have been brought up and resolved

  ‣ Requests for additional resources (formal written)

  ‣ Transfer of the project to "maintenance" mode

  ‣ Lessons learned and evaluation of the project

Complete the chart to incorporate these items into the project communication plan.

What	Method to use	To whom	When	Why
Changes to the original plan				
Vendor contract review or changes to the contract				
Interim milestones completed and other successes				
Conflict or overlapping with other projects				
Issues that have been brought up and resolved				
Interim milestones completed and other team successes				
Request for additional resources (formal written)				
Transfer of project into "maintenance" mode				
Lessons learned and evaluation of the project				

Exercise answer

What	Method to use	To whom	When	Why
Changes to the original plan	Major change: meeting Minor change: E-mail Update project plan and WBS; Issue formal report.	Major change: sponsor, stakeholders, team, resources, and supervisors. Minor change: team, stakeholders.	Promptly, as necessary. Best to communicate as soon as you know, even before the change is implemented.	To keep everyone in the loop. (Changes can affect other projects or the final product.) To avoid surprises, wasted effort. To improve efficiency.
Vendor contract review and changes	Formal written contract. E-mail New contract, if appropriate. Discussion/meeting with those impacted and team.	Stakeholders. Vendor. Business office. Manager of the budget. Sponsor and team.	At the beginning of the contract and promptly, if there are any changes. Review again mid-contract and at close.	To confirm requirements and deadlines are met. To track items affecting budget. Informational.
Interim milestones completed and other team successes	Project report. Update WBS. Announce some successes in staff meetings. Verbal praise. E-mail praise.	Project manager and sponsor. Team. Organization.	Status meetings. Ongoing as milestones occur. Some staff meetings.	To balance communication so everything isn't a problem. To keep people in the loop. To avoid surprises. To show progress to the team and boost morale. To update stakeholders on status.
Conflicts or overlap with other projects	Meeting with project managers. E-mail updates.	All project managers. Sponsor.	Monthly updates and as necessary.	To avoid extra work or potential project failure. To resolve conflicts. To share information.

What	Method to use	To whom	When	Why
Issues that arose and how they got resolved	Meeting notes. Discussion with those outside the team who are impacted. Issue log (project document). Post on the Intranet.	Project manager and team. Other project managers. Any others impacted. Keep on record. Share with sponsor.	Throughout the project. During and after a problem.	To hold discussion to identify who needs to know. To let others know how problems were resolved. To keep everyone up-to-date. To apply solutions or decisions made to future projects. Knowledge.
Request for additional resources (formal written)	Meeting. E-mail and formal written.	Project Manager to sponsor or budget manager. Project manager to department heads or supervisors.	Throughout the project, as needed. Give as much lead time as possible	To seek collaboration to keep project on track and maintain quality. To deal with unplanned issues.
Transfer of project into "maintenance mode"	Formal written procedure. Staff meeting. Verbal report.	All staff. All stakeholders.	Before project is implemented. Again at end of project.	To inform staff what to anticipate and who will take questions. To avoid missing important details/next steps.
Lessons learned and evaluation of the project	Informal written report at end of project for future reference. Determine at meeting. File on Intranet.	Team members, sponsor, and other project managers. Staff.	After the project ends. Scheduled meeting. Summary of issue log.	To improve future projects. To help people doing ongoing work

RECOMMENDED READING

D'Aprix, Roger. *Communicating for Change: Connecting the Workplace with the Marketplace*. San Francisco, Calif.: Jossey-Bass, 1996.

D'Aprix, Roger. *The Credible Company, Communicating with Today's Skeptical Workforce*. San Francisco, Calif.: Jossey-Bass, 2009.

Jensen, Bill. *Simplicity, the New Competitive Advantage in a World of More, Better, Faster*. New York: Perseus Publishing, 2000.

Kotter, John P. *A Sense of Urgency*. Boston, Massachusetts: Harvard Business School Press, 2008.

Kotter, John P. *Leading Change*. Boston, Massachusetts: Harvard Business School Press, 1996.

Kotter, John P., and Rathgeber, Holger. *Our Iceberg Is Melting*. New York: St. Martin's Press, 1996.

28

Identify Risks and Opportunities

"Is there any way I could have avoided these problems?" asks the Project Manager. "Seems like I am putting out one fire after another. It doesn't leave me any time to pursue opportunities."

"You'll avoid 90 percent of potential problems on your project—and uncover opportunities as well— with a little up-front risk management," advises the Facilitator.

What is risk management?

Risk is the possibility of loss. While creating the project plan, the project manager anticipates future events that could cause the project to lose money, time, resources, quality, or materials. *Risk management* is identifying when and where these can occur in a project and planning to minimize their impact. By anticipating the risks and what the response will be, the project manager maintains control, makes better decisions, and wastes no time keeping the project on track.

It is important to identify possible risks at the early stages of a project. Without assessing the risks, the project itself may get the go-ahead, when, if the risks had been assessed, the project would have been found to be unfeasible or too risky. The costs to the organization of a failed project are greater than any extra time or effort taken to assess the risks.

Is it possible to anticipate every risk? No, this is unrealistic and cumbersome. It is more profitable to identify as many risks as possible and then focus on the critical ones, those that affect activities on the critical path or those most likely to occur. Note that new risks need to be identified throughout the project as activities are carried out, as new technology is introduced, and as external events touch the project.

There are five steps you can take to manage risk. Use them to control your project and keep the project from controlling you.

Step 1: Define where and how much risk you are willing to accept.

Because is not possible to address every risk that you identify during a project, it is important to understand the areas most important to your team, your customers, and your sponsor so that you can focus your attention and resources appropriately.

To get started, think about the triple constraint of time, cost, and scope. (See Lesson 19.) For example, are you willing to risk going over budget? How much over? Are you willing to risk spending additional staff time? How much more?

Take five minutes to identify a few areas where you are willing to accept risk. Be sure to specify how much you are willing to assume. Also, identify areas where you are *not* willing to assume any risk (if there are any). For example:

▸ We are not willing to risk going over budget.

▸ We can accept delays to the project delivery date if they are not over 3 months.

- We will not risk personnel shortages. We have allowed funds for additional staff time if needed.

- We are not willing to risk poor quality of search results.

- We will not risk delays in the project to implement new tech developments for the current version.

Step 2: Identify risks and opportunities.

The most likely sources of *risk* depend on the complexity of the project, the funding sources, the duration of critical tasks (the longer a task takes, the more that can go wrong), dependencies (the weather can be one), etc.

Do not forget to identify *opportunities*. What things could go right? And if they do, how will you take advantage of them? For example, if the project costs less than anticipated, can you use the money for something else?

Identifying risks and opportunities is not solely the responsibility of the project manager. In fact, it is smart to involve other people. Consider talking to the sponsor (who should have given you some information about risks in the business case), your team members, or other people who have worked on similar projects. Brainstorming can be used effectively to generate ideas.

Some of the risks for our Web redesign project include

- Introduction and availability of new technology that, if found to be beneficial, could delay the project and require additional funding.

- Delay from reliance on one specialized designer who is committed to other priority projects in the organization as well as this one.

- Creating over-complexity by personalizing every customer account transaction, exhausting testing resources and customer support.

- Duplication of key numbers so that search results contain irrelevant references.

What about opportunities?

- ▶ Developing a sophisticated key number system so a more expensive search engine is not needed.

- ▶ Determining an innovative process to keep the Web site up-to-date and avoid the expensive undertaking of redesigning every three years.

- ▶ Developing new products that arise as a result of innovation.

Step 3: Decide which risks you will respond to.

There will always be many risks associated with any project. Some are more likely to happen than others. Some will have a bigger impact if they do happen. Your team has to decide which risks are worth focusing on and which to set aside. These decisions will be somewhat subjective because they are based on your experience and your risk tolerance.

Rate your risks on a scale of 1 to 10 for their probability of occurring and the impact they will have (1 = low, 10 = high). Based on this information and your threshold for risk, pick one risk you want to focus on. For example, here is the list of risk items resorted by priority. The first risk has the highest potential to impact the project in a negative way.

1. Duplication of key numbers so that search results contain irrelevant references.

2. Planning to use old technology. Introduction and availability of new technology later in the project could delay the project and require additional funding.

3. Creating over-complexity by personalizing every customer account transaction, exhausting testing resources and customer support.

4. Delay from reliance on one specialized designer who is committed to other priority projects in the organization as well as this one.

Step 4: Decide how you will respond.

Project managers have options for handling any risk or opportunity. The response you choose will generally fall into one of the following categories.

For risks

- ▶ Mitigate: Reduce the probability that the risk will occur.
- ▶ Transfer: Make another party responsible, e.g., buy insurance or a warranty.
- ▶ Accept: Do nothing. "If it happens, it happens."
- ▶ Avoid: Eliminate the risk by eliminating the cause.

Here is how these strategies might be applied to the risks identified in our Web redesign project:

1. Duplication of key numbers so that search results contain irrelevant references.

   Mitigate by proofing and review to make certain there are no duplicates.

2. Planning to use old technology. Introduction and availability of new technology later in the project could delay the project and require additional funding.

   Avoid. We will only use the latest technology available.

3. Creating over-complexity by personalizing every customer account transaction, exhausting testing resources and customer support.

   Mitigate: Every request for personalization must have a corresponding approved testing resource and customer support plan.

4. Delay from reliance on one specialized designer who is committed to other priority projects in the organization as well as this one.

   Mitigate: Give the designer longer lead times. Negotiate priority on the other projects.

For opportunities

▸ Exploit: Add work or change the project to make sure it happens.

▸ Enhance: Increase the likelihood that the opportunity will happen.

▸ Share: Allocate ownership to a partner who is best able to achieve the desired result.

▸ Accept: Do nothing. "If it happens, it happens."

How will we respond to the opportunities?

▸ Developing a sophisticated key number system so a more expensive search engine is not needed.

Exploit. Make certain that the key number system is implemented.

▸ Determining an innovative process to keep the Web site up-to-date and avoid the expensive undertaking of redesigning every three years.

Enhance. Use collaboration to increase the likelihood that an innovative process to keep the Web site up-to-date is determined.

▸ Developing new products that result from innovation.

Accept. We will accept new products as they meet customer needs and are developed.

Step 5: Know when you will respond.

Part of the job of the project manager and team members is identifying the *trigger* for your risk. Think of the trigger as the warning that the risk is about to happen. Throughout your project, you should be watching triggers so you know when to activate your risk response. Talking about the status of risks and triggers is an excellent topic for team meetings.

Consider the triggers for the risks previously identified:

1. Duplication of key numbers so that search results contain irrelevant references.

    Trigger: Proofing process identifies use of duplicates or initial test search results show results that are not relevant.

2. Using old technology. Introduction and availability of new technology that, if found to be beneficial, could delay the project and require additional funding.

    Trigger: Result of attending a conference showing new technology.

3. Creating over-complexity by personalizing every customer account transaction, exhausting testing resources and customer support.

    Trigger: Lengthy programming code documents. Many errors in the coding. Missed deadlines for sections of code.

4. Delay from reliance on one specialized designer who is committed to other priority projects in the organization as well as this one.

    Trigger: Missed meetings. Requests for more time to finish tasks. Stressful responses.

Monitor risks throughout your project.

You should monitor risks throughout your project, not just during planning. Use the five steps whenever you identify new risks. As your project progresses, remember to

▸ look for risk triggers

▸ monitor the noncritical risks

▸ identify and plan for new risks

▸ make sure that risk plans are executed effectively

▸ make sure original assumptions about risks are still valid as your project changes

▸ reevaluate risks to be sure there are no new critical ones

In a nutshell ▶ ▶ ▶

Communication: Involve others in the identification of risks and triggers. Brainstorming can be used effectively to generate ideas. Be clear about what amount of risk the project can assume. Validate that this is approved by the stakeholders.

Collaboration: Mitigating risks involves collaborative conflict resolution to find win-win solutions for responding to risks. Resolving how to respond to a risk at the planning stage develops trust and comfort with interdependency.

Project Management: Effective use of triggers as well as a clear response plan will give the project manager control of most uncertainties.

EXERCISE

What are the risks of not creating a risk management plan?

Exercise answer

1. When the negative event occurs, the project manager will be unprepared and will have to scramble to determine what caused it and what to do.

2. The project may be jeopardized by delays and increased costs.

3. The team will spend time needed to complete activities to do problem solving instead.

4. Poor decisions may be made because they will be made under the pressure of deadlines and without support.

5. The project itself may get the go-ahead when, if the risks had been assessed, it would have been found to be not feasible.

6. Opportunities may not be recognized or exploited.

7. The project manager risks overlooking triggers that would warn her of trouble ahead.

29

Wrap Up the Plan

"Here's the plan. Want to look it over before I submit it for approval?" asks the Project Manager.

"Have you looked it over?" responds the Facilitator. "You've spent a lot of time working out the details. Step back and take a big picture view. Does the plan achieve the project goals? Is the plan realistic? Are you confident your approach can deliver the project on time, on budget, and meet expectations?"

Taking another look

You have worked carefully on all the sections of the plan. Do all these pieces work together to deliver your project on time, on budget, and meet expectations?

The project manager and the planning team have

- ▶ defined the scope requirements
- ▶ determined an approach
- ▶ created a work breakdown structure
- ▶ built the activity list

- charted the network diagram and critical path
- estimated resources
- planned the schedule
- developed the budget
- established quality standards
- crafted the communication plan
- identified the risks, opportunities, triggers, and responses

It is time to look at the plan elements from an overall perspective.

Does this plan work—will it achieve the project goals? For example, if the overriding goal of the project is moving the organization to adopt Web First as the core of its operations, are there any activities or work plans that do not use or lead the organization toward Web technology or processes? When the risk management plan was drafted, was it considered a risk if any plan outcomes were not Web First compliant?

Is it realistic? It may have been several weeks or months since you started the plan. Have there been any changes? Consider:

Do you have commitments from the resources you based your estimates on? Are they still available?

Has anything happened in the organization that would push for an *earlier delivery date* on your project? Has a special event been planned that requires your project be finished sooner than originally estimated?

Has there been a change in the organization's priorities that would *affect your funding?*

Did you identify any risks that require you to *adjust your approach?*

Are all the *testing sessions you need to do to meet your quality standards* covered in your schedule?

Have prices or wages increased since your resource estimating was done?

Has your organization *adopted any new business practices or processes* that have to be followed? For example, will a new bidding process requirement lengthen the time it will take to choose a vendor? Is this activity on the critical path? If so, your project may be delayed.

Making adjustments

If adjustments need to be made to one area of your plan, think of how those changes might affect the other areas of your plan. Remember the triple constraint of *time, cost,* and *scope* discussed in Lesson 19. If one area is changed, the other areas must adjust to accommodate.

▸ If you find wages have increased, your estimate for the cost of resources will rise. Are you now over budget?

▸ To bring your resource cost down you may eliminate a senior staff person and replace her with a less costly junior staff person. Will this change lengthen the time it takes to get the work done? Will training be necessary? This will add cost and lengthen duration.

▸ If your plan is now over budget and will be delayed, you may need to adjust scope. Is there a feature that was dependent on the senior staff person's work that could be shifted to a later version? This would bring cost and time back into balance.

Review the critical path

Many adjustments are made as the plan unfolds. If any adjustment is made to an activity that is on the critical path, account for it in your critical path flow diagram. These adjustments will alter the time it takes to complete your project. If critical path items are overlooked—or not accounted for—you risk being unable to deliver your project on time. Even if tasks are not on the critical path, review their dependencies. If a delivery date is affected, how will that affect activities that depend on that delivery?

The wisdom of your planning team

The planning team should see the plan in its final, formal state. Use the wisdom of your planning team for a final reality check. They can verify estimates, confirm that the work packages have all essential elements, advise if there have been changes in their work environment or in the organization, and reconfirm their commitment to the project.

In a nutshell

Communication: The plan itself is a formal communication document. It will be used as a baseline and road map for the project. The project manager will use it to determine if activities are on target and if costs are under control. The plan is a living document that describes the deliverables of the project, when they are due, and how they will be measured.

Collaboration: The final plan is the result of collaborative work. It clearly must state and achieve the project goals—the outcome of the shared vision of the stakeholders. Any elements that do not lead to achieving the shared goal must be identified as a risk or ruled out of scope.

Project Management: Taking the big picture view of the plan, using the wisdom of the planning group, and ensuring that the plan is feasible and realistic is required of the project manager. If an adjustment is made, consider the effect on the triple constraint: Balance scope, cost, and time.

EXERCISE

1. Which factor is the most important in making the project plan realistic?

    a. The estimates were made by workers who did similar work in the past.

    b. The sponsor has given resource and funding support to the project.

    c. The project manager has done three projects more complex than this one.

2. Which factor is the most important in making the plan achieve its collaborative goal?

    a. The team members support the plan.

    b. The stakeholders reviewed the final plan.

    c. The scope statement was crystal clear.

3. Which factor is the most important in making the plan feasible?

    a. The risk management plan is thorough.

    b. The activity list is thorough.

    c. Scope, quality, cost, and time are in balance.

4. Which factor is the most important in making the plan acceptable to the sponsor and stakeholders?

    a. The risk management plan is thorough.

    b. It is clearly written and well documented.

    c. Once each section was complete, no further changes were allowed.

Exercise answers

1. *a.* The estimates were made by workers who did similar work in the past.

2. *b.* The stakeholders reviewed the final plan.

3. *c.* Scope, quality, cost, and time are in balance.

4. *b.* It is clearly written and well documented.

30

Gain Approval for the Plan

"The approval meeting is all set. What if the stakeholders don't approve the plan? What are my options?" asks the Project Manager.

"Understand the stakeholders' concerns before going into the meeting," answers the Facilitator. "Be prepared to show how your plan addresses their expressed and even unexpressed concerns."

Formal approval

Formal approval of the plan is the signal that the business case will be put into action. The plan has proved that the business case is feasible, and the project manager has agreed to deliver its requirements on time, on budget, meeting quality standards, and with the resources committed to it. The project will be funded by the organization and supported by its stakeholders.

Preparing for formal approval

Be prepared to address common concerns and arguments of those who will make the decision. Anticipate expressed as well as unexpressed concerns and speak to both. Following is a list of concerns, unexpressed concerns appear in parentheses.

Concern that there is a *better time* to do the project. (This may be the desire to put off committing to the organizational change.) This concern may be answered by highlighting elements from the business case that show the benefits and necessities of doing the project now, or what the organization will lose by putting it off. For example, we must improve our search results or risk losing our customers.

Concern that *more information and/or research must be provided* before the plan can be approved. (This may be fear of failing, perhaps based on past experiences.) This concern may be answered by explaining that the plan is a living document that is not cast in stone. Options and changes are considered throughout the project. Proceeding now will allow these options to unfold. Hesitating will not, and you run the danger of not seeing them at all.

Concern with *committing resources and funding.* (This may be the hesitation to take action or make uncomfortable trade-offs.) This concern may be answered by highlighting the benefits to the organization(s) the outcome will bring. These are addressed in the business case. (See Lesson 7.)

Concern that the *schedule is unrealistic.* (This may reflect the uncertainty of balancing this project with existing work.) This concern may be answered by explaining who was involved in the estimating process and why you believe the schedule to be accurate. It is also helpful to highlight how you plan to handle the transition period when productivity drops. (See Lesson 1 on managing organizational change.) This concern may also reflect the fear of committing to a timeline when the project has unknowns. This unexpressed concern can be addressed by talking about the expectations and priority of scheduling and quality.

Concern that there will be *proper control* of the project—particularly if it is a collaborative project. (This may be the desire to remain independent and in control or lack of trust in the project manager.) This concern is addressed by the confidence, openness, and professional presentation of the project manager and the thoroughness of the plan documents, particularly the communication plan. (See Lesson 27.)

Concern that the plan is *lacking important detail*. (This may reflect lack of trust in the project manager.) Understand the interests of your approvers and make sure those areas are covered. You want your plan to touch on all aspects of the project, so if something is identified that you missed in your plan, be thankful. Better to address it before your project has started than to scramble and account for it later.

Remember that the goal of this meeting is to make sure you have a plan in place that will deliver a successful project. It isn't a rubber stamp meeting. Take advantage of all the knowledge and experience you have in the room. Be prepared to engage the team and approvers in taking a close look at the plan. Encourage discussion and feedback and be genuinely interested in comments. Give each one serious consideration. They are giving you their input because they, too, want the project to succeed.

Prepare the plan as a formal document and include an executive summary of the key goals, scope, approach, budget, quality, risk, and communication plan. Address these concerns and any others that may have surfaced during the planning period.

Plan a formal approval meeting and distribute the planning documents 48 hours before the meeting.

Agenda for the meeting

Here is a successful agenda for a project plan approval meeting.

Participants: Stakeholders

Purpose: To seek approval for the project plan

Consensus or decision needed: Approval for the plan

Agenda

- Each participant briefly gives their strategic interest in the outcome of the plan
- Project manager outlines the shared goal and how the plan achieves it
- Go/No-Go analysis
- A straw vote to determine where the group stands
- Options, if there are reservations about the plan
- Seek approval
- Next steps

How to handle each agenda item

Here is practical guidance to help you prepare for and conduct the plan approval meeting.

Purpose: to seek approval for the project plan

Preparation: Send copies of the plan document with the agenda to the meeting participants at least 48 hours in advance of the meeting. Be clear about the purpose of the meeting and indicate who will be at the meeting. Ask participants to read the plan before the meeting and come prepared to discuss any reservations.

At the meeting: Establish the purpose of the meeting at the beginning and briefly introduce the agenda items. It is also helpful to have the agenda items listed on a flipchart:

A flipchart at this meeting is beneficial because it

- gives prominence to the agenda;
- gives prominence to the ideas shared. Participants become more comfortable with sharing ideas when they see their ideas recorded;
- creates a central focus that draws the participants away from looking at each other to the topic at hand. They become more comfortable with the process;
- keeps the ideas central and brief (it is important that the scribe be able to record just the main point in a concise, clear manner);
- brings movement and action to the meeting as the topics are handled; and
- provides color for emphasis or interest.

Each participant briefly gives their strategic interest in the outcome of the plan (the product)

Preparation: In the call to the meeting, indicate you will ask the stakeholders to share their strategic interest and to come prepared. Indicate the time allotted for each one to speak. Give an example. "I will ask the Sponsor to share how the plan addresses the strategic goal (from the business case) of moving the organization to Web First."

At the meeting: Go around the table and ask each stakeholder to share their interest in the project with the group. Begin with the sponsor, who will share the business or organization's interest. Remind participants of their time limit. This is not a time for discussion, but for sharing and listening. Ask the scribe to record the main point each one makes on the flipchart. If the speaker is interrupted, ask that he be allowed to finish and move to the next speaker. At the end of this sharing, allow a brief time for questions if any clarification is needed. This exchange is not to introduce new information, but to reaffirm that each person's strategic interest is met in the project plan.

Project manager outlines the shared goal and how the plan achieves it

Preparation: Distribute a clear executive summary—the main points described briefly at a high level—with the plan. (See Time-Savers at the end of this Lesson for a sample executive summary of the plan.) Prepare a flipchart that lists your main points. Consider your audience and be sure the plan matches their working styles. (See Lesson 2.)

At the meeting: Refer to the flipchart as you highlight how your plan will successfully achieve the goal. Be clear, concise, and confident. Be aware of any unexpressed concerns and address them as well.

Go/No-Go Analysis

This is a group activity that provides the opportunity for analysis and discussion to determine the feasibility of going ahead, or not, with a project. Selected participants will complete sections of a matrix before the meeting, and the results are used as the basis for discussion.

Sample matrix

	Disadvantages	Advantages
Go		
No-Go		

Preparation: Ask two participants to fill out one row (the advantages and disadvantages of going ahead with the project) and bring their results to the meeting. Ask two different participants to fill out the second row (the advantages and disadvantages of not going ahead with the project). The project manager should also be prepared to share ideas during discussion.

At the meeting: The four participants will share their analysis: Record their findings on the flipchart; open the discussion to the group; and record others' ideas. Avoid getting bogged down in extended or circular discussions.

A straw vote to determine where the group stands

Preparation: Work with your gatekeeper so you can move into the straw vote in the time allotted. Prepare to lead the group in the straw vote.

At the meeting: Go around the table and ask participants where they stand in regard to the project plan. Does it appear to be a go or a no-go? Ask them to voice any reservations. Have the scribe record these on the flipchart.

Options, if there are reservations

Preparation: Prepare for reservations or requests and be able to offer options and rationale. The most common requests will be for the project to be completed in less time or for less money. What if a condition for approval is to finish the project in less time? Prepare to explain realistically what options are available to the stakeholders if the time allowed for the project is shortened.

▸ What features might be dropped or delayed (reduce scope).

▸ Which additional resources may need to be funded (increase cost).

▸ Which quality standards might be lowered (reduce quality).

At the meeting: Be articulate and knowledgeable. Answer the concerns and respond to the requests sincerely. Be realistic. Be prepared to explain how estimates were determined and who has given the project resource commitments. Offer options that are realistic and be prepared to present any risks associated with their requests.

Seek approval

Preparation: Review the rules for consensus and the techniques for gaining consensus. (See Lesson 6.)

At the meeting: Gain a sense of the group's position. If the plan is generally accepted, seek consensus.

Next steps

Preparation: Be prepared to make revisions to the plan and allow yourself time after the meeting to do this. Know how long it will take, so that you can speak confidently to the group. If the plan is approved, be prepared to explain the next step which is the Kickoff Meeting. (See Lesson 31.)

At the meeting: If revisions need to be made to the plan, explain how long it will take and schedule another meeting for final approval. If the plan is approved, explain that the next step is the Kickoff Meeting. Ask for any feedback on the communication plan and assure the group you will follow it.

No matter the outcome, thank everyone for their participation and tell them when they should expect to hear from you.

In a nutshell ▷ ▷ ▷

Communication: Communication between the project manager and stakeholders must be open and realistic. Preparation and past performance are key. Address expressed and unexpressed concerns honestly without becoming defensive. Determine that the communication plan meets the needs of the stakeholders and that it is followed.

Collaboration: An important aspect of gaining trust is the ability of the project manager to make sure that the interests of the stakeholders are heard and addressed. Reaffirm the shared goal. Use the Go/No-Go analysis to show the benefits of the plan and to bring any uncertainties to the surface so they can be handled.

Project Management: There is a good chance that the stakeholders may ask for conditions before they will approve the plan. These may include doing the work in less time for less money and fewer resources. If these conditions are accepted, be prepared to explain the effect on scope, time, and cost constraints.

EXERCISE

Which of the following concerns might be held by a stakeholder but be *unexpressed*? How might the project manager bring them out in the open and deal with them impersonally?

1. Current projects in the organization will be delayed because staff resources will be reassigned to the new project.

2. Work flow will be disrupted and staff productivity in general will drop.

3. Work that is considered now to be a priority in the organization will have less value or will be eliminated because it is not considered to be Web First.

4. Decisions will be made without my being consulted or notified.

5. If I don't agree to the project, I will be seen as uncooperative.

6. The project will overspend to get all the features that are sure to crop up.

Exercise answer

Concerns that may be *unexpressed* and how to bring them out in the open.

2. Explain up front that the project (new projects in general) is bringing change to the organization and that as the organization transitions to this change, productivity is expected to drop. Once the transition is completed, productivity will increase to a higher level than before the change.

3. This concern might reflect the fear of change. Ask the sponsor to clearly identify the business reasons for the project, especially how the organization is responding to the needs of the market. A clear vision will show what the change will be and help others see their contribution and value to the project and to the organization.

5. Collaborative projects achieve the shared goals of the stakeholders. Each stakeholder is encouraged to identify how the plan will achieve his or her strategic interest. If conflicts need to be resolved, it will be through collaborative resolution, not cooperation. Encourage discussion of reservations to the plan to seek the win-win outcome. Without it, the project is not fully supported.

Sample: Executive Summary of the Plan

Web Redesign Project: Executive Summary

This document formally records and details the history, scope, approach, timeline, risks, and other deliverables for the Web redesign project.

Our strategic vision is to have the Web the core of our operations and ensure that our development and processes are Web First.

Customers reply in surveys that they are unhappy with the speed of our site, quality of search results, and other functions. Our site is not based on the latest technology, the design does not consistently reflect our brand, and customer service functions are not personalized. Our internal processes assume that content will first be prepared for print and then posted to the Web.

The scope of the project is to rewrite our program in .net bringing speed and the latest functionality, tag our content so that it is quickly searchable and results are relevant, personalize our sales outreach and responses to customers, redesign the entire site so that it reflects our brand identity, individualize what we offer to customers, and create new processes that will ensure our content is developed and produced Web First. All features will be customer tested before being released. Quality standards are medium for approvals and high for final release.

We will begin in October 2009 and expect the entire project to be completed in 3 years. We will break the project into 6 versions. Each will be its own project. The first version will include the elements that have the highest priority and those that will add the most value to the organization.

We will largely do the work in-house, but we will contract for technical programming. The in-house work will be done by teams representing all departments, using collaborative conflict resolution and communication methods. We will use best practice project management methods.

The project plan gives the details of the project and how it will be implemented. Some highlights from this plan

▸ Budget: We estimate it will cost $120,000. This includes internal staff time of $80,000 and contract programming of $40,000.

▸ Changes: All changes will be managed. None will be accepted unless approved by the sponsor.

▸ Risks: Risks are identified and plans to deal with them are specified.

▸ Communication: The plan includes a detailed communication plan. We will use a red, yellow, and green highlighting system to alert stakeholders of the status of all major work packages.

▸ Monitoring: The team will meet weekly to monitor status of the schedule and to resolve any problems.

▸ Assumptions: We assume the collaboration of stakeholders for decisions and support. We assume support from supervisors for release time of programmers and designers. We assume that the organization will support new processes. We also assume support for 6 months after the release to transition the new processes.

Web Redesign: Executive Summary
Version 3 Update

This document addresses revisions made to the Web redesign plan as we move into launching versions 3 and 4 to our site.

After meeting with the IT and marketing staff, we will commit to completing versions 3 and 4 (out of 6) of our site in September and November, respectively. The first release is scheduled for September 26 to meet our deadline for delivering the Top Tips product to our customers. This release will include

- the introduction of Top Tips
- the introduction of revised newsletter
- a page dedicated to information about becoming a contributor
- revised text on the about us page
- revised look for the search result pages
- revised rules for displaying featured content
- revised primary law home page

The remaining work will be released in early November. This release will include

- a revised store and e-commerce area
- a fully revised primary law area
- a revised subscription home page
- revised navigation across the site
- revised home page for the site
- a new customer service area

To meet these deadlines, we are reprioritizing our time, cost, and quality balance so that hitting deadlines has the highest priority. We will lower the quality of the design to be sure the pages are designed according to schedule. Because the November release includes our e-commerce system and our primary law research area, we will not compromise on testing time. These areas are complex and need to be tested thoroughly before they are released.

If needed, we will outsource some of the technical programming work. Outsourced programming work tends to be between $60 and $90 per hour. Contracted work will be capped at 40 hours to stay within budget.

The IT and design staff will meet weekly to review the schedule and deal with any questions. In addition, the current web team will continue to meet to review wireframes and make any remaining decision. Status reports will be distributed at each meeting.

Sample: Go/No-Go Decision Matrix

Go/No-Go Decision Matrix		
Project Name:		
Project Lead:		
The Question:		
	Go	No-Go
Advantages		
Disadvantages		

For guidelines in using this form, see *Project Management Demystified* by Sid Kemp, particularly pages 301–304 on brainstorming and decision making.

QTI Go/No-Go Decision Matrix Template 2004–01. Excerpted from *Project Management Demystified* by Sid Kemp (McGraw-Hill, 2004) © QTI, Inc. 2004. www.qualitytechnology.com

Uses:

For any yes/no decision, either for an entire project, or for a single feature.

Steps:

1. Before the meeting
   - ▶ The project manager prepares the question
   - ▶ Two other people each prepare one column, advantages/disadvantages of going ahead or not
   - ▶ All meet, agree on terms, respond to each others' ideas.

2. At the meeting
   - ▶ Project manager presents the question
   - ▶ Each preparer presents his/her side, including both advantages and disadvantages
   - ▶ Open to additional ideas
   - ▶ Get straw vote/sense of the meeting
   - ▶ Move to a decision

3. After the meeting
   - ▶ Include those who disagree in the ongoing work

QTI Go/No-Go Decision Matrix Template 2004-01. Excerpted from *Project Management Demystified* by Sid Kemp (McGraw-Hill, 2004) © QTI, Inc. 2004. www.qualitytechnology.com

31

Hold the Kickoff Meeting

"I want to get this project off to a good start," says the Project Manager. "Any suggestions?"

"Start at the end," says the Facilitator. "Have the right people in the room and make the vision clear to them. If they can see the end product and how it fits into the strategic plan, the team will be motivated to get there."

Introductions

Formal approval of the plan ended the work of the planning team. The *kickoff meeting* introduces a new team to the project, the *implementation* team. Some of the team members also may have served on the planning team, and they will bring knowledge from that experience. However, the team members will be new to each other as a team and the project manager's initial focus will be as much on building the team relationships as introducing them to the project.

Here are objectives for a productive kickoff meeting. It's about introductions:

1. Introduce an organized, relaxed, productive meeting/working style to the team.

2. Welcome the team and introduce the sponsor.

3. Introduce the project outcome with a clear vision.

4. Introduce the team members to the project and to each other.

5. Describe the next steps.

6. Evaluate the meeting.

1. Introduce the meeting style

The kickoff meeting introduces the project manager's meeting/working style to the implementation team. This team will work together for many months executing the plan, and the first meeting will set the tone for meetings to follow. An organized, timely, productive meeting—well prepared and executed—inspires confidence that the project will be carried out on time, on budget, and will meet quality standards.

Although the style with which you run the meetings may be your own, it is important to always follow a few basic meeting principles. These principles will set a positive tone and ensure successful and productive meetings.

Prepare an organized, realistic agenda and send it out 24 hours in advance of the meeting. Include the executive summary of the plan with the agenda.

Arrive early and prepare the room. Be sure that there is enough seating, that the room is comfortable (temperature and lighting), and that you have any equipment you need. Have a flipchart available.

Start and end the meeting on time even if all members have not arrived.

Stick to the agenda topics and time limits.

Follow the Rules of Conduct for Meetings (see Lesson 11).

Encourage participation from all members and provide opportunities for interaction.

2. Welcome the team and introduce the sponsor

Show enthusiasm for the project by welcoming and thanking the team members for their participation and commitment to the project. Introduce the sponsor and ask her to highlight the benefits this project brings to the organization. Point out the commitment and priority the organization has given to the project by providing resources, time, and funding. Explain that the project is a collaborative effort, requiring input from all levels of the organization at all stages of the project. Acknowledge the collaborators. Be clear that discussion and ideas are encouraged and welcomed throughout the project.

3. Introduce the project with a clear vision

The sponsor will describe the shared vision of the project—the end result of the team's work as if it were already in place today. The team members should be able to see their roles in making this vision come to life. The main goal and guiding principles of the project should be clear: For example, when the Web redesign project is finished, the organization's products and processes will be developed and produced using Web First methods. Clarify *why* that is a shared goal of the collaborators.

Allow time for team members to ask the sponsor questions. Be open to suggested changes and note them for consideration. Each suggestion will be weighed against the projects goals and guiding principles at a later time. Define any terms that may be new or unfamiliar to team members.

4. Introduce the team members to the project and to each other

Ask team members to share how they see themselves in relation to the project and what part each one plays in accomplishing the vision. Have each team member introduce who they are, where they work, and how their skills and experience link them to the project. Include what they hope to gain by working on the team. This can include both personal/professional goals as well as goals for their department. It is important for the sponsor and project manager to hear this. It is a good opportunity for the team members to understand the project and identify any areas where their goals conflict with the project's goals. Go around the table to let each member participate in this sharing. Record their responses on a flipchart. This is your first step in relationship building on your team. Resolve any conflicts in goals one-on-one and outside of the meeting.

5. Describe the next steps

Indicate that your next meeting will be soon and will introduce the plan in detail. The meeting will define how you will work together as a team to bring the vision to life.

6. Evaluate the meeting

Ask each participant to share what went well and what could be improved for the next meeting.

In a nutshell ▶ ▶ ▶

Communication: The kickoff meeting is a forming stage for the new team. It is also the opportunity to introduce the project sponsor and the implementation team. Communication is introductory and geared toward relationship building. Define any terms that may be unfamiliar. Provide opportunities for each participant to speak and encourage them to do so.

Collaboration: Encourage the team members to talk about how they fit into the structure of the plan and to share what they are bringing to the project—skills and experience—as well as the benefit they will reap from the project outcome. Provide opportunities for them to realize that their individual needs will be met through collaboration. Allow time for team members to ask questions of the sponsor.

Project Management: Team meetings are among your most valuable tools as a project manager. Master these seemingly simple but critical meeting and facilitation skills. The kickoff meeting sets the stage for your project and is your first step in building your team's commitment to it.

EXERCISE

Here are agenda topics for a kickoff meeting. What time limits would you assign to each topic on the agenda? How long would you advise the meeting to be?

1. Welcome the team and introduce the sponsor.

2. Introduce the project outcome with a clear vision.

3. Introduce the team members to the project and to each other.

4. Describe the next steps.

5. Evaluate the meeting.

Exercise answer

Consider an hour and a half for this important meeting. This will provide time for team members to ask questions and for the sponsor to respond.

It is important to focus first on the relationship of the project to the organization and the relationship of the team to the goals of the project and to each other.

1. Welcome the team and introduce the sponsor (10 min)

2. Introduce the project outcome with a clear vision (30 min)
   20 min to present the vision
   10 min for questions

3. Consider a break here (5 min)

4. Introduce the team members to the project and to each other (40 min for a team of 6)

5. Next steps and meeting evaluation (5 min)

SECTION IV

▼
▼

Executing

Vision without action is a dream. Action without vision is simply passing time. Action with vision is making a positive difference.

~Joel Barker

Lessons

32

Introduce the Plan to the Implementation Team

"Finally," says the Project Manager. "We can put the plan to work. The new team seems excited about the project. Some were on the planning team and already have shared with me how they are going to approach their work."

"Enthusiasm is what you need," says the Facilitator. "It's great to get to the project tasks, but don't skip the team past the forming stage. You have a new team and a new plan. Introduce them to each other."

A new team

The *implementation team* is a new team. The members will devote time and skills to the day-to-day work of the project. They will receive work assignments, work with deadlines and constraints, engage in problem solving, be asked to make changes, and celebrate victories. The project manager is their functional supervisor while they are on the project, assigning tasks and monitoring the quality of their work.

Some of the members have been on the planning team, while others may be new to the project and to teamwork. It is likely that they have not worked together as a team. They will need to develop the trust to communicate, collaborate, and share the project work as a team.

As you prepare for your early meetings, revisit Lesson 11. These principles apply for any new team and help you recognize the stages of team development. Focus first on relationship building, including taking the time for icebreaker activities and gaining consensus on the rules of conduct. Just as you need to master the basics of meeting management, master the basics of team building, including coaching your team members on how to be a productive team member, the stages of team development, and the meeting roles, such as gatekeeper.

What about storming? Your team will move from forming to the power struggles and discordant behavior that signal storming. Help them to work through this stage as they develop trust. This process is detailed in Lesson 16.

A new plan

Team members will have been introduced to the project at the kickoff meeting. (See Lesson 31.) Subsequent meetings continue the introduction to include the plan itself and how the team will work together to implement the plan.

In planning agendas for these early meetings, consider the needs of the team members:

> ▸ *Who will be at the meeting?* If the project is large or complex, the work will be done by smaller subgroups, and only subgroup leaders will be at the meeting. Others involved in the detail work will be getting direction from their subgroup leader. The subgroup leader will be writing detailed activity plans every two weeks and will hold meetings to guide and monitor his own subgroup. At your implementation meetings, subgroup leaders need to be at the level of the big picture, understanding where their work fits in, their scope requirements, budget, quality

constraints, what affects their deadlines, how the testing and approval process will work, the process for making changes, problems and issues, etc.

▶ *Are the members familiar with each other? With you?* Those unfamiliar need to be comfortable expressing themselves, listening, depending on and trusting each other.

▶ *Are any members experienced in working on project teams?* Are they familiar with the stages of team development? Do they know the structure and vocabulary of a project plan? Those new to project work need to learn the basics of teamwork and project implementation.

▶ *Are any of the members stakeholders who approved the plan?* What is their level of commitment to the project? Those who are new to implementation need to know what is expected of them.

▶ *Have any of the members been involved since the beginning of the project?* Those who are experienced and have been involved since the beginning of the project need to get to know their new teammates and understand how the implementation work is now different from the planning work.

▶ *What is their style of learning?* Those who are procedural want to know "what do I need to do?" They need directions. Navigators want to know the context, how it works. They need to understand the vision and goals. Revisit Lesson 2 and help your team members identify their own learning style and work with that of others.

Planning the meeting

Purpose

The purpose is to introduce team members to each other and to teamwork. During the meeting the team members will

▶ Share any new insights learned at the kickoff meeting on what *they* bring to the project team.

▶ Build a shared vocabulary of project planning terms and other terms that may be unique to the project work.

▶ Learn the major sections of the plan, including the change management plan, final delivery date, and the dates to complete deliverables and major milestones.

▶ Be introduced to a collaboration skill: Developing trust by sharing concerns.

Building the agenda

Initial team meetings are 80 percent relationship building and 20 percent task. How might this be applied when the *task*, introducing the plan and getting the project rolling, is the compelling topic? Here are some tips:

▶ Distribute the agenda 24 hours in advance of the meeting. Let the members know that they will be asked to share their understanding of why they are on the team. Note that this was also covered in the kickoff meeting, but it is not mere repetition. Not everyone may have been at the kickoff meeting. In addition, team members may have had new insight or understanding after the meeting was over, etc.

▶ Plan a fun, quick icebreaker to start the meeting. For example, ask members to sit next to someone they do not know or have not worked closely with and find out one thing they have in common. Share this with the group. See Lesson 11 for more suggested icebreakers.

▶ Ask team members to share any new insight from the kickoff meeting, why they have been assigned to the project, and if they have been given a specific responsibility. This will provide an introduction to the scope of the project.

▶ Prepare a flipchart before the meeting of common team-building and project plan terms, such as consensus, forming, storming, norming, scope, milestone, WBS, risk management, quality standards, communication plan, etc. At the meeting, ask for a quick show of hands as you read each term, to indicate if the team members are familiar with the term. This will signal to you and to the team members where they stand on the basics and how quickly you may be able to proceed. Explain that as you proceed, these terms will become familiar to them.

▸ Prepare a flipchart of the high-level scope and major milestones of the project. *Keep this a brief outline.*

▸ Plan a collaboration activity that will help develop trust. Here is an excellent one:

> Hold a round-robin discussion and ask, "What about this project worries you?" Give team members the time to put their concerns on the table and onto a flipchart so everyone knows what the issues are. It sounds negative, but it is, in fact, a positive relationship builder. The team often finds solutions along the way. They begin to feel united as they realize everyone has the same concerns and will be working to solve them. It is also a good time for the project manager to show her support for team members—that she understands what the difficulties might be and is committed to working through them.

▸ Assign a team member who is experienced to be the gatekeeper, to keep the agenda on track. Start and end the meeting on time.

Here is a sample agenda for this introductory meeting.

Icebreaker (10 min)

Team member new insights (5 min)

Project and team terms (10 min)

High-level overview of the plan scope and major milestones (15 min)

Collaboration skill: Developing trust by sharing concerns (15 min)

Next steps and meeting evaluation (5 min)

The clear focus is relationship building. The purpose of introducing the plan is achieved. In subsequent meetings, continue to build the relationships and team/collaboration skills and gradually devote more time to tasks.

Follow-up meeting

The agenda for a follow-up meeting might be:

Icebreaker/team-building training (15 min)

> Example: Each person receives one of the team rules of conduct on a sticky note. Ask members one at a time to paste theirs on a flipchart in the order that they think is most important. They may ask for input from the group while doing it.

Plan details, includes defining terms (30 min)

> Send the detailed plan and the definition of terms as handouts with the call to the meeting.

Collaboration skill: Consensus (10 min)

> Example: "Do you agree that the rule of conduct at the top of the list is the most important one?"

> Or, to follow up from the concerns discussion, "Do you agree we can complete the project by the deadline?"

Next steps and meeting evaluation (5 min)

As the team learns more about collaboration, meeting skills, and team skills, productivity and task accomplishment will increase. Discussions will be focused and relevant. Terms will be familiar. The team will feel a sense of accomplishment as meetings achieve their stated purpose and as members see their work valued—accomplish its purpose.

In a nutshell

Communication: A new team forms. Communication during early meetings is geared toward introducing the members to each other. Agendas and meeting activities are 80 percent relationship building and 20 percent task.

Collaboration: Use team-building skills to develop trust. Build a collaboration activity into each meeting to help you and your team master collaboration skills. Consensus and the rules of conduct for meetings are important tools to hone for making decisions and handling conflict in future meetings.

Project Management: Planning meeting agendas and holding productive meetings are two of the most important skills of the project manager. Focus the initial meetings on establishing trust and on understanding the project plan.

EXERCISE

Plan an agenda for a follow-up meeting to introduce the communication plan to the team. The meeting length is one hour. Include agenda topics and time limits. The team is still in its forming stage.

Exercise answer

Purpose: Introduce the communication plan

Agenda:

1. Icebreaker: (20 min)

    Assign each team member a form of communication (have them draw a note out of a dish with the communication type on it). For example

    > e-mail
    >
    > memo
    >
    > formal report (such as business case)
    >
    > casual face-to-face meeting
    >
    > formal staff or department meeting

    Open with this instruction: I would like to tell all staff that they can take the day off tomorrow. Using the form of communication you drew, share what that form of communication will look like and what it might say.

    Take a quick survey: "Which do you think is the most effective and efficient form of communication?"

2. Details of the communication plan (30 min)

3. Collaboration exercise: Consensus (5 min)

    Consensus item: "Do you agree that use of [the communication style from the survey answer] would be the most effective and efficient communication type to tell staff to take the day off?" Unless all agree on how it will be communicated, no message can go out saying that everyone gets the day off.

4. Next steps and meeting evaluation (5 min)

TIME-SAVER

Handout: Definitions of Project Management Planning Terms

Definitions of Project Management Planning Terms

Business case: The business justification for the project: how the project is expected to move the organization forward.

Scope: What the project will deliver: its features and requirements as outlined in the business case. For example, as sponsor indicated, we are redesigning the Web site to improve functionality for our customers and staff. This is complex, so we are going to plan and deliver the work in versions. You received the plan for Version 1.

Approach/WBS: How the work breaks down in manageable chunks or phases.

Milestone: The due date for a major chunk of work.

Schedule: When the work will be done and who will do it, including how long each task is estimated to take and how much it is estimated to cost.

Quality standard: How we will measure that the work is done and that it meets expectations.

Risk management: How we have considered uncertainties and what we will do if specific risks happen.

33

Manage Subgroup Leaders

"How do I know what the subgroups are doing?" the Project Manager asks. "Are they on track? Will they meet their deadlines? Are requests for changes going directly to them? Are they making their own changes without my review? Are they maintaining quality standards? I can't be at all of their meetings."

"Sounds like you want the assurance that activities are progressing as they should without becoming a micromanager," says the Facilitator. "You can achieve accountability with your subgroup leaders using communication, collaboration, and project management."

Subgroup leaders: Who they are and what they do

For complex projects, the project manager must focus on the big picture and manage at the level of a work package or deliverable rather than hurrying around overseeing day-to-day tasks. She must identify potential problems, manage changes to the project plan, watch for risks and opportunity triggers, and manage the relationship and coordination between deliverables.

In most cases, many tasks and activities are required to complete each deliverable. Who is responsible for making sure that work is completed? For large projects, that role often falls to subgroup leaders. Subgroup leaders are responsible for one or more deliverable. They are often experts in an area working under the direction of the project manager and adhering to the project plan, including scope requirements, major milestones, budget, and quality standards. Their role is expanded to plan, report on, and meet the milestones within their own activity schedule. They are accountable for producing their deliverables.

The Web redesign project has the following subgroup teams, each with a leader:

- ▶ IT
- ▶ Design
- ▶ Content
- ▶ Customer Experience
- ▶ Search/Browse

Subgroup leaders often lead their own smaller teams to create their deliverables. These teams operate under the same team principles as the larger teams. Their deadlines are often short, their work is focused in one area and is often dependent on the completed work of other teams. The Customer Experience user testing group, for example, cannot do its work until design and programming are completed.

Each subgroup leader creates an activity list for each deliverable they are assigned. Most likely, a substantial part of the activity list was made during the planning process. These activities were listed to help estimate the project schedule. In general, the activity list includes the activities that will span a two-week period. As these activities are carried out, the subgroup leader plans the activities for the next period. The leaders report the results of these activities to the project manager who integrates them into the larger plan.

The project manager's meetings are opportunities for the subgroup leaders to share their progress and concerns, receive assignments, get problems solved, learn of any changes, and celebrate victories. Because groups are dependent upon each other, accountability is crucial. Communication, collaboration, and project management are keys to their success and build trust.

Meetings with subgroup leaders

Communication

Communication tools for meetings that project managers hold with subgroup leaders include:

▸ Agenda. A carefully prepared agenda will signal to the subgroup leaders what to prepare for the meeting.

▸ Project plan. The project plan document provides the big picture milestones, goals, quality, and schedule. It reminds leaders how, where, and when their work fits into the plan.

▸ Guiding Principles document. A list of the guiding principles will also be posted on the meeting room wall for quick reference. (See Lesson 13.)

▸ Group leader's activity list. The group leaders work from their detailed lists and use them to update the group. These are helpful for answering questions, identifying time delays, other problems, and even opportunities. The subgroup leader should *not* report the completion of *each* activity, but whether or not the entire deliverable is on track and any issues that the rest of the team may need to know.

▸ Meeting minutes. These are the record of action items and decisions whose outcome may affect following meetings. It is helpful to review the action items at each meeting to verify they are being completed.

▸ Flipcharts. These keep meetings focused on the purpose and main points and signal to participants that what they have said was heard and recorded.

Collaboration

The project manager and subgroup leaders will share their progress toward meeting the project goal. If there are concerns or issues to work out, the project plan and guiding principles documents will be foundational to decision making, managing any changes, and reaffirming priorities. As the work progresses, the project manager should assess whether or not the work of subgroup leaders meets the shared goals. For example, in the Web redesign project, the project manager should consider whether deliverables are meeting the goal of Web First.

Project management

It is important to use team meetings wisely. Focus the attention of the team at the right level for their role in the project. Meetings are used to problem solve and monitor potential risks, changes, and conflicts in scheduling. The project manager focuses on deliverables. The subgroup leaders focus on activities and bring relevant issues to the team. (See Lesson 21 for a discussion on creating and using activity lists.) It is rarely helpful to use the team meeting to review activities. It is helpful to have a flipchart of the deliverables, marking off those that are finished. If any subgroup work is falling behind, the subgroup leaders need to learn what is happening and how to get the plan back on track.

Meeting focus

Focus the meetings on these key points:

What has been accomplished?

> Expect and require specific evidence of what actually has been done in measurable terms. Examples might include: Completed 3 out of 4 customer tests. Or 56 of the 75 programming units have been completed. Keep these updates brief. It should not be a laundry list of each activity completed, but a summary that confirms the schedule is on track.

> If work is not being completed, the project manager should have been informed in advance with reasons given.

What will be done next and how does the work further the project?

Again, require brief but specific, measurable accounts of the work to be accomplished before the next meeting or to satisfy the next milestone.

Identify how that work accomplishes the goals of the project. This is an important check for the project manager to be sure the subgroups are making good decisions that will accomplish the project's goals.

Are there any issues?

Are there resource issues? Is work not completed by one group causing delays for another work group? Are there issues to consider when looking ahead, including concerns about shared resources? These are important concerns the group will air and resolve.

To help focus the group, the project manager can use a flipchart that displays the WBS (including deliverables), checking them off when completed.

Accountability

The subgroup leaders are accountable for their deliverables. The project manager does not micromanage the work of the subgroups but does hold the leaders accountable for accurate reporting, meeting goals and milestones, for notifying her of any issues or concerns, and committing to teamwork. The project manager will follow up as early as possible with individual group leaders who are not meeting their responsibilities to remedy any negative circumstance and get the project back on track.

Reasons are accepted—excuses are not

It is the project manager's job to anticipate and solve problems. You do this with the help of subgroup leaders. Stress to your subgroup leaders that if a deliverable deadline will be missed, they must give you notice and a reason *before* the deadline occurs. By knowing that a deadline is in danger, you and the subgroup leader have an opportunity to correct it. Notifying you after the fact that the deadline was missed and giving you an explanation for the missed deadline is equivalent to providing an excuse and takes away your ability to solve the problem. Be clear that you can deal with reasons. You cannot deal with excuses.

In a nutshell

Communication: Consistent, persistent use of basic communication tools, including the agenda, project plan, WBS, meeting minutes, and flipcharts, helps focus discussion and builds team skills.

Collaboration: To build trust, the foundation of collaboration, the team members must demonstrate accountability. Require specific reports of measurable activities completed and require that leaders notify you in advance if a deadline is in danger of not being met. This will promote accountability.

Project Management: The project manager does not micromanage. She holds the subgroup leaders accountable by requiring specific reports on the status of their deliverables. Team meeting time focuses on identifying and solving problems and making decisions that keep the project moving forward. If there are any issues or if activities are not on time, on budget, or meeting expectations, she follows up immediately. Reasons are accepted. Excuses are not.

EXERCISE

A subgroup leader reports that his group did not complete a work activity on time. What steps should the project manager take next?

Exercise answer

The project manager should hold the group leader accountable without trying to micromanage. Steps include:

1. Remind the group leader that you must know if work is not going to be finished *before* the deadline occurs. You can deal with reasons and try to get things back on track. You will not accept excuses.

2. Require the leader to give you a plan within 24 hours detailing how he will get the work activity on track.

3. Determine whether or not the plan is realistic and feasible.

4. Confirm whether or not this work is holding up other work and endangering other deadlines.

34

Supervise Your Project
and Team

*"What supervisory skills do I need the most?" asks
the Project Manager. "Am I supervising the project?
Those are administrative skills. Or am I supervising
the team? Those are people skills."*

*"You need both," answers the Facilitator. "Both are
predominately people related. Most of all, you need
to build trust."*

Administrative and functional supervision

The project manager has dual responsibility: administrative supervisor
for the project and functional supervisor for the team members.

To supervise the project, the manager is an *administrator* who

▸ sets deadlines and monitors progress toward meeting them

▸ assesses risks to the project and makes plans to mitigate the risks

▸ removes obstacles that would block the success of the project

▸ solves small problems before they become big ones

- makes certain that contracts are fulfilled
- communicates with stakeholders
- ensures that the project conforms to the shared vision and goals and meets requirements and quality standards
- provides good documentation

To supervise the team, the manager delegates and evaluates work assignments and creates an atmosphere that allows team members to do their best work. The project manager is also a *functional* supervisor who

- sets and measures performance standards for staff
- provides education and training as appropriate
- builds team camaraderie and trust
- resolves conflict, especially conflicting priorities between supervisors
- makes decisions
- celebrates victories
- documents performance for personnel records

Administrative oversight of the project requires strength in project skills such as organization, time management, and attention to detail, whereas *functional* supervision may be assumed to be people skills. Both types of supervision, however, are heavily people oriented, particularly in collaborative initiatives that drive organizational change.

The essential supervisory skill is the ability to trust and to inspire trust. Supervision that accomplishes both the administrative oversight of the project and the development and support of team members is based on trust that is established through communication, conflict resolution, and project management. Supervision is ineffective without trust. Lack of trust fosters micromanagement. The project manager does not have time to, nor should she, monitor every detail of the work done on the project as if she were doing it all herself. This will dampen morale and lead to burnout. Likewise, if the project manager is blindly trusting and does not rely on facts and experience to exercise oversight, the project risks cost overruns, delays, scope creep, and poor quality.

Supervising collaborative projects and teams through trust requires building relationships, removing obstacles that stand in the way of success, focusing on facts and actual results, and accepting responsibility.

Build relationships

Trust is developed through taking the time and making the effort to build relationships. This is particularly essential for the success of collaborative projects that must move beyond cooperation to interdependence. When team members feel trusted, they feel they are accepted, listened to, have the skills they need, and are valued. Follow the 80/20 rule in relationship building: Spend 80 percent of time on developing new relationships and 20 percent of time on the task. Get to know your team members and let them get to know you. Here are some tips for building strong relationships among team members:

▸ Reach out to team members, other supervisors, stakeholders, significant vendors, etc. Face-to-face meetings are important because 55 percent of communication is nonverbal—for example, facial expression, body language, tone of voice. Keep an open-door policy and encourage team members and others to share their concerns.

▸ Express your own needs and goals and draw out others to express their needs and goals.

▸ Be clear about expectations, priorities, deadlines, assignments, and agreements.

▸ Communicate so that the recipient understands what is being communicated. This requires attention to working styles and active listening.

▸ Control your emotions and respond rather than become defensive when faced with changes and unexpected behaviors. If you need to vent, do so with someone else and at a later time.

▸ Accept your own working style and the styles of others.

Remove obstacles that stand in the way of your team's success

Project managers need to trust that the work is being done to quality standards and will be on budget and on time. Be alert to warning signs that a team member may be struggling or that an activity is at risk and then take action. Some typical obstacles that get in the way include:

Conflicting priorities. When a team member has both a functional (project) supervisor and an organizational administrative supervisor, priorities and work assignments can compete for time and attention. These should be worked out between the supervisors. (See Lesson 10.)

Conflicting or fuzzy goals. As work progresses on the project, team members may be faced with new assumptions and differing expectations by stakeholders, especially if there has been a change. It may result in extra steps that seem unnecessary or in confusion about what to do. If a deadline approaches and you are hearing "we're still trying to figure it out," then take action to clarify. Use the key elements and guiding principles document to bring changes in line with the goals of the project.

Staff shortages. Illness, vacations, leaves, etc., can pull a key person off the project. The project manager should have a backup plan for staff shortages on key activities so they do not become obstacles. (See Lesson 23.)

Vendor issues. Vendors may not deliver the quality of work or deliver on time. This may happen if there is a personnel change and the new representative is not familiar with the contract. The requirements of the contract need to be made clear, along with the consequences of poor performance. (See Lesson 38.)

Lack of skills or training to do the work assigned. Either be sure that the team member has the skills or provide training and the time to learn.

Perfectionism and poor quality. Both are ineffective uses of time. Perfectionism encourages excessive rework before the deadline, while poor quality results in the need for rework after the deadline. Agree on measurable standards and approval points that control for each.

Focus on facts and actual results

Project managers need to trust that estimates and reports are accurate to predict correctly what is likely to happen in the future. This helps to remove uncertainty and leads to better decisions. When dealing with vendors, team members, or others, it is important to focus on facts and actual results.

▸ Hold regular status meetings, require reports, and issue updates to the schedule.

▸ Keep documentation that is accurate, timely, and concise.

▸ Problem solve to get to root causes and remove the obstacles.

Accept responsibility

Project managers and team members must be able to trust that each accepts responsibility. This is demonstrated in the end results and in positive and supportive communication:

▸ meeting deadlines and standards

▸ foregoing excuses or blaming others for poor performance or delays

▸ taking initiative to alert the team to delays or problems

▸ asking for help or training when needed

Give constructive feedback

Giving feedback reinforces performance that meets the objectives and standards of the assignment and gives guidance to correct performance that is short of the mark. Team members benefit from both positive and negative feedback; if given in a constructive manner, it will be welcomed. Here are some tips:

▸ Be specific about what was done well and what needs improvement. Explain why. Include next steps. Use examples:

Positive feedback example: "John, I have the test results. It shows that the code you wrote for the browse list shortened the search time by three minutes. That's exceptional. What do you think of using the same approach for the overall search feature? We'd like to cut the time on that, too."

Negative feedback example: "Sarah, when I reviewed the testing schedule, I saw that the customer testing procedure is missing the audit measure for password security. Please explain why it wasn't included. How will you make sure all measures are included before the testing procedure is finalized? We have only one opportunity to get the testing done and stay on track."

▸ Determine the appropriate time and place for the feedback.

Give feedback as soon after the situation as possible, allowing yourself time to gather any data you need so that your feedback will include specifics.

If you are angry, you will first want to get control of your emotions. It is helpful to give yourself time to calm down and to talk it over with your supervisor or mentor before you talk to your team member. Do not be tempted to send a response by e-mail if you are angry. If you must communicate by e-mail, ask your supervisor to review it—and give you feedback—before you hit "send."

Determine the appropriate place for the feedback. Face-to-face meetings are usually preferred. For negative feedback, plan a face-to-face meeting in a confidential space.

▸ Use the word "and" (rather than the words "but" or "however") when giving both positive and negative feedback at the same time. Otherwise, you risk negating the positive feedback. For example: "I tried the master page for the store. Your design for the check-out process made it very easy to use. *And* I also tried to find the place to enter the discount code but didn't see it even though I knew it had to be there. How can you make it more visible?"

Difficult conversations

Project managers face difficult conversations throughout the project. Don't put them off. These conversations are necessary and, if handled well, usually result in better understanding and more trusting relationships. Examples of difficult conversations include

- meeting with a vendor who has not fulfilled his contract or is late,
- talking with a supervisor about extra work that is required to keep the project on schedule because of an unplanned resource shortage,
- asking stakeholders for an increase in funds to cover the need for extra programming, and
- confronting a team member who has missed several meetings and explaining that it affects team morale.

Before having a difficult conversation, prepare for it. Review the facts and consider the conversation from both perspectives: yours and theirs. Acknowledge any part you may have played in contributing to the difficulty. Plan to simply state the facts and ask for clarification. At the meeting, speak to the issue at hand and explore how it can be resolved. Agree on specific action that will be taken and a date that it will be reviewed. Document this conversation. If the behavior does not improve and there needs to be another conversation, document this second meeting and give a copy to the team member. A third conversation may have serious consequences, depending on the policies of your organization.

For an in-depth study of this topic, review the excellent resource *Difficult Conversations: How to Discuss What Matters Most,* by Douglas Stone, Bruce Patton, and Sheila Heen.

Trust is earned

The authority to make commitments, hold meetings and require attendance, set standards, and delegate assignments is granted by the project. Trust, however, must be *earned.* It is earned by consistently being yourself, accepting your working style and those of others, and adopting a communication style that results in understanding each other. Recognize accomplishments as well as trouble spots. Maintain a standard for team meetings that is productive, encourages participation by all, and progressively allows the team to develop into a high performance, innovative group—perhaps not needing your supervision at all!

In a nutshell ▶ ▶ ▶

Communication: Supervision requires communication: meetings build relationships; documentation and reports aid administrative oversight. The ability to give constructive feedback and have difficult conversations is a key communication skill for supervisors.

Collaboration: The foundation of supervision is trust. Lack of trust leads to micromanaging. Blind trust leads to poor oversight. Build trust through relationships and back it up with consistently relying on facts and actual results.

Project Management: Project managers have dual supervisory responsibility: to administer the project and to be functional supervisors of team members. Both rely heavily on people skills that hone the ability to spot warning signs and remove obstacles that stand in the way of project success.

EXERCISE

The project manager is both an administrative and functional supervisor. Use the following table to assess the risk to the project of assigning a critical task to a team member at each skill level. Describe the following:

1. For each of the skill levels noted in the chart below, what risk does the project manager need to address?

2. What steps would you take to mitigate that risk?

3. What steps would you take to remove obstacles that would keep the team member from performing his best?

4. How would you build trust?

Guide for determining training and support that may be needed for team members to perform their tasks. Useful for setting expectations for estimating purposes. Also useful for assessing risks to the project.		
Skill level	**Training/Skill status**	**Competency**
No knowledge	Has not begun to develop this skill.	
Basic (Apprentice)	Has begun training in this skill.	Has basic competency. Still needs to be shown what to do and how to do it. Needs fairly constant supervision or support.
Proficient (Journeyman)	Can perform independently what he or she has been taught to do.	Has proficient competency. Needs only occasional support.
Mastery (Expert)	Can innovate and is ready to teach others.	Expert competency.

Exercise answer

No Knowledge

1. There are several risks to the project: delays, cost overruns, poor quality.

2. First, a team member at this level would not be assigned to a critical path task. Consider outsourcing the task to someone who is experienced.

3. It might be beneficial to this person to assist a more experienced worker to learn the skill. Later in the project this person may be able to fill in, if there is a need.

4. Assign the team member appropriate tasks at her skill level. Provide training and encouragement.

Basic

1. Risk is that the team member may not receive the supervisory attention needed, either from the project manager or from his organizational supervisor. The project risks delays, cost overruns, or poor quality. The team member may experience stress from feeling isolated or overwhelmed.

2. Do not assign a basic-level worker to a critical path task unless there is a commitment to provide the supervision and any training needed.

3. Assign the team member basic-level tasks and gradually increase the level of difficulty as she gains experience. Do not assign responsibility for the entire work package.

4. Have an open-door policy. Reach out to the team member by stopping by the work area and chatting. Have shorter turnaround times for tasks and give positive feedback.

Proficient

1. The project manager should be able to rely on this team member to dig into the task and perform efficiently. There may be a risk that the team member will not ask for guidance or for the order of priorities and do unnecessary work or the wrong work.

2. Make sure that tasks are clearly described and that expectations and goals are set.

3. Verify that any dependencies for this task are complete so this team member can work productively.

4. Get to know this team member's style and give direction and feedback that will have a positive impact. (See Lesson 2.) Set shorter deadlines in the initial stages of the work and adjust as confidence is gained on both sides.

Mastery

1. The expert team member will be given major responsibility. A risk is that she may be pulled away from the project or leave the organization, or that she will stick to familiar patterns and processes and not move to the new style of doing things.

2. Have a backup plan for this critical task. Have a trusting relationship with the team member's organizational supervisor so that you will be given advance notice of any change in her availability. Ask her how she will approach her work and provide guidelines for any new approach.

3. Have this team member work with a team member at the basic level to move that person up to proficiency. If there is a new approach to learn, give her time and support to adjust to the new way.

4. Have an individual meeting with her. Acknowledge her mastery and enlist her help in moving the team to the new way.

RECOMMENDED READING

Buckingham, Marcus, and Curt Coffman. *First, Break All the Rules: What the World's Greatest Managers Do Differently.* New York: Simon & Schuster, 1999.

Buckingham, Marcus, and Curt Coffman. *Now, Discover Your Strengths.* New York: Simon & Schuster, 2001.

Stone, Douglas, Bruce Patton, and Sheila Heen. *Difficult Conversations: How to Discuss What Matters Most.* New York: Penguin Books, 1999.

35

Delegate Tasks and Authority, Not Responsibility

"I'm delegating assignments," the Project Manager reports. "I'm being clear that people are accountable for completing the tasks. It's their responsibility to get them done."

"Delegate tasks and authority," says Facilitator. "It's the project manager's responsibility to see that the project deliverables are met. Responsibility is not delegated."

The authority to delegate assignments

Whether you are a project manager or subgroup leader, you will be delegating work, and the authority to accomplish it, to team members. What is the basis for this authority?

▶ Authority to delegate assignments is given to the project.

▶ The project is given authority by its priority.

▶ The priority of the project is determined by its business value.

▶ It's important to note that if the project manager fails to make assignments, the project itself will make the assignments through requests from others. If the project is a priority, the work must get done. These assignments are likely to be last minute and unorganized, causing stress and confusion.

▶ The project manager is responsible for getting the project done. She needs to be proactive. If she suspects there is going to be trouble with resources, she needs to face the problem as soon as possible and look for solutions.

Project and team leaders are functional supervisors of team members and a partner to the administrative supervisor of the team member. Unless the team member is assigned to the project at 100 percent effort (on a full-time basis), he will be juggling other assignments as well this project's. Consider the needs of the team member and their administrative supervisor when making assignments.

Here are some tips that will maintain good relationships with both team members and their other supervisors.

Project leaders do

▶ Communicate the priority of the assignment to the team member and his supervisor. This will allow both supervisors to prioritize work for the team member.

▶ Clarify the project (what are the details?).

▶ Clear time with the administrative supervisor first. Give the supervisor a clear understanding of what is being asked (what are the goals?).

▶ Give plenty of lead time and a firm deadline.

▶ Ask the team member for time estimates. Acknowledge that the person doing the work has expertise and can estimate time and help set expectations.

▶ Collaborate with the administrative supervisor, who should take into account that the team member will be assigned other work to do. Look for opportunities to help adjust the regular workload.

▶ Distribute good agendas in advance. Avoid surprises by giving a heads-up to the team members and administrative supervisors.

Project leaders avoid

▸ Administrative and functional supervisors having different priorities, with the team member being put in the middle.

▸ Giving short notice or no communication.

▸ Lack of clarity about how much time the team member needs to be available for a project.

▸ Assigning work to team members who lack the skills to do it.

▸ Failing to set priorities.

▸ Indecision.

Giving the assignment

When delegating assignments, include the following:

1. The action to be taken:

   Include the date the assignment is given as well as the action that is needed. Describe the action as a result: for example, program log-in screen for home page.

2. The goals of the project that apply to the assignment and the priority:

   Goals of the Web redesign project that apply (from the business case)

   > log-in time that meets customer expectations

   > costs stay within budget

   > customer help is self-serve; functions are easy to use and intuitive

   Priority

   > This task is on the critical path. Must be completed on time.

   This helps the team member understand the project manager's expectations and gives both the project manager and the team member doing the assignment a common basis for evaluating the work that is done. If appropriate, include any guiding principles that apply.

3. Instructions and authority needed to complete the assignment:

This includes the due date, the budget allotment for the work, who will be approving the work and when, and any other instructions needed for the assignment.

Web Redesign Project Written Request Form		
Action/Assignment/To	Goals/Priority	Instructions/Authority
To: IT programmer	Fast log-in.	Budget allotment is 15 hours, including corrections after testing.
Date: Sept. 1, 2009	Costs stay within budget.	Deadline for final log-in screen Oct. 30, 2009.
Action: Program log-in screen for the home page and store	Customer help is self-serve. Functions are easy to use and intuitive.	First draft approved by PM/ team at Oct 1 meeting.
	Priority: critical path activity.	User testing session Oct 15 at 10:00 a.m. Final approval by PM/ sponsor Oct 25.

Assignments may be given verbally at the team meeting or at individual meetings. Always follow up with the written request form. It is also helpful to copy the team member's supervisor. If assignments are given during a team meeting, they should be recorded in the action items section of the meeting notes form. A sample meeting notes form is included in the resources section at the end of this lesson.

Maintaining responsibility

The team member is accountable for completing the task on time per the requirements and instructions. Be clear that if there is any reason the task will not be completed on time, the project manager must be alerted *in advance*. The project manager is ultimately responsible and determines a way to get the work done or makes adjustments that will not affect the overall schedule. If changes are requested during work, for example, if user testing reveals a flaw in the design or programming method, the project manager should be informed, especially if it will add hours to the task.

Informing a project manager in advance that a deadline is in danger will be uncomfortable for the team member. The project manager should take this into account and develop a working style that invites even bad news. An open-door policy, nonjudgmental communication style, curiosity, and a problem-solving atmosphere will encourage members to approach the project manager without fear. This will allow for best results from both the team member and the project manager.

Remember, 55 percent of communication is nonverbal. It is also prudent for the project manager to stop by the team member's workstation occasionally for encouragement and casual conversation. This will give the project manager a sense of the workload and stress on the team member.

Note that approvals are scheduled into the task so there will not be surprises at the final approval. If the project manager has been clear about the goals of the project and the work meets these goals, it will be evident by the first draft and the work can proceed or corrections can be made.

In a nutshell ▶ ▶ ▶

Communication: Clarity, early notice, and follow-up are important when delegating assignments. The method and result should be formal: a meeting and written delegation sheet. Communicate the task, priority and goals, and the authority to do it. Communication from the team member is also important, and the project manager should be approachable. Be alert to and seek nonverbal communication as well.

Collaboration: The project manager is a functional supervisor and a partner to the team member's administrative supervisor. Collaboration between supervisors is important to meet the goals of the project assignments and the organization as a whole. Clearly identifying the project goals that relate to the assignment gives direction to the assignment and signals the business value and priority of the assignment.

Project Management: The project manager delegates the tasks but maintains responsibility for the project completion. Communication is essential, allowing plenty of lead time for assignments and clear instructions, dates, and authority. If she suspects there is going to be a problem getting the work done, she needs to be proactive and find solutions.

EXERCISE

Which of the following tasks can be delegated? Which should not be delegated?

1. Converting an action item from the meeting notes to a task assignment sheet.

2. Designing the interface for a Web subsite.

3. Arranging to have five customers test the order section of the online store.

4. Negotiating extra time from the supervisor to catch up a work assignment.

5. Asking the sponsor to approve a change in design that will save time and add convenience for the customer.

6. Getting confirmation on the progress of an assignment from a team member when there is concern about the deadline being met.

Exercise answer

1. Do not delegate. The project manager should make the assignment herself to ensure that the information is complete.

2. Delegate.

3. Delegate.

4. Do not delegate. This should happen at a meeting between the two supervisors; do not put the team member in the middle.

5. Do not delegate. The project manager evaluates all change requests before they go to the sponsor.

6. Delegating is not advisable if there is concern about the deadline being met. It is better for the project manager to note the nonverbal as well as the verbal communication.

TIME-SAVERS

Template: Work Assignment Sheet

Work Assignment Sheet

Action/Assignment/To	Goals/Priority	Instructions/Authority

© 2010 Change Leadership Network, University of Michigan, Institute of Continuing Legal Education

Template: Meeting Notes (Minutes)

Meeting Notes	
Project Name:	**Notes Distributed:**
Leader:	**Notes Prepared By:**
Date of Meeting:	

Meeting participants

Absent

Date of next meeting

Agenda topics

Purpose(s) of meeting

Action Items

Action required	Assigned	Due	Status

Decisions

Discussion

ICLE thanks Marianne Clauw for permission to reprint this meeting notes template.

RECOMMENDED READING

Edmondson, Amy. "Do I Dare Say Something?" Harvard Business School. Working Knowledge, http://hbswk.hbs.edu/item/5261.html.

Fisher, Roger, Ury, William, and Patton, Bruce. *Getting to Yes: Negotiating Agreement without Giving In, Second Edition.* New York: Penguin Books, 1991. (Lesson 35)

Stone, Douglas, Bruce Patton, and Sheila Heen. *Difficult Conversations: How to Discuss What Matters Most.* New York: Penguin Books, 1999.

36

Measure Your Progress Using Baselines

"The project end date seems so far away," says the Project Manager. "Anything can happen between now and then. How do I make the end points real and control the steps along the way?"

"Your project scope, cost, and schedule were approved in the plan," answers the Facilitator. "These are the baseline measures that will tell you where you should be at any point in the project. Set these up so they are clear and easily compared with where you are that day. Don't forget quality. You have measures for that as well."

Establishing project baselines

To evaluate and communicate the status of a project, the project manager must know where the project should be at any point in time. These starting points are recorded and approved in the project plan and become the baselines for the project. The project manager measures the progress of the project against these baselines. Any changes that are approved will result in new baseline measures. Baselines are valuable tools. They

- alert the project manager if the project is off target and needs corrective action
- clearly identify scope creep and its effect on schedule and cost
- give the project manager a basis to make realistic projections
- provide a record of the changes or versions a project has undergone so they can be analyzed

Establish baselines for the following areas of a project:

Scope. This includes the requirements and measures from the scope statement.

Cost. This is the budget and resources allocated for the project.

Schedule. This is the start and end dates for the deliverables. Use the Work Breakdown Structure (WBS) for a list of these deliverables. (See Lesson 20 for more information on the WBS.)

Quality. These are the quality standards. (See Lesson 26 for more information on creating quality standards.)

The baseline measures are locked in at the beginning of project execution to give the project manager a point of reference as work progresses. The baseline is taken from the approved plan. This gives the project manager a tool to measure how the project is progressing against the original estimates. When there is an approved change to the plan, the baseline is adjusted accordingly. The new baseline will become the point of comparison.

If the project *isn't* meeting the baseline, the project manager needs to consider what actions to take to get the project on track. In general, if a project is falling behind schedule, if no action is taken, the project manager can expect the project to continue falling behind at an equal or greater rate. This is the project manager's cue to step in early and correct whatever problem is causing the project to fall behind.

What are the most likely reasons a project will miss the mark?

Unclear or unexplained assumptions about scope, quality, and cost requirements. When there is not clear communication between the people who created the vision, those who created the plan, and those who are executing the project, it is not uncommon to have inaccurate assumptions about what the project includes, how the product should work, and what quality standards it needs to meet. If the execution team underestimates the requirements, rework will be needed down the line. If they overestimate the requirements, they are spending time reaching unnecessary goals or standards.

Unrealistic estimates in the budget and schedule. Unrealistic budget and schedules can be avoided during the planning process by getting input, when you can, from those who will do the work and from experts who have experience. The schedule may also be thrown off by not allowing time for adequate discussion and assuming that decisions will be easy.

Unforeseen difficulties. You will most likely encounter a few unexpected problems throughout your project. You can keep a project on track by having a plan in place to work through the difficult issues. For example, determine who is the ultimate decision maker, establish a quick method of getting customer feedback, and weigh the problem against your guiding principles to see if an obvious solution presents itself. Your project may have built-in contingency time in the schedule to allow for unforeseen events.

Scope creep. This is the accumulation of seemingly minor changes that do not result in the plan being adjusted. Everyone wants your project to be a success and as good as it can possibly be. It is tempting to add "small" changes that will make your end result even better. Rather than adding the new item to that release, start planning a version 2. This will keep your current project on track and make certain that new items are prioritized and weighed against your organization's strategic plans.

Using the baselines as locked-in starting points, the project manager will be able to identify issues with scope, cost, schedule, or quality and maintain control from the beginning of the project.

Here is a sample baseline schedule for the *Build* phase of the Web redesign. (See Lesson 26 for an example of a quality baseline.)

Deliverables	Resource	Estimated/ Actual time/cost	Estimated/ Actual schedule
Documentation of new site and directory structure	Margaret	20 hr	Start 1/5 End 1/9
Set of .net master pages and shared code			
Draft CSS for Web styles	Gary	40 hr	Start 1/5 End 1/23
Code that is shared across pages			
Top-5 list	Brad	20 hr	Start 1/19 End 1/23
Featured content	Leslie	40 hr	Start 1/19 End 2/2
Related resources	Leslie	20 hr	Start 1/19 End 2/2
List of recently added content	Brad	20 hr	Start 1/23 End 2/2
Search and browse area	Marilyn	60 hr	Start 1/26 End 2/13

In a nutshell

Communication: At the beginning of the project, your planning team worked together to establish the baselines when the schedule was created. Your implementation team agreed to the schedule during your initial team meetings. The baseline is a record of what you agreed to and a tool to identify when the project is falling off track.

Collaboration: Your team worked together through the planning process to agree upon a baseline. When approved changes are made to the project, it is important to work together to revise the baseline. Remember to consider all of the project constraints (scope, time, and cost) when revising your baseline.

Project Management: Your project baseline is an excellent tool for maintaining control over your project. It helps quickly identify emerging issues. When you notice a project is not meeting the project baseline, take a proactive role in finding the solution. Remember to consider scope, time, cost, and quality, when considering options that will correct the problem.

EXERCISE

List at least five warning signs that your baseline would help you identify and correct.

Exercise answers

1. Cost of development for one deliverable is over what was budgeted.

2. Quality check of work shows that requirements for a deliverable were not met.

3. Deadline for a deliverable was missed because of unforeseen problems.

4. A check against the requirements list shows the developer added functionality that was not originally planned.

5. Shifts in resources to correct the baseline may put future deadlines at risk.

37

Stay Focused and Informed with Status Reports

"What did you want to know about the redesign project?" asks the Project Manager. "It's moving right along. Everything's on track. There's nothing really to report."

"Nothing is really something," responds the Facilitator. "Stakeholders expect to hear from you on a regular basis. You will want them to trust you for any news—good or bad. Manage those expectations with good communication channels."

Status reports are part of the communication plan

Status reports are an important and effective tool. They keep the project manager focused and the team and stakeholders informed. However, status reports also have the reputation of being unnecessary overhead and a waste of time. Use your time wisely and make your status reports count by reporting only what matters. Small projects may require less reporting than large complex projects. The project manager collaborates with the stakeholders and team to determine who will receive the status report, how often, where it is stored, and what information will be most useful to keep the project on track.

Building trust

Stakeholders trust the project manager to keep them informed about the project. A good rule of thumb is that no stakeholder likes to be surprised. They expect to be the first to hear good news or bad. They want to know if there are any issues or concerns that would delay the delivery date, push costs to exceed budget, affect quality, change the scope, or add risk to the project. They need to know the status so they can make good decisions about what action, if any, they need to take. For example, if the project is on schedule, they may begin marketing efforts or begin planning for the next project. If the project is not on schedule, they may be able to provide more money, secure more resources, or decide that the project should be dropped.

A formal status report helps to convey this information. Report regularly, at least monthly, if things are on track. If there are serious issues or problems, inform stakeholders right away and follow up at least biweekly.

Report enough detail to give a clear picture of status—be specific, use plain English, and be concise. Include:

- ▸ what has been accomplished to date
- ▸ any variances from the budget, schedule, or quality standards
- ▸ what will be done in the next reporting period
- ▸ any issues or problems that arose since the last reporting period
- ▸ what was done about issues or problems
- ▸ any recommendations or changes

Color coding is effective

Many project managers find that a color-coded system is effective. They report green when the project is on track, yellow if there is a concern and an area needs to be watched or corrected, or red if there is a serious concern and immediate action is needed. This system is a quick reference for the stakeholder to see that the project manager is assessing the health of the project and taking control. It also builds trust.

Color coding, however, does not replace the report on the items just listed. It only signals to the stakeholders where they might want to pay special attention.

Reporting variances

A *variance* is an instance when your actual schedule is different from your baseline. It is important to encourage your team to report and discuss variances. These conversations can identify problems, identify solutions, and help the team work together to keep the project on track.

Reporting variances to stakeholders also alerts them to possible issues with a project. Stakeholders can be part of the solution. They can provide additional resources, remove roadblocks, or increase funding. It is important to keep them informed throughout the project.

An example of variance reporting is included in the status report template at the end of this lesson.

Reporting tips

Consider both the needs of the receiver and the type of information to be shared. If the news is *bad*, deliver it immediately, in person. First tell the sponsor then call a meeting to tell the stakeholders. Do not exaggerate (alarm) or sugarcoat (minimize). Explain:

▸ what the situation is, including why it happened

▸ what you intend to do about it or what you recommend

▸ what resources you need

▸ when you will report again to follow-up

If the news is *good* (for example, you completed a major milestone in the project), share the praise and arrange to celebrate with the team. An e-mail is appropriate for sharing good news with stakeholders.

To build trust, use a format that is

Consistent. Use a template to report information in the same way so trends can be spotted and progress is easy to measure.

Easy to scan. Stakeholders are busy. Be clear and concise. Use text where appropriate and break up the text with some bullets. Use tables where appropriate. Color coding is easily scannable.

Strategic. Provide key information about the project that will meet the expectations of the stakeholders and maintain their trust, such as:

a concise executive summary of the status at a glance, including high-level budget summary

measures of the outcomes of key elements in relation to meeting their goals

any changes or issues that are causing you to rethink any area of the project

progress and performance of interim deliverables on the project, with explanation for any variances

The following behaviors will *erode* trust. Avoid these:

Turning reports in late. Be on time every time with the reports.

Assuming the news is old and stakeholders have already heard it. Report all new information since the last report. This provides context and a reference for future use.

Using technical or "project" vocabulary. Use plain English and define terms that will be unfamiliar to those not involved in the work itself.

Generalizations. Be specific as to which deadlines were met, where the budget stands, what the quality standard was, etc. The format of the report should make this clear and easy to update each reporting period.

Faulty facts and figures. Double-check your calculations, formulas, and variances. Double-check the critical path items. Confirm schedules for resources, especially if there will be vacations or resource shifting.

How to set the stage for honest, realistic, complete reporting

Project managers receive status reports from their team members. The reports are then incorporated into the formal status report. Here are guidelines to set the stage for honest, realistic, and complete reporting.

Everyone has good intentions and no one likes to deliver bad news. Project staff may honestly feel that problems can be solved or that individual delays can be overcome without management intervention. It may just seem easier that way. To combat this situation, a project manager needs to focus on reporting the completion of milestones and any variations from the baseline. (See Lesson 36 for more information on creating a project baseline.) For example, the project manager may ask whether or not the milestones will be completed on time. If not, what is the reason and what is needed to get the project back on track? The project manager must set not only the rules for status reporting, but also the stage for honest and realistic reporting through the following four steps:

1. Combine reporting methods for an effective blend of meetings and written status reports. Staff members may be even more reluctant to deliver bad news in a meeting, and a written report, even a brief one, can provide a much-needed "heads-up" to a project manager.

2. Formal status reporting is not a replacement for personal communication. Informal discussions and impromptu brainstorming should always be encouraged. Important information can sometimes be uncovered at the most unexpected times.

3. Pave the way for open communication. Be sure to include standardized questions in your status report format that are designed to focus on identifying problems and solutions. A starting point is to look at the most important things in a project. It will vary project to project, but here are a few typical criteria for project reporting.

    Has the scope of any project task changed? (Yes (include plan for change)/No)

    Will any major activity or milestone date be missed? (Yes (include plan for corrective action)/No)

    Are there any new or emerging risks or opportunities? (Yes (include plan for mitigating, exploiting, avoiding, etc.)/No)

    Are there any unsolved technical problems? (Yes (include plan for corrective/preventative action)/No)

    Are there any unresolved user review/approval problems? (Yes (include plan for corrective/preventative action)/No)

    Are there any likely variations in budget expenditure? (Yes (include plan for corrective/preventative action)/No)

4. Avoid micromanaging. Asking for too much detail isn't a good use of people's time and can leave your team feeling they are not trusted.

What about changes to the plan?

Project managers are problem solvers. If concerns arise, decide what you will do about them, seek recommendations, and offer options. Be realistic. Include any changes in the status report.

Status report template

See the Time-Saver section for a sample status report for the Web redesign and for the status report template.

In a nutshell

Communication: Status reports are formal communication from the project manager to the stakeholders and other team members. The reports need to be consistent, clear, concise, and accurate so stakeholders will know what their next move should be—whether or not things are on target and no action is required, or if they should get involved.

Collaboration: Consistent, timely, accurate status reports build trust. They should accurately reflect the status of the project and neither exaggerate nor sugarcoat problems. If the message is bad news, it should be delivered immediately and in person.

Project Management: Status reports help the project manager stay focused at the work package level and keep the stakeholders informed. A color-coded scheme works well. Green indicates things are on target. Yellow is a signal there are areas to be watched. Red indicates trouble that could jeopardize the project.

EXERCISE

How and when might a project manager report the following situations regarding the project?

1. Version 1 of the project is completed on time, on budget.

2. Labor costs for the project are at 75 percent. The labor for the project is 50 percent complete. Projections indicate the labor costs will be 10 percent over budget at this rate.

3. A request by a stakeholder will add to the scope if approved.

4. The results of user testing indicate the failure rate of the search results is missing the quality standard by 20 percent. Quality search results are the highest priority in the project.

5. All milestones for the reporting period have been met.

Exercise answers

1. This is green status in a regular status report. It can also be a time for celebration, and a special message via e-mail would be appropriate.

2. This would be a yellow alert on the regular status report and reported in the issues and actions section of the report. At this time the project manager might take action to bring the costs in line or justify the overage. It is also a warning to determine the reason for the overage in labor costs and bring it into line or formally increase the budget.

3. The sponsor approves changes to the project. This would prompt a meeting with the sponsor. The result of the meeting would be reported in the next regular status report.

4. This is a red alert. Search results are the highest priority and work must be done to get better results. This may add cost and time to the project.

5. This is green status. It is noted in the regular report.

TIME-SAVER

Sample: Project Plan Status Report

Report Date: April 2009	
Project Name: 2009 Web redesign—Version I	**Project Leader:** Carol **Project Team:** IT, design, customer experience, content, usability
Strategic Goal: Make Web First the core of our operations	**Budget:** $150,000 **Initiation Date:** 2009 **Planned Completion Date:** 2010

Executive Summary: Version 1 Status: Green

Version 1 will meet launch date of July 1.

Accomplished since last reporting period: Completed design, programming, testing for customer account area. Approvals received.

To do next reporting period: User support testing. Launch site.

Budget status: Green

	Budget	To date	% Complete	Project end
Labor internal	1,200 hours	500 hours	50%	1,100 hrs
Labor external	$50,000	$10,000	20%	$50,000
Materials	$100,000	$25,000	25%	$100,000

Outcomes

Measure of key elements—Version 1	Baseline	Target	Measure	% Target
Fast, relevant search results	500 errors	2 errors	2 errors	100%
Fast log-in	1 min	1 sec	1 sec	100%
Consistent branding: **status yellow**	1 in 10 pages	1 in 3 pages	1 in 5 pages	60%
Content key numbers assigned	None	All	All	100%
Self-serve customer experience	Ordering only	Ordering and private account	Ordering and private account	100%

Any issues or changes that are causing you to rethink the project

Change	Effect on project
Request for an additional subsite by courses	Will add a version and extend project four months. Meeting with sponsor 6/1.

Deliverables and major milestones (these are the work packages from the Work Breakdown Structure)

Milestone	Planned date	Actual date (reason for variance)
Wireframes	4/15/2009	5/1/2009: Stakeholder approval took longer than expected; future meetings have been scheduled in advance to make sure everyone is available.
Programming	6/1/2009	Still on track. We are outsourcing another piece of the project to make up lost two weeks.
Testing	7/1/2009	
Training	7/15/2009	
Launch	8/1/2009	

Template: Project Plan/Status Report

Project Plan/Status Report

Report Date:	
Project Name:	**Project Leader:** **Project Team:**
Strategic Goal:	**Budget:** **Initiation Date:** **Planned Completion Date:**

Executive Summary: Status: Green, Yellow, Red

Accomplished since last reporting period:

To do next reporting period:

Budget status: Green, Yellow, Red				
	Budget	To date	% Complete	Project end
Labor internal				
Labor external				
Materials				

Outcomes

Measure of key elements	Baseline	Target	Measure	% Target

Any issues or changes that are causing you to rethink the project

Change	Effect on Project

Deliverables and major milestones (these are the work packages from the Work Breakdown Structure)

Milestone	Planned date	Actual date (reason for variance)

38

Manage the Vendor Contract Successfully

"The vendor says he will come back and finish the last small section of programming code next week. Everything else is done. In the meantime, I'm going to submit the invoice for payment so it can get on the books before our fiscal year closes," says the Project Manager.

"Payment is made after the work is done and approved," cautions the Facilitator. "There will be no incentive to complete the work, or fix it if it's faulty, if the vendor has already been paid."

Vendor relationships: What is the vendor's incentive?

The vendor relationship reflects a match between the labor and materials that are needed for the project and the skills and experience of the vendor providing the service or goods. It is a business relationship characterized by good faith and backed up by a written contract. The vendor wants to get more work from you, needs good references, and wants to get paid on time.

The vendor relationship begins with finding the match, continues through administering the provisions of the contract, and closes with finalizing the contract and other documents, including approving the final payment. Even beyond completion of the contract, you may be asked to provide references for this vendor to other companies or organizations that need similar work.

Finding a good match

Finding a good match includes

▶ taking the time to get informed about what is needed and the best suppliers of that need;

▶ creating a clear requirements description;

▶ being realistic about cost, particularly any added cost for changes, and availability;

▶ drafting a contract that is clear and enforceable;

▶ confirming there are no conflict-of-interest issues; and

▶ matching your needs by making reference checks to verify actual prior results of potential vendors.

General guidelines for selecting a vendor

Vendors require clear, complete specifications to estimate time and cost accurately. This information will also be spelled out in your contract, so be sure your specifications, including quality standards, are as complete as possible. Do not assume a detail is too small and do not assume the vendor will infer your basic requirements. Although your requirements might be "common sense" for your organization, they are not necessarily common sense for others.

Vendors should also be clear about their own requirements. For example, if the job is to convert text to an electronic format, will mathematical equations be accepted? What about text that is in a foreign language? What about text that is handwritten or incomplete?

Before selecting a vendor, ask potential vendors to provide references and other proof of their quality and quantity of work on similar projects. When selecting a vendor, follow the policies of your organization to avoid conflict of interest. In many organizations, even the appearance of a conflict of interest, for example, accepting gifts or free services from a current or potential vendor, is discouraged.

Request for proposal (RFP)

If costs of the work to be contracted will be substantial (some companies define $5,000 or more as substantial), companies may require competitive bids from at least three vendors and select the one with the lowest cost. Competitive bids are sought in a fair bidding process in which all bidders are given the same specifications and asked to respond with a written proposal by a set date. No bidder is given an unfair advantage by knowing in advance how much you are able or willing to pay for the work done; any bidder with such knowledge would be disqualified.

This bidding process can begin with a request for information (RFI), a formal document asking vendors to describe their services and capabilities so that you can decide how to frame your RFP.

The RFP is a formal invitation to vendors to bid on your project work. It lists information about your company and project and gives detailed requirements of the work to be done, including any stipulations. It also asks for disclosure of any conflicts of interest and references. The more clear your RFP, the better your vendor evaluation procedure will be, and the better your chance to match your project needs with the appropriate vendor. Many samples, examples, and guidelines for RFPs are available on the Internet.

What if the vendor makes a mistake on the bid in your favor?

If you receive a bid that is clearly too low, should you "take the vendor up on it?" That is almost always a bad idea. You will either get a frantic call from the vendor later on (in which case you may have chosen the wrong vendor), get the wrong product (because the vendor didn't understand the specs), or spoil the relationship for the future. It is advisable to discuss the low bid with the vendor. Does it have a new material or process that greatly reduces the costs? Is the method or material untried and therefore a possible risk? Is the vendor lowering its bid to get your contract? Will the vendor meet your requirements and quality standards? If the vendor's incentive is to get your business, ensure that your needs will be met. This includes gaining confidence that the work will be done per your contract specifications.

Contract guidelines

Most contracts of material value are written or reviewed by legal counsel, and this is advised. Written contracts generally include:

▸ Clear requirements specified in writing, including date due and quality standards.

▸ Penalties or recourse if the requirements are not met, for example the penalty assessed for substitutions, such as paper substitutions for printing.

▸ Detailed cost or "cost not to exceed" amounts if vendor charges are based on time and materials.

▸ Specifications for the process you and the vendor agree upon for completing the project and the added cost of any changes. Be sure you are clear about extra charges if any changes are requested during the work. How will changes be authorized and by whom? Will they be charged by time and materials? Or by a fixed charge? Will the costs escalate if there are more than a fixed number of requests?

- Contract stipulation that one contractor is in charge, even if there are subcontractors. If vendors share a contract, for example if one vendor does printing and another vendor does mailing and they agree to work with each other under one printing/mailing contract, stipulate that only one vendor is responsible and will be held accountable for the work done by both companies.
- Regular audits of the work throughout the project.
- Clear designation of who owns the programming code (or intellectual property).
- How payment will be made.
- How loss or damages will be recompensed.
- Warranty provisions.
- Insurance and indemnification clauses.
- Termination provisions—notice, opportunity to cure, etc.
- Security clauses, if applicable, regarding what happens to data transferred for use in development: for example, the vendor must delete the data after the project is complete and cannot use it for anything else.
- Nondisclosure and noncompete stipulations.

A note about types of payment

The contract states how costs will be calculated and payment made. There are three typical methods:

Fixed cost. The vendor estimates all costs and provides a detailed breakdown for approval. Final cost for the project may not exceed this amount and will not be less. The vendor's profit is in the difference between vendor's quoted cost and vendor's actual cost. This method puts the risk on the contractor for all the costs and provides an incentive for the contractor to be efficient. It may also encourage the contractor to cut corners so be sure that your standards are clear. Fixed cost agreements require less administrative work for the project manager.

Time and materials. The vendor estimates the cost for labor and materials and stipulates that you will pay the actual costs, regardless of the estimate. Your cost could be higher or lower than the estimate. It is advisable to include a "not to exceed" clause in these contracts. The vendor must get approval for any costs beyond the "not to exceed" amount. This method is used when there are unknowns and the vendor is not able to provide exact estimates for duration or materials. Time and materials agreements require more administrative work for the project manager to verify the vendor is being efficient and cost effective.

Purchase order. A purchase order is issued by a company's procurement office through a purchase requisition request. It stipulates the terms for and amount of payment. It is the legal agreement that the purchase of goods or services has been authorized and will be paid for per the terms of the contract. Purchase orders are usually required for purchases over $5,000, depending on the company. Some orders are required at $2,000.

Administering the contract

Administering the contract includes understanding the details of the contract that the project manager will administer and providing oversight. The project manager must be thoroughly versed in all provisions of the contract and able to hold up approval of payment if the contract obligations are not met. Administering the contract includes the following activities:

▸ Setting and communicating expectations and measures of quality standards to the contractor.

▸ Regular meetings and reports/approvals to monitor the vendor's work quality and progress.

- Assessing progress toward completing project milestones per the agreement, including checking the quality and timeliness of the work.

- Resolving any problems, conflicts, or changes that could impact the successful completion of the work.

- Orderly record keeping, including records of invoices matched against actual work done, documentation of any changes or disputes and their resolution, logs of hours worked corresponding to project activity, delivery dates and details (including inventory counts) of materials delivered, and samples of materials or products.

- Determining the cause and impact of any delays on your critical path and taking appropriate action to keep the project on schedule.

Contract completion

Before the final payment is made, verify that each of the stipulations in the contract is fulfilled to your satisfaction.

- What has been promised was delivered complete, per the requirements in the contract.

- Invoices are accurate and reflect completed work. There should be no final payment until you are satisfied that the work is finished to the performance standards stipulated in the contract. It should be clear that the final payment reflects the total amount due.

- Invoices are approved by the project manager before they are paid. Both the vendor and your business office should follow this procedure so that invoices submitted directly to your accounting department are not automatically paid on preauthorized, open, purchase orders.

- Any work orders are closed out to prevent future invoices being paid inadvertently.

- Any registrations for warranties are completed.

- Any data the vendor received from you as part of the project has been deleted or destroyed, if applicable.
- The contract, with your project history, is filed or submitted to your business office, as appropriate.
- The vendor receives a formal acceptance of the work.

Include lessons learned from working with vendors in your lessons learned meeting. (See Lesson 45 for more information.)

Working with your business office

Most business systems require that the project be tracked and invoices or other documents be clearly identified by the project name and an accounting code that corresponds to the project. Accounting systems also provide a place to write a comment or note. Keep careful records. Apply the proper accounting code and back it up with a comment referencing the project. This notation allows the project expenses to be quickly retrieved and summarized by the system. The accounting report is a convenient and official reference for all project expenses. File the final expense report with the contract and other project documents.

Provide comments, or notes, with the invoice to allow you or a manager of a future project to search the system and get a simple, complete report of the project expenses without having to locate each invoice document separately.

Here are examples of comments that provide good search results. Note that including the reference "Web redesign" at the beginning of the comment field will cause the search to automatically list them together. This is very helpful when your project is large and has more than one account number to assign.

Web redesign first user survey postage

Web redesign programming for .net conversion

Web redesign frame drawing test copy

Vague or general comments will not help you determine at a glance if all invoices are accounted for or if the invoice may have been inadvertently assigned to the wrong account number. Perhaps a postage expense charged to your project was actually for another project. You would not be able to tell this quickly without searching the system further. Avoid writing general comments such as:

Invoice 1/1/09

Blank (no comment)

Web content

Postage

What if a dispute arises?

If the vendor has failed to meet its contractual obligations, discuss it in a formal meeting. Prepare for the meeting by assembling relevant documents, including work product examples. Present the contract stipulations and show what is and what is not meeting the contract. Expect the contractor to want to meet his obligations and approach the meeting in that light. Agree on specific steps to be taken and set a date for them to be finished. Document the proceedings of this meeting and copy all parties. If problems persist, seek legal counsel.

Your goal is to have all vendor contracts fully performed when the project is finished. It is costly and time-consuming to follow up with a vendor who has not fulfilled the contract completely, is late submitting invoices for payment, or must correct a mistake that has not stopped the project from launching but is not up to standards.

In a nutshell ▶ ▶ ▶

Communication: Business relationships are formal, characterized by a formal bidding process, contract, and formal business meetings. Properly review and approve documents, including invoices and warranties, before any payment is made.

Collaboration: Business relationships are also partnerships that fulfill shared goals. If there is a dispute, attempt to resolve it in good faith, expecting both partners to meet their obligations. Partners should be held accountable.

Project Management: The contract documents, related invoices, warranties, and maintenance agreements need careful, orderly, attention. Invoices are approved and paid only when the work has been delivered and meets requirements.

EXERCISE

In the following situations, which courses of action would you advise
the project manager to follow and which would you advise her to avoid?

Situation	Follow	Avoid
The vendor has done very satisfactory work on several past projects. You would like a couple of quick items done and ask for a quote. The vendor says no problem, no need for a contract for these small items. A handshake agreement is okay.		
The vendor is very late submitting the last invoice. Its accounting department is short staffed, and this has delayed sending the invoice. The vendor wants to give you the cost over the phone and have you pay directly.		
You are unhappy with the quality of work your vendor has supplied. You want to bring it to the company's attention immediately. You call and arrange for a formal meeting to find out why the vendor has not met obligations.		
You have an excellent relationship with your vendor. You see no reason to go to the extra aggravation of putting a clause in the contract for the penalties of not fulfilling the contract.		
You are pressed for time getting everything together for the final launch of the Web redesign, but you take the time to carefully code the final invoices and write a clear comment on each one so they are easily searchable in the system.		

Exercise answers

Avoid situations that would place you in a personal rather than a business relationship. This adds risk to the project and gives you no clear recourse if there is a problem.

Situation	Follow	Avoid
The vendor has done very satisfactory work on several past projects. You would like a couple of quick items done and ask for a quote. The vendor says no problem, no need for a contract for these small items. A handshake agreement is okay.		X
The vendor is very late submitting the last invoice. Its accounting department is short staffed, and this has delayed sending the invoice. The vendor wants to give you the cost over the phone and have you pay directly.		X
You are unhappy with the quality of work your vendor has supplied. You want to bring it to the company's attention immediately. You call and arrange for a formal meeting to find out why the vendor has not met obligations.	X	
You have an excellent relationship with your vendor. You see no reason to go to the extra aggravation of putting a clause in the contract for the penalties of not fulfilling the contract.		X
You are pressed for time getting everything together for the final launch of the Web redesign, but you take the time to carefully code the final invoices and write a clear comment on each one so they are easily searchable in the system.	X	

39

Evaluate All Changes to Your Project's Scope and Plan

"I don't know what happened," laments the Project Manager. "I am in danger of missing the deadline to deliver Version 1 of the Web redesign. We decided to make a couple of small changes that threw off the project. I knew it was a bad idea, and now we're a month behind. I'm putting my foot down. From here on out, no more changes."

"Hold on," says the Facilitator. "Change isn't always bad. A change can save your project just as easily as it can sink it. The trick is in separating the good from the bad and communicating the decisions to your team and stakeholders."

Managing change throughout your project

Managing change starts while you are creating guiding principles as part of the initiation process. It is a good idea to include a guiding principle that commits your team and stakeholders to evaluating each change request according to the project goals and requirements. This sets the stage for a logical evaluation process that will sort out the good ideas from the bad. Your guiding principle might read "requests for additions or changes to the project scope will first be evaluated on their strategic merit." (See Lesson 13 for more information on establishing guiding principles.)

Managing change continues during project planning as you create the process to evaluate change requests throughout the project. Gaining consensus between the stakeholders and the team on this process before moving to project execution will help everyone know what to expect when a change is requested. Consider using this as a consensus item during the kickoff meeting.

Without an agreed-upon process for evaluating change requests, it can be difficult to assess whether or not a change should be incorporated. The tendency is to allow "scope creep," i.e., to repeatedly agree to changes without evaluating them first. Because the requests seem as if they might result in a better end product, project managers often find themselves allowing unnecessary changes. The cumulative effect of these changes—even if minor—will delay the project, tax resources, and possibly move you away from the project's goals.

During project execution, your job as a project manager is to identify and evaluate changes quickly (according to your change management plan). The evaluation process will eliminate scope creep and make sure you are approving only the most necessary and feasible changes. It also guarantees that the change is being fully incorporated into your project plan.

In addition to identifying and evaluating change, you should address the root cause of many common changes. For example, pay close attention to staff resources and stay in contact with their supervisors to be certain you have the staff time you need when you need it. This communication can prevent a change to the schedule.

Identifying changes

It is unrealistic to expect the project scope and plan to remain constant throughout the project. Remember, a project is progressively elaborated. As new information unfolds and stakeholders realize more clearly what they want, the scope will be adjusted. The plan is adjusted throughout the project to account for changes to scope, respond to risks and opportunities, and keep the project aligned with the baseline schedule, cost, and quality requirements.

Be proactive in identifying changes throughout the project, especially at the beginning when changes are generally less costly and quicker to make. Changes will generally fall into one of three categories:

1. *Corrective action:* In this instance, a change is needed to the plan to bring the project back in line with the schedule, budget, quality, and scope requirements. These changes are generally identified by measuring progress against the project's baseline. (See Lesson 36 for further discussion on baseline.)

2. *Preventative action:* These changes to the plan or scope will prevent an emerging problem or take advantage of an opportunity. The problems are identified by reviewing the risk and opportunity assessment. (See Lesson 28 for more discussion on risks and opportunities.) These changes can also come from stakeholder or team member requests. For example, in talking with a customer, the project sponsor has identified a potential addition to the project that would meet a new customer need.

   Pay attention to the number and severity of scope change requests. If you are getting requests frequently, ask your sponsor to review the business case and vision. The problem may actually be a change that is affecting the business case. If so, step back and rework the business case and vision. If you don't, continuing with project execution will most likely result in wasted time and money.

3. *Defect repair:* These are typically changes to the plan that account for the time and cost of reworking a deliverable that did

not meet specifications. These changes are typically identified as the quality control process is executed throughout the project. (See Lesson 26 for more discussion on quality control.)

Evaluate each change to avoid scope creep

As a project manager, you must be sure to evaluate each change against the project goals and their effect on your project plan. Incorporating frequent changes without this evaluation is often referred to as scope creep. Projects suffering from scope creep are often difficult to plan and control and are seldom completed successfully because the cumulative effect of these changes is hard to predict.

When evaluating each change request, use collaborative win-win communication techniques so that the implementation of the change meets the goals of both the stakeholders and the organization. Work with the requestor to understand the request and his goals. Make sure the requestor clearly understands the project goals and schedule. This most often starts a discussion that results in a greater understanding or appreciation for the project or in identifying solutions that make the change possible. Use this information as you and your team evaluate how the change will affect your project.

To evaluate adopting a change, measure it against the shared goals described in the business case and vision. Be prepared to ask the requestor these strategic questions:

▸ What has changed strategically since the business case or vision was written?

▸ Does the request fit into the vision for the project or does it require a change?

▸ Is the change acceptable to those stakeholders who will be affected by its outcome?

▸ Does the application of the request further the goal of the project or is it a new goal?

▸ Can this change be saved for a future version of the product?

Look at the impact of the change. How will it affect your project constraints (scope, time, cost, quality, customer satisfaction, risk)? How would the current project priorities shift to accommodate this change?

Look for options. What is the best way to incorporate the change? What will have the least impact and the least risk? (Be careful when trying to lessen the impact, it can be easy to jeopardize the quality of the end product.) Is the project still feasible? What is the risk of accepting or not accepting the request, and does the request introduce new opportunities and risks?

After weighing all aspects of the request, the project manager must finally recommend to accept or not accept the change.

Document the change request and the result

Document the change request and your decision in the *change log*. A change log is simply a spreadsheet that tracks requests and the decisions made about them. It's an excellent reference for why you chose to or chose not to implement a request.

If you decide to implement the change, update the project plan. You need to consider the schedule, scope requirements, risk assessment, quality plan, etc., to make sure you are fully assessing how the change affects your project.

Web page	Decision	Requested	Date requested
Online Books Product Homepage	In the navigational links on the left of the product homepages, the link should say "Online Books" instead of "Books."	Charlie	2/26/2009
Book landing page and content page	In the books' table of contents (both the landing pages and the left navigation in the content) the Forms and Appendixes should not be an expanding list.	Charlie	2/26/2009
Pages indexed for search	To solve the title searching problem, anything that is indexed in our search should not have our company name in front of it. Anything that is not indexed in our search, (i.e., homepage, results, store and product homepages, etc.) should.	Charlie	2/27/2009
How-To Kit content page	Top-5 function should not be present.	Charlie	3/11/2009
Online Books table of contents page	The Related Resources function should not be included on this page.		3/13/2009
Online Books main page	The Related Resources function should not be included on this page.		3/13/2009
Content pages	Content Area Title bar—minimum size 140 pixels height—can grow as necessary and must be at least 10 pixel padding along the bottom.	Charlie	3/13/2009
All books content pages	We are adding a print function to our online book content. This change should be made across all online books.	Charlie	3/17/2009

Communicate your decision

Notify all the people who need to know about a change, including team members (if they haven't already been involved with it), other project managers, and sponsor.

Be sure to tell them why the change was or wasn't accepted. If it was accepted, make sure you explain how the change impacts the project and their roles and responsibilities. Refer them to the updated documents log.

Handle "change reactions"

Manage the emotional reaction that changes can bring. A responsive approach can neutralize a negative change reaction such as anger, confusion, surprise, or fear. Take steps so team members or stakeholders do not feel isolated or overwhelmed. Use proactive communication, engage those affected by the change to commit to making it a success, follow the established approval process, and adjust the plan appropriately.

Controlling scope creep with versions

If your scope calls for releasing the project in versions, keep a list of requirements in priority order for each version. When additional requests come in, evaluate each one on its merits and, if appropriate, add it to the requirements list. When planning begins for the next version, the entire requirements list is reviewed and reprioritized so that the next version takes the project a step closer to its strategic goal.

In a nutshell ▶ ▶ ▶

Communication: Communicate with stakeholders and team members throughout the project as you identify and evaluate changes. Be sure that everyone who needs to know about the change is notified using appropriate communication channels. The channels should be spelled out in the communication plan.

Collaboration: Evaluate each change against the project's goals. This process can reduce the conflict associated with change. Continue collaboration as you decide how to implement the change to prevent people from feeling isolated or overwhelmed. Follow the accepted approval process for all changes.

Project Management: Changes occur throughout the project. Creating guiding principles and a systematic process for managing them will help you handle change requests effectively during project execution and avoid scope creep. By proactively identifying, preventing, and evaluating changes, you minimize their impact and their effect on your team.

EXERCISE

How might each of these requests be handled so that they do *not* jeopardize the project?

1. Request for change because of incomplete or inadequately described requirements list.

2. Request for extra time to research and test new technological developments that will enhance the features of the project.

3. Request to change the project to align with a change in the vision for the overall organization.

4. Request to include new products being developed in another area of the organization.

5. Request for a new feature that, if implemented, will please a customer.

6. Request for additional time to get a feature perfect before it is shown to the testers.

7. Request to change the scope because the original time and cost limits were unclear.

8. Request to decrease the time needed to complete the project (agree to an unrealistic deadline) to please influential stakeholders.

Exercise answers

These are recommendations:

1. Review the requirements list with the team and confirm that definitions are complete, agree with the business case and vision, and the team has a shared understanding of what these are. Determine if the request fills a gap. If so, it should be added to the scope.

2. Evaluate the request by finding out more about the new technology and whether it looks promising. It could be included in a future version. If the technology looks promising, assess how your current

work can be structured to take advantage of these features, if the conversion can be made.

3. If the vision changes, take the time to evaluate it against your project. Make adjustments in your plan to correspond to the revised vision, if needed.

4. Evaluate the request by determining whether the new product might have been overlooked in the requirements list or not described. Consider adding to the list for a future version.

5. Explore the request with the requestor. If it is based on a suggestion of one customer, it does not alone merit a change. If it highlights an incomplete requirements list or corresponds with high customer demand (such as from survey data) you may want to adjust the plan if it does not alter scope. You can also add the suggestion to your list for a future version.

6. Require that the deadline in the plan be met and the work go to testing. Perfection can never be reached. If perfection is a standard, the project will never be finished.

7. Analyze the request based on time and cost. If necessary, make the adjustment. It is better to make the adjustment early in the project and deal with realistic estimates than to have the project run over budget or be delayed.

8. Explain how decreasing the time needed to complete the project will add cost or reduce the scope of the project. Ask what the stakeholders would like to be removed from the project in order to meet the shorter deadline.

TIME-SAVER

Template: Project Change Log

Project Change Log			
Project Name:			
Project Leader:			
Project Team:			
Change requested	**Decision**	**Requested by**	**Date**

RECOMMENDED READING

Kotter, John P. *A Sense of Urgency.* Boston, Massachusetts: Harvard Business School Press, 2008.

Kotter, John P. *Leading Change.* Boston, Massachusetts: Harvard Business School Press, 1996.

Kotter, John P., and Rathgeber, Holger. *Our Iceberg Is Melting.* New York: St. Martin's Press, 1996.

40

Help Your Team Members Manage Their Time

"I don't have enough time to get everything done."
The Project Manager sighs. "How can I get more
time?"

"We already have all the time there is," responds the
Facilitator. "How is it possible to get more?"

24 hours = 1,440 minutes or 86,400 seconds

Each of us has all the time there is—24 hours each day. That can be bro-
ken down to approximately 1,400 minutes or approximately 86,000 seconds. Do we really need more time? Even if we think we do, we cannot
have more time. Nor can we save time today to use tomorrow. Each day
is a new and complete 24 hours. Instead of more time, what we really
need is to control the time we already have by knowing what we do with
it and by making the most of it.

Where does all the time go?

When talking about time, the term "spend" is often used, as in, How do you spend your time? This same term also is used when referring to money. Think of time, like money, as a precious resource that you want to count. Unlike money, you cannot save it and use it the next day. Coming face-to-face with how you actually spend your time is the first step in managing this scarce resource.

Peter Drucker, in *The Essential Drucker,* advocates creating a log of how you think you are spending your time for a typical week and then actually recording your time for a two-week period or for a month. Compare how you *thought* you would spend your time to the actual record. If you are like most leaders, you will be surprised at the difference. What were your priorities? What was actually getting your attention—and your time?

Time management—putting time and attention on your priorities

Stephen Covey, in *The Seven Habits of Highly Effective People,* recommends categorizing your activities into four quadrants: what is urgent and important (putting out fires that will allow you to meet a deadline), what is important but not urgent (planning, documentation, reporting), what is urgent but not important (e-mails, drop-in meetings), and what is not urgent and not important (surfing the Internet, gossiping).

Analyze where you spend your time. Do you spend most of your day putting out fires even when you allocate the time for planning? Do you respond repeatedly to e-mails as they stream across your computer screen even while you are trying to write an executive report? How often do you spend two hours in meetings that are scheduled to last one hour?

Spend the time you have effectively

Leaders should focus on those things that are important but not urgent. For example, time spent on planning and risk management will result in anticipating problems and determining a plan of action before these become fires to put out. Time spent on documentation and reporting will give team members the information they need so they can work efficiently. Time spent preparing an excellent agenda will pay off in a meeting that accomplishes the purpose efficiently.

Decrease time spent on activities that are urgent but not important. Get control of e-mails by responding to them twice each day instead of allowing them to interrupt your concentration. Discourage drop-in meetings by scheduling times for "office hours" and by encouraging staff to make appointments.

To get significant blocks of uninterrupted time, Drucker advises leaving the building to work off-site when planning or doing other important activities. When you are interrupted, it may take 20 minutes to return to the level of concentration you reached before the interruption.

Spend no time on not urgent, not important activities.

Many project management skills and tasks rely on time management

Using time wisely signals respect for others' time, contributes to good relationships, and establishes trust. Knowing how to effectively allocate time is demonstrated in such skills as setting and communicating priorities, realistic estimating, planning agendas, and evaluating the effect of changes. Some of the tasks that involve time management are listed here. Note that in most cases, the project manager also uses strong communication skills to allow her team to make the best use of its time.

Manage the project schedule. Know where you are in the project and the amount of time required at that point.

Conduct meetings that accomplish their stated purpose and give clear guidance for action items.

Write clear guidelines and expectations regarding requirements that, when followed, result in work being approved without time spent on rework.

Provide good working documents that are accessible to team members and stakeholders. Keep them up-to-date so they don't spend time looking for the latest version.

Develop guiding principles that help you make the tough calls quickly throughout the project work. Don't spend time spinning your wheels or rehashing old arguments.

Adjust the plan, if there is a change. Factor in the effect the change will have on scope, time, resources, cost, and quality. Give advance notice to supervisors and team members if there is a change in assignments so they can manage their time.

Work with your team to make realistic time estimates.

Resolve conflicts using collaborative methods. This results in quick, innovative problem solving.

Proactively identify risks, opportunities, and responses so plans are in place when a risk or opportunity is triggered. This reduces the time spent putting out fires.

Make decisions when needed, rather than putting them off and delaying project progress.

Dealing with deadlines

The plea "I just need more time" often crops up when deadlines loom. "I ran out of time," or "another member didn't finish her work on time, so I couldn't finish mine on time," are responses commonly heard after deadlines have passed. Turn these conversations away from the issue of "time" to the real issue of what is causing the delay by identifying the problems that have their root in time management and translating them into effective time-management solutions.

If you understand that you cannot create more time, you will help your team to make better use of the time they already have and to accept responsibility for keeping their time commitments. Here are some typical time-related arguments and how they might be reframed to focus on solving problems and improving efficiency. The project manager's goal is to help the team member identify the source of the delay or missed deadline. To put focus on how to complete the task efficiently, it helps to restate the problem to remove time from the argument and deal just with the activity.

Time argument	Time argument reframed
"I need more time to write this amount of programming code."	"The time estimate allotted for this task is appropriate. Are you working without interruptions so you can finish the code in large blocks?"
"I need more time to redo this design. They approved my concept but it wasn't perfect."	"Time for revision was allotted in the plan. You used all the time to do the concept. Are you asking for reviews before the final concept is required to make sure you are on track? Are you spending extra time seeking perfection for just a concept?"
"The supervisor said she didn't give this work priority. She needs more time unless you want to pay for overtime."	"Do I (the leader) or you (the subgroup leader) need to develop a relationship with the supervisor that is based on trust and communication?"
"They didn't do their part on time, so I couldn't start my part. I need more time."	"Are you making it clear in the status meetings when you will be starting your part so the project manager and the person responsible for holding you up are aware of it?"

The power of compounding

Even small amounts of time spent unproductively, or small additions to the project, when repeated and totaled, can have a significant compounding effect. Very often, the effect is time-consuming. Let's look at communications, 90 percent of the project manager's time.

Here is a formula to calculate the communication channels needed for a project: $N*(N-1))/2$, where N = number of stakeholders. If you have

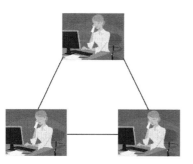

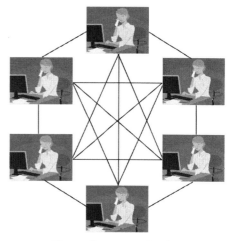

Lines of communication
between 3 people

Lines of communication
between 6 people

5 stakeholders, you have 5 times 4 divided by 2, which is 10 channels. What if you just add one stakeholder? That would be 6 times 5 divided by two, which is 15. (Consider this when selecting your team. Smaller may be better!)

What if your meeting is 10 minutes late getting started? If you have 6 participants, the total effect is losing one hour of productive time. If the meeting runs long by 10 minutes because it started late, that is another total hour lost for those who don't return to their other assignments on time. If one person holds up a different meeting because your meeting made her late, then it further compounds the loss of productivity.

Be alert to procrastination

You have to get started before you can finish. *Procrastination* is the inability to get started and generally results from the fear of failure, burnout, perfectionism, or the inability to make decisions. It manifests itself as putting off doing a task, wishful thinking, or waiting until conditions change for the better before tackling an issue. The effect is that the person pushes the task to its time limit, usually trying to finish it in a rush to meet a deadline. No time is left to deal with emergencies, unforeseen obstacles, mistakes, etc.

One sign of procrastination is clutter. If your e-mail box is overflowing, the piles of paper on your desk overlapping, your files disorderly, you may be putting off taking action or making decisions until they become a crisis—for example, your computer crashes or it takes you half an hour to locate an important document.

Defeat procrastination

Take action. This includes breaking the task into smaller chunks that are manageable and can be accomplished quickly. This provides a small victory (positive reinforcement) and the incentive to move on to the next task. Make a list and be sure to cross off what has been accomplished.

Make immediate decisions, handle items, and move on. Deal with e-mails at first reading, rather than setting them aside to respond to later. Handle a paper once and either file it away or send it off to its next destination.

Focus on meeting quality standards and requirements rather than being perfect.

Set feasible goals and achieve them. Then reward yourself. This will improve self-esteem and defeat the fear of failure.

Make time for yourself. Avoid burnout by making time for yourself a priority. Evaluate requests for your time and learn how to say no successfully. If you are feeling constant stress, seek support.

Heed the wisdom of the ages

A penny saved is a penny earned.

~Benjamin Franklin

A journey of a thousand miles must begin with a single step.

~Lao Tzu

Time is the coin of your life. It is the only coin you have, and only you can determine how it will be spent. Be careful lest you let other people spend it for you.

~Carl Sandburg

What may be done at any time will be done at no time.

~Scottish proverb

In a nutshell

Communication: When the conversation is about the need for more time, rephrase it to help your team member uncover and resolve the actual problem.

Collaboration: The complexity of collaborative projects can compound the effects of poor time management. Take the time to understand where your time is actually spent so you do the planning work that allows others to spend their time effectively. Make sure your priorities are what get your attention.

Project Management: Many project management skills have their foundation in time management and communication. Focus on mastering these skills. When time appears to be the problem, look for the root cause. It could be a legitimate change to the project, an inaccurate estimate, procrastination, or a lack of efficiency and good time management. Uncover the cause and work with your team member to resolve it.

EXERCISE

As Peter Drucker suggests, make a log of what you think you will do each day of the next week or two. Then record your time as you actually spend it.

Answer these questions:

1. What were the differences between how you thought you would spend your time and what you actually did?

2. What would you like to change about how you are spending your time?

3. What is a simple plan that will help you achieve that goal?

4. What would stand in the way of your achieving your plan?

Try this group exercise

Revisit the balloon game. Follow the general instructions for one round of the game. (See Lesson 9.) Stop when the group is exhausted or most of the balloons are on the ground.

Let the group analyze how they might be more effective if they try again. Let them work out a plan. They will work together to keep the balloons in the air effortlessly. They will find that they can handle twice as many balloons without stress or more resources when they spend some time up front making a plan.

RECOMMENDED READING

Covey, Stephen R. *The Seven Habits of Highly Effective People: Powerful Lessons in Personal Change.* New York: Fireside, 1989.

Drucker, Peter F. *The Essential Drucker.* New York: HarperCollins, 2001.

41

Solve the Right Problem at the Right Time

*"Our team meetings have become less productive,"
reports the Project Manager. "We are working well as
a team, and we identify problems and offer solutions
quickly, even if it means we don't stick to our original
agenda. Trouble is, the problem doesn't stay solved. It
comes back, and we waste meeting time solving it all
over again."*

*"Problem solving can spring up in a meeting like a
weed and take over quickly," warns the Facilitator.
"To solve a problem, pull the problem-solving activity
out of regular meetings and plant it in its own
meeting. Prepare to dig deep."*

"We are problem solving"

Recognizing unplanned problem solving in team meetings is one of the
most valuable meeting management skills to develop. It is particularly
important for the project manager and the gatekeeper to be skilled at

spotting when problem solving is taking over a meeting. In many cases, when attention turns to problem solving, team members are either lacking the information they need to make good decisions or the right people aren't in the room. At the very least, your meeting agenda is thrown off and you will not achieve the real purpose for that meeting. Here are the warning signs of unplanned problem solving:

▸ The topic is not on the agenda.

▸ There is high interest in discussing the topic—generally because it is a cause of frustration.

▸ A lot of different opinions are being expressed without any structure to evaluate the opinions.

▸ The phrase "we need" crops up when the problem is described.

When unplanned problem solving takes over the meeting, use this phrase to stop it: "We are problem solving." This becomes the signal to *stop* the discussion and get back to the agenda topic.

If the team has identified a problem, note it on the flipchart and in meeting minutes as a parking lot item and make a plan to deal with it at a later meeting.

Solve the problem for good

If a problem has been identified, it is best to have a separate meeting focused on solving it. Be sure you invite the people who can solve the problem (they may not be members of your team) and give them the information they will need to prepare.

Use the following steps to permanently solve the problem.

1. *Define the problem statement.* Albert Einstein was quoted as saying that if he had one hour to save the world, he would spend *fifty-five minutes defining the problem and only five minutes finding the solution.* This points to the first and most important question to ask in the problem-solving process—what *is* the problem? When people define a problem they are usually describing its effect—the pain or

frustration they feel as the result of the problem. They then offer a solution. For example,

▸ Every time I do a search I have to wait two minutes for the results and then sift through 100 irrelevant items. We need a faster, more reliable search engine.

▸ Our meetings always run late and we don't accomplish anything. We need to quit having meetings.

▸ Last-minute requests are throwing off our schedule and will delay the project. We need a rule that we will not accept requests after the final cutoff date.

In these examples, the "we need" solution becomes the problem to solve. Then the team is off and running pursuing what they assume is the solution.

How can we get a new search engine?

How can we work without holding meetings?

How can we write a rule that will be accepted and followed?

This circular problem solving does *not* produce results. The real problem is neither identified nor solved, the meeting time is wasted, and resources are wasted pursing the wrong solution—and even after the assumed solution is implemented, the problem persists.

2. *Look for the root cause of the pain or frustration*; that is the *real* problem. One method to get to the root cause is to ask "5 Whys." Here are 5 Whys applied to the problem of meetings running late:

   1. Why do meetings run late?

      Because we can't get through the agenda.

   2. Why can't we get through the agenda?

      Because we take meeting time to solve urgent problems that are not on the agenda.

   3. Why do we take meeting time to solve urgent problems?

      Because they need to be solved quickly and everyone is here to give input.

4. Why do the problems become urgent?

> Because decisions are delayed by waiting for everyone's input.

5. Why do we wait for everyone to be present to give input?

> Because we make all decisions using consensus.

The *root cause* appears to be taking unscheduled time to abide by the team's agreement to use consensus to make all decisions.

The remaining steps to solve the problem become more clear and effective:

3. *Identify approaches to resolve the problem* and choose one. (Remember to evaluate solutions against strategic goals, project requirements, and constraints.)

4. *Use your change management plan* to implement the solution you choose. (See Lesson 39 for managing changes to the project.)

5. *Check back frequently* to be sure your solution is solving the problem.

The problem-solving meeting

Before the meeting:

> ▶ Devote problem solving to its own meeting. Structure the preparation and agenda to follow an effective problem-solving procedure. Make sure the correct people are attending and that they have time to prepare.

> ▶ Provide objective background information. Use facts and figures to describe and substantiate the problem. Avoid assigning blame. Keep the communication positive and future oriented.

At the meeting:

> ▶ Be clear about the purpose.

> ▶ Create an atmosphere of trust and sharing that encourages creative thinking.

- ▶ Follow a process. This will keep the team productive. Take steps to engage all team members in the process.

- ▶ Don't rush the creating of the problem statement. It may take more than one meeting to reach an understanding of what the real problem is.

- ▶ Get consensus on the problem statement.

- ▶ Brainstorm options. If the solution is not obvious, the team will brainstorm options and approaches and chose the best one. This may need its own meeting. *Tip:* When the problem is uncovered, the solution is usually obvious. If the solution is *not* obvious, consider that you might not have uncovered the real problem. You need to keep digging for it.

After the meeting:
- ▶ Follow through with the agreed approach to solve the problem.
- ▶ Evaluate its effectiveness.

What if the problem persists after the agreed solution has been implemented?

If the problem persists, dig deeper to define the root cause. Take the lessons learned from the first attempt and use them to succeed in your next attempt. Ask the team the following questions:

Did we hurry through the process?

Do we need to gather more facts? Is there more we need to know?

Were there assumptions we did not question?

Did we listen to everyone's input objectively?

Again, as Peter Drucker advises, "the right answer to the wrong problem is very difficult to fix." (*The Daily Drucker*). Have you uncovered the real problem?

What if the problem—or the solution— is out of the team's control?

If it seems the problem or solution is out of your control or is larger than your project, consider what you can control and act on that. You may not be able to control all decisions, but you *can* control your response to those decisions.

Perhaps the testing schedule was made weeks before the project schedule was finalized to secure commitments from volunteer testers. The actual schedule for testing cannot accommodate the dates that were made weeks ago because the work is not ready. Now the volunteers are no longer available to do testing. Making the appointments and securing the volunteer testers was and is out of your control. What *do* you control? Perhaps you control extra funding to hire testers. Perhaps you can provide a testing room off-site or on a weekend that is convenient to the volunteer testers.

Look at the strategic goals and project requirements. Testing is a project requirement. Encourage your team to find a positive response and choose a solution that will move the project forward. If the decision was not the right one, work in a positive way to provide objective information so a better decision can be made.

Most important, avoid assigning blame or looking for a person to blame. A chronic problem is rarely a person. It is almost always a faulty process.

In a nutshell

Communication: "We are problem solving" is a key phrase to apply when your team is off and running to solve a problem not on the meeting agenda. Any team member can apply this phrase. The leader and gatekeeper should be especially skilled in keeping the meetings on track.

Collaboration: Problem solving is a valuable collaborative skill. A positive outcome is best reached when team members are open in their discussions, able to self-disclose and question assumptions, look forward to solutions rather than assign blame, and are able to reach consensus on the problem statement and approach.

Project Management: Problems arise throughout the project process. Using an efficient process to solve them is valuable for the team and for the project. Evaluate and decide whether the problem is a risk to your project's success and is worth the time to solve. Prepare for problem-solving meetings by providing objective background information. Use the change management plan to incorporate the solution into your project. Evaluate solutions to confirm that the problem was, in fact, solved.

EXERCISE

In the example (p. 401) using the 5 Whys to identify a root cause of a problem, what options might the team offer to solve the problem of meetings running late? The team makes all decisions using consensus and takes unscheduled time when decisions are urgent.

Choose the best option and analyze whether it will, in fact, solve the problem.

Exercise answer

1. If consensus is required for all decisions, allow time on every agenda for consensus activity "just in case."

   > This does not ask the question, Why does the team require consensus for every decision?

2. Revisit the agreement that consensus must be used to make all decisions.

   > This leads the team to problem solve by further asking Why? Why do we feel we need to use consensus for all decisions? Is it a trust issue?

3. Call an extra meeting or provide a regular meeting just to make decisions.

   > If the decision is a major one, this would be appropriate. Asking team members to attend extra meetings can lead to resentment.

4. Gain input on decisions through e-mail and quickly gain consensus at the meeting.

   > This may be appropriate for simpler decisions. It does not speak to the larger issue of why consensus is needed for those simpler decisions.

RECOMMENDED READING

"Drill Down: Breaking Problems Down into Manageable Parts." Mind Tools Ltd., http://www.mindtools.com/pages/article/newTMC_02.htm (details about the 5 Whys and other problem-solving methods).

Drucker, Peter F. *The Daily Drucker*. New York: HarperCollins Publishers, Inc, 2004.

McNamara, Carter. "Basic Guidelines to Problem Solving and Decision Making." Free Management Library, http://www.managementhelp.org/prsn_prd/prb_bsc.htm.

Michalko, Michael. *Cracking Creativity: The Secrets of Creative Genius.* Berkeley, Calif.: Ten Speed Press, 1998.

Shibata, Hidetoshi. "Problem Solving: Definition, Terminology, and Patterns," http://www.mediafrontier.com/Article/PS/PS.htm.

42

Make Decisions That Align with the Project Vision and Goals

"How will I know I am making the right decisions?" asks the Project Manager. "What if there is an emergency or a risk to the project?"

"You have already determined much of what you will do," answers the Facilitator. "Those decisions are in the risk plan. Think of decisions as realizations rather than choices to be made. They come from insight. Fuzzy vision about the project or organization will cloud this insight."

Dealing with uncertainties in the plan

Projects face many uncertainties before and during the execution phase. The project manager assesses these uncertainties, predicts them, and creates a plan for how they will be handled. This provides a rational environment for decision making and a framework for responding positively to situations.

In making the risk management plan, the project manager has already anticipated what might change, issues that may arise, and other uncertainties or vulnerabilities in the project. While it is not possible to anticipate all uncertainties, the discipline of thinking them through and crafting a plan of action if they arise gives the project manager an important advantage. The plan includes triggers to alert the project manager of the risk, the decision, and the actions to take.

The risk plan was made with input from the planning team. The plan was also reviewed and approved by the stakeholders, clearing the way to make assessments and take appropriate action.

What are the decisions and who are the decision makers?

Decisions are made at different levels in the organization and in the project. At the highest level, decisions determine the mission, ethics, and vision of the organization. Who are we? What is our purpose? What are our core values? What are the priorities for the organization? Who are our customers?

At the lowest level, they involve day-to-day choices associated with performing tasks. What is expected of me? What is the procedure I am to follow? What authority do I have to determine how I will do a task and whether or not it is done correctly?

Decisions must be aligned with and flow from the mission and vision of the organization or they will be ineffective. For example, even at the task level, work must conform to the quality that defines the brand identity of the organization. This will govern decisions about how the work is to be done and at what cost.

Here is schematic of the flow of decision making:

↓ Mission of the organization, including its ethics

    Determined by the governing board with the Director

↓ Vision of the organization

    Determined by the Director, with the governing board and input from staff and stakeholders

↓ Guiding principles

    Determined by the Director, with the governing board and input from staff and stakeholders

↓ Goals/priorities

    Determined by the Director, other executives, stakeholders

↓ Policies

    Determined by the Director, stakeholders, product developers, managers

↓ Rules/responsibilities

    Determined by managers, team leaders, bylaws, consensus

↓ Tasks

    Determined by supervisors, team leaders, team members

Decisions flow from goals

When the correct decision is unclear, seek clarity in the goals, guiding principles, vision, and mission of the organization. Seeking clarification from rules or processes will be unsatisfying. A decision based on a rule that is not enforceable or outdated will be a poor decision. Decisions based on a process may be locked in the argument "this is the way we have always done it." Decisions that stem from goals, guiding principles, and vision will move the organization forward and challenge complacency.

When decisions are delayed or seem to be a struggle, there may be conflicting goals. Determine the shared goal first. Decisions about how to reach that goal will follow. If goals continue to be conflicting, then the vision is fuzzy. Step back and make the vision clear.

Fuzzy vision

If the vision is unclear to the decision maker, what flows from the vision, such as the strategic plan, will get increasingly murky. When you cannot clearly see the end result, you are forced to make decisions based on short-term goals and deadlines rather than on the strategic direction. Often short-term goals conflict with your strategic plan. Policies will fluctuate and change with circumstances. Rules will seem arbitrary and unenforceable, and tasks will seem burdensome.

Project decisions

At the project level, decisions flow from the business case, vision, and guiding principles of the project. If there is fuzzy vision, the project team will struggle with conflicting goals and the pressure to cooperate. Clear vision will lead to the win-win outcome of collaborative decision making. Here is the flow of decision making at the project level.

↓ Project vision, guiding principles, key elements, priorities

Determined by sponsor, stakeholders, project manager

↓ Project plan

Determined by project manager, planning team, stakeholders

↓ Rules and responsibilities

Determined by project manager, stakeholders and subgroup leaders

↓ Subgroup tasks

Determined by subgroup leaders, teams

Making good decisions

Good decisions follow from

A clear vision for the organization and the project

A clear, communicated vision understood by all stakeholders and team members is the best tool for good decision making. The adage, "if you don't know where you are going, then take any road to get there," applies to the organization or project that lacks a clear vision.

Guiding principles

Some guiding principles flow from the vision while others are a reflection of the core values and culture of the organization and stakeholders. Principles are agreed to at the beginning and are often posted on the meeting room wall. They are a valuable reference and anchor for making decisions throughout a project. For example, if the guiding principle is "we will create all products so they can be displayed on the Web First," then a choice between a print-only product that is cheaper to make in the short term or a more complex Web interface product that has long-term gains and aligns with the vision becomes a straightforward decision.

Clearly defined roles and responsibilities

A clear determination of who is authorized to make decisions should be agreed to at the outset of the project. When a crisis arises, who has authority to act is already determined. This avoids confusion, saves time, and prevents uninformed decisions.

Willingness to support long-term goals over short-term gains

Good decisions generally come from taking the long view. Short-term gains are tempting and often argued by finance departments and managers under pressure to meet targets or balance budgets.

Agreement on the shared goal of the collaborative partners and trust that all will support it and work to achieve it

Committing to reach the shared goal of the collaborative partners will move the project forward and lead to a win-win outcome. If there are conflicting goals, decisions will be unsatisfactory. Decisions made for the sake of being cooperative will not challenge fuzzy vision or conflicting goals. In the long run, the decision may prove to be a poor one.

Good, objective data that lead toward insight and away from emotionalism

Good, objective data that is clearly presented can lift the team from a crisis mode to a problem-solving mode. Combining this data with a process for making a good decision can move the team from emotionalism to logic and clarity. For example, providing accurate time and cost estimates needed to implement a proposed change can give the decision makers the information and assurance they need to make a sound decision.

Looking at the information from different perspectives

The Go/No-Go decision matrix offers a structure and process to analyze input for decision making from different perspectives. This tool is particularly effective when different stakeholders take differing perspectives—as represented by the two columns here:

Go	No-Go
Advantages	Advantages
Disadvantages	Disadvantages

(Instructions on using the Go/No-Go decision matrix can be found in the Time-Savers section of Lesson 30.)

Win-win orientation for resolving conflict

The win-win orientation allows the team to focus on the goals of the stakeholders and the project. It requires communication and comfort with sharing what is important to the individual or the organization. The decision or outcome of this type of discussion may result in an approach that neither side may have considered.

Embracing change

The desire to keep things the way they are leads to complacency. To see what is changing and how it may affect you, Peter Drucker, in his book *Managing in the Next Society,* advises managers to "look out the window and see the changes that are taking place." This forward-looking approach is necessary to anticipate changes and make decisions that take advantage of opportunities. It encourages decisions that are responsive and positive, rather than negative reactions.

Future orientation that includes the ability to hold others accountable

A good decision will be one that is executable. It must be understood that all who agree to the decision are accountable for making it happen and following through with their agreement.

Ability to gain consensus

Gain consensus on decisions that require team support to be implemented. If a decision requires consensus and the leader and team members do not know how to participate in the consensus process, it can be delayed. Good decisions result from full participation by those involved in the decision. This includes background preparation, speaking up, and listening constructively. The team leader or project manager can and should develop the skills to encourage the discussions needed to build consensus.

Workplace and team culture that encourages the open exchange of ideas

A culture that encourages staff to speak up without the fear of negative consequences encourages the open exchange of ideas. These ideas provide insight that is important to good decision making. Team meetings rather than individual discussions between a team leader and individual team members provide the best environment for the exchange of ideas. The meetings allow team members to hear all the ideas and add their own thoughts and perspectives. This collaborative approach generally results in a better, more comprehensive decision and a greater understanding among team members.

Recognizing problems early and taking action to remedy them before they have an adverse effect on the project

Watching the project plan, including measuring progress against the baseline and recognizing the triggers that signal risks and opportunities, is important. Decisions made proactively—as soon as an issue is identified—often can be made more quickly and with less consequence. The risk and opportunity assessment is particularly useful because it already contains the decision on how to proceed when a trigger emerges. (See Lesson 28 for more information.)

Positive attitude

A positive attitude is reflected in the ability to listen with an open mind, the willingness to share ideas, and the commitment to the goal of the project, including the desire to see the project completed successfully. These are elements of trust and support change initiatives by seeking the win-win solution. Decisions based on collaboration will likely not be compromises. Cynicism rarely results in good decisions. It refuses to see the opportunity or embrace the change. It argues for itself without focusing on shared goals. It has no vision. It disengages others. (See Lesson 10.)

Decisions can be delayed by

Unclear expectations

Know where you are in the project and what the expectations are for that stage. During research stages, expectations are generally broad. For example, the sponsor might be looking for examples and general concepts that will help the organization make decisions. Providing concepts can include finding similar products, drawing sketches on paper, or writing a description. Further along in the product development process, the expectations will be different. For example, the sponsor might want to see a saleable product as the end result. The final product will include clean design, will function properly, and be accessible on the Web site. Both the sponsor and team should question the expectations to be sure they know what they are.

Procrastination

Procrastination is often the inability to make a decision. A well-written scope statement and requirement list removes the doubt that often prevents people from making decisions. A well-described risk plan forces the procrastinator to consider the uncertainties and determine what will be done about them. The other project management documents, such as the business case, vision, guiding principles, and schedule are helpful in minimizing procrastination. These documents help set the priority and deadlines of a project.

Perfectionism

If you wait until you have all the information you need to make a decision, there is a good chance the decision will never be made. Project managers must balance gathering enough information with moving the project forward. In most cases, the project manager is making the best decision possible with the information available at the time. Consider the risks of proceeding without all of the information. In most cases, the risks are acceptable, can be prevented, or can be mitigated by planning ahead.

Insufficient or inaccurate information

Keep the plan and plan documents up-to-date, including any input from subgroup managers. Require regular status reports. There are sure to be changes throughout the project that affect the project plan, including the schedule (new baseline), risk and opportunity assessment, and change log. Documenting what has happened and anticipating risks will keep the information viable. Again, over- or underestimating will lead to poor decisions. (See Section II for more information on the project plan.)

The approval process

A confusing or undefined approval process will cause delays and frustration. If decisions are made at the wrong level, they are often overruled, causing rework later in the project. If there is only one decision maker and he is away, the request may sit on his desk until he comes back.

You can also waste time making some decisions in a group that are more appropriate to be made by an individual. For example, when you have two design options that meet a requirement and both are in line with the project goals and guiding principles, the final decision is often subjective. It makes the most sense to assign the decision to the subject matter expert. In this example, the decision would be left to the designer.

In a nutshell

Communication: Decisions are often recognized rather than made. They result from insight that comes from listening, looking out the window and seeing the changes going on, as Peter Drucker advises, and the open interchange of ideas. In the risk management plan, the project manager shares insight about what may affect the plan and provides remedies.

Collaboration: Clear vision and shared goals are the basics of collaboration. Avoid fuzzy vision, which leads to conflicting goals and the pressure to cooperate or compromise to meet deadlines and move forward.

Project Management: The risk and opportunities plan, including the triggers and responses to them, is an important tool for good decision making. Uncertainties have already been anticipated and how to respond to them determined. The change management plan is also important to the decision-making process. It helps you determine how to carry a decision forward when it results in a change to your project. This allows responsive, controlled management of, rather than reaction to, crises.

EXERCISE

Peter Drucker advises executives to "look out the window" to see what is changing. As a project manager who must anticipate changes and corresponding risks, look out your window and record what you see that is changing. How might these be seen as triggers that should be included in your risks and opportunities plan?

Exercise answer

Is the workforce aging? Or are more tech workers requesting off-site locations? If you have to replace a worker, will you find the tech skills you need for your project? Will it require more training to bring them up to speed? Will you be able to offer remote working capabilities?

Are business professionals listening to portable devices? Does your project offer the feature of easily downloadable content? Will it need to change?

RECOMMENDED READING

Drucker, Peter F. *Managing in the Next Society.* New York: St. Martin's Press, 2002.

43

Build a High-Performing Team to Resolve Conflict

"The team seems to be acting like a real team," says the Project Manager. "They used to be my source of conflict," she jokes. "Now they want to enforce the rules and resolve their conflicts. I see signs of trust."

"Sounds like the team has moved past storming to the norming stage," responds the Facilitator. "They're on their way to becoming a high-performing team."

Signs of norming

The norming team displays trust as evidenced by agreeing on rules and behaviors and how the team will work. Team members are tolerant of individual differences and support each other. Their communications are more relaxed and thoughtful. They learn more quickly and are moving into problem solving. They want to be proactive about issues that affect the project.

At this stage, the task/relationship balance shifts to focus on the tasks at hand. Team members have more responsibility, task subgroups will form, and the leader will delegate leadership responsibility to those ready for it. The group is proud of its accomplishments and is easily motivated. Celebrations become important as tasks are completed.

The leader of a norming team

  ▸ moves more quickly to the tasks; the task/relationship ratio is 80 percent task and 20 percent relationship building;

  ▸ supports open communication as well as addresses and helps the team resolve conflicts;

  ▸ encourages the team to problem solve;

  ▸ delegates tasks and leadership duties;

  ▸ helps the team to determine if consensus is necessary or not; and

  ▸ makes certain that reporting is accurate and well documented.

As the team masters problem solving and is productive, it becomes a high-performing team.

Signs of high performance

The high-performing team is interdependent. Team members value the high productivity their team's effort achieves, and they let go of individual competitiveness. Team members have the ability to trust one another, respect feedback, and listen constructively. They value resolving conflicts and seek win-win solutions. They hold each other accountable and also support individual efforts to achieve the project goals. High-performing teams welcome cross-departmental involvement and the improvement that changes can bring to a project.

The leader of a high-performing team

  ▸ serves a more participatory role as the team members work together to productively report, problem solve, and resolve conflict;

  ▸ delegates tasks and authority;

  ▸ trains leaders by having members serve as team leader, including preparing agendas and meeting notes, and running meetings;

- develops partnerships and collaborates with other teams; and

- encourages the team to take on organizational problems as well as project problems; for example, how the project can foster strategic change within the organization.

The high-performing team resolves conflicts and innovates

As the team develops, it faces conflicts at every stage.

- Forming-stage conflicts are identity related. What is my place on the team? Will I do well?

- Storming-stage conflicts are control related. Whom can I trust? How will my ideas get implemented?

- Norming-stage conflicts are learning related. How do we solve this problem?

- Performing-stage conflicts are project related. What is the goal we need to achieve? What is causing this conflict?

The high-performing team efficiently resolves individual conflicts and moves to project and organizational conflict resolution. Through this mastery the team is able to innovate. Discussions are respectful and thoughtful. Listening spurs insight. The pull to cooperate is replaced by the understanding that shared goals are the means to conflict resolution. Striving to achieve shared goals often requires innovation.

Collaborative conflict resolution

In collaborative conflict resolution the "hard-wired" conflict reactions that stem from fight-or-flight defense strategies are replaced with the win-win resolution strategy. The win-win is the result of interaction.

- Avoidance is replaced by reaching out to learn the goal of the partner or team member.

- Compromise is replaced by valuing the goals for each side and reaching a shared goal that meets both needs.

- ▶ Accommodation is replaced by defending what is needed to achieve the goals of the project.
- ▶ Competition is replaced by listening for what will achieve a win for both partners.

Skills of the high-performing team that foster innovation

Brainstorming, especially with the understanding that there are no wrong ideas

Comfort with interaction, face-to-face sharing of ideas, and real listening

Ease with sharing ideas—even if they are not "perfect" (perfect is actually discouraged)

Problem solving—the search for the underlying organizational goals and what is important to the user and the project

Motivation and high morale that spurs creativity

Ability to learn quickly; acceptance of change and new ideas

For example, during the Web redesign project, we discovered a large number of errors and inconsistencies during our quality-checking process. These errors cost both the designers and developers a significant amount of time during a tight schedule. The mistakes caused tension between the design and development departments to run high, with the designers saying "why can't the developers get it right?" and the developers saying "with all these versions and inconsistencies, how am I supposed to know what to do?"

The design supervisor and IT supervisor met to discuss the problem. They narrowed the problem down to the process used to pass the design from the designers to the developers. The process that was used in the past fit well with the designers' normal work flow, but did not fit well with the normal development processes in IT.

Neither department could afford the time they were devoting to making corrections. They agreed it was time to look for a better approach. As they discussed the problem, the supervisors agreed to a common goal. They wanted a process that guaranteed a quality site but resulted in less inconsistency and fewer rounds of corrections.

Next, the supervisors talked about the needs of each department.

▸ The *designers* wanted to maintain a paper process to fit with their normal work flow. The printed pages they handed to the developers contained handwritten notes that would be hard to duplicate with software.

▸ The *developers* preferred electronic copies so that they could easily share pages and work on different parts of the same Web page at the same time. They often worked out of the office, so passing printed pages back and forth was problematic.

▸ Both groups needed a way to collect and communicate design changes throughout the design and development process that could be applied across all pages as necessary.

▸ Both groups wanted to minimize the multiple versions of pages and end up with one master copy.

Focusing on the common goals and the needs of both departments led to a simple solution:

▸ The design department still produces print wire frames and handwritten notes. But now the pages are scanned to create an electronic copy stored in a central location that anyone can use.

▸ The original print copy is maintained by the designers as the master copy.

▸ Changes to the pages are either made to the master and the page is rescanned or communicated through daily updates to a change log.

These simple changes had a big impact on the quality of work and the relationship between the work groups. The process for passing information was clear, the confusion around finding the latest version was gone, the needs of both groups were respected, and the shared goal was met.

This process is still being improved, but it is no longer in the hands of the supervisors. Team members are now comfortable discussing and implementing possible process changes on their own. They work in a way that considers the working styles of both groups and respects the complexity of both the design and development tasks. The supervisors have increased trust in each other and their staffs and are comfortable letting communication proceed and decisions be made without their involvement.

In a nutshell ▶ ▶ ▶

Communication: Interaction is the communication skill that fosters innovation. It is often the result of collaborative conflict resolution. This skill is developed through team building and effective meeting management.

Collaboration: Interdependence, trust, and comfort with feedback lead to the ability for team members to drop fight-or-flight conflict resolution patterns and learn to seek the win-win.

Project Management: The high-performing team is the most productive. The project manager is able to delegate, the team accomplishes tasks quickly, and collaborates with other teams.

EXERCISE

Fill out the table to include the behavior a leader might exhibit to help her team with these common issues.

Stage	Major issue	Leader behavior
Form	Trust; What are we doing? Where do I fit in?	
Storm	Conflict; control (power struggles)	
Norm	Agreement on the norms—how the team will work	
Perform	High productivity	

Exercise answer

Stage	Major issue	Leader behavior
Form	Trust: What are we doing? Where do I fit in?	Introduce/vision: Prepare well for meetings. Introduce goals and purpose; help members get to know each other; understand the charge (mission) of the team; establish the ground rules.
Storm	Conflict; control (power struggles)	Explain/teach: Openly acknowledge the conflict; examine your own response to conflict; reinforce positive conflict resolution (collaboration); do not become authoritarian; revisit the goals, rules; focus on process (how will we accomplish our goals?).
Norm	Agreement on the norms—how the team will work	Participate/coach: Support the work of the team; provide feedback; focus on tasks (what do we need to do?); develop leadership in team members.
Perform	High productivity	Delegate/observe: Allow team to work; prepare for setbacks if there is a change (someone leaves or is added to the team).

SECTION V

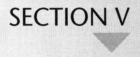

Closing

Follow effective action with quiet reflection. From the quiet reflection will come even more effective action.

~Peter Drucker

Lessons

44

Tie Up Loose Ends by Following the Closing Process

"We have final approval and we're launching the redesigned site," announces the Project Manager. "Everyone is excited and ready to celebrate. The site looks great—we exceeded expectations! The Sponsor says she's already signing us up for a new project. We can't wait!"

"Congratulations!" says the Facilitator. "Before you move on, be sure to tie up any loose ends. Make sure you agree on how long you will provide support and how bugs and training will be handled. And don't forget to hand off the maintenance of the project."

When does the project end?

By definition, a project is a temporary endeavor that has a beginning and an end. Delivering the final product is an exciting, emotional event, and team members often are either sad to be leaving the project or excited to be moving on to new projects. But is the delivery—including the celebration—the end of the project? Usually not. Postdelivery tasks are usually required, and it is helpful to identify them so they get attention. They also provide structure and order to the handoff of the new product or service to those who will accept the new responsibilities for it.

Project closing tasks include:

▶ The approval and delivery of the product. This can be a formal process that requires a signoff from the sponsor and stakeholders. How this is to be handled will be included in the project plan.

▶ Celebrating the project and team successes.

▶ Defining and assigning postdelivery responsibilities. These can include

Providing customer support, especially if new technology was introduced and customers need assistance or training. Determine how long the project will cover this support and when it will be turned over for routine customer support. This can be a week or a month, depending on the complexity of the new technology.

Providing training. There is usually a need to train staff and customers, including stakeholders. There should be a training plan that provides training documentation and the estimate for support. This may include new processes that staff will need to follow or changes in staff routine. Sufficient time and technical support is needed for staff to adjust to the transition.

Fixing bugs and glitches. Programming and design time should be allocated to fix bugs and glitches that may not have been caught in the testing processes. Determine at what point these will no longer be considered a responsibility of the project and will be handed off for routine maintenance. This can be a week or more depending on the complexity of the new technology. Make certain that staff are assigned for fixing bugs and glitches and are not pulled away to do new work.

- Closing vendor contracts. Include any notes about performance that would be helpful to future project managers.

- Assembling final documentation. This includes a comparison of the final schedule and budget estimates to the actual schedule and budget. It should also include your change log.

- Creating a final Lessons Learned document. (See Lesson 45 for more information on documentation and lessons learned.)

- Releasing staff to other projects and providing performance evaluation notes for their supervisors or personnel file. These performance notes should include any new skills or responsibilities the team member acquired as a result of the project work as well as their overall contribution to the project success.

- Communicating to customers, staff, and stakeholders that the project is completed and drawing their attention to its benefits and features.

Transferring responsibility for day-to-day operations of the new product or service

Transferring responsibility for day-to-day operations of the new product or service to staff is often the signal that the project has ended. It moves the new product or service into the regular routine of business. The project team may be very excited about the new product or service they have planned, implemented, and delivered. They are eager to hand it off and use their new skills and knowledge on new projects. Those receiving the product, process, or service, however, may not be as excited. They may express the emotions associated with change including

Anger (spelled f-e-a-r) at the change in their routine or added work. Customer Service staff may anticipate a flood of calls for assistance by customers who find their old password does not work on the redesigned site, for example.

Concern that they will not have answers for customers and the customers will be angry or inconvenienced.

Reluctance to move away from a comfortable pattern of working to unfamiliar, uncertain processes that may still have bugs or glitches.

Fear that their needs will go unrecognized or be lost in the praise for the new product or service.

Unwillingness to move away from areas in which they hold expertise to new areas where they are still learning basic skills.

It is helpful to provide order and structure to this transition time between the project team's devoted effort to complete the project and the regular staff's acceptance of the new technology and processes. Communication, training, and support, including conflict resolution, are the keys.

Communication

Communication is extremely important at this stage. Take these steps to make your communication efforts effective:

▶ Start early. Encourage the sponsor to share the business need, vision, and goals for any corresponding changes with the entire organization.

▶ Share significant progress at your regular all-staff meetings.

▶ Select an ongoing team, such as your core management team, and provide them with regular status reports throughout the project. Share how the project may introduce change to your organization and to their departments. Ask the managers for their support and for feedback from their staff on what would make the transition a smooth one for them.

▶ Communicate the big picture. Help all departments to see how the project touches each of them and how interdependent they will become. Help them work out communication channels with each other to coordinate the changes and set up new processes that take advantage of efficiencies.

▶ Stay ahead of the rumor mill. If there are glitches or bugs, staff should expect to hear the news and how it will be handled directly from you.

- ▶ Make the transition a news item in your newsletter or bulletin board. Share stories, praise, concerns, triumphs, failures, lessons learned. Use humor, for example, by creating a "bug off" report to share progress on finding and fixing bugs in the system.

- ▶ Reinforce the new vocabulary: terms, processes, and forms. Expect to hear—and help to translate—the new language.

Training

Training and support are also extremely important. Short, consistent, regular training sessions that support the learner and the learning process are more effective than intensive, information-packed, one-time training sessions that leave the staff person on his own to apply the new skills.

ICLE converted to a new business system and had the typical intensive introduction to the system before it was activated. We also required all users of the system to start attending a half-hour training session each Monday morning. The goal was to support all of the users and to make sure that everyone was adhering to the new processes the system required. We planned to hold these Monday morning sessions for only six weeks, but it has been 10 years and they are still going strong. The users do not want the meetings discontinued—this is the place where valuable information is shared and staff learn from each other.

Documentation is an important aspect of training. Use general overviews, screen shots, step-by-step instructions, and keep it up-to-date. Make it easily accessible on your intranet so everyone always has access to the latest version. (Revisit Lesson 2 on working/learning styles when developing your training plan and documents for tips on connecting with navigator and procedural learners.).

Support

One aspect of support is to have skilled staff available for a period of time after the project release to answer questions and deal with problems. This support is included in the project and comes to an end according to the plan and budget. Make it clear to staff, especially supervisors relying on this support, when it is scheduled to end and how the project will be folded into their regular work plans and supervision.

Another aspect of support is dealing with the emotions that surface when change disrupts the routine and bumps people out of their comfort zones. Techniques that helped your team weather the storming phase of team development are useful at this time.

- ▶ Encourage staff to express their concerns and listen to them.
- ▶ Focus on the process you will take to move through the transition.
- ▶ Celebrate achievements along the way.
- ▶ Be inclusive—we are all doing this together. We are all on the same team.
- ▶ Be proactive. Some staff will develop the new skills more quickly than others and may become impatient at how long it takes others to change. Ask them to help the others develop their skills.
- ▶ Allow time for staff to learn the new way. How long this should be depends on the complexity of the change.

Revisit Lesson 1 on managing organizational change, particularly the effect of change on productivity. Remind staff and supervisors that it is normal to have lower productivity following the introduction of a change and give them time to adapt.

In a nutshell

Communication: Communication is important at every phase of the project, and especially when the project ends. Develop effective communication channels that begin early and continue through release of the project. Make effective use of organization-wide staff meetings and managers' meetings to share news and to ask for feedback.

Collaboration: Acceptance of the new product or service within the organization is important for its success. The transition from the project team to regular staff should include how to handle conflicts that arise when change is introduced to the organization. Communication, training, and support are keys. Make the transition from the team to the regular staff a coordinated, collaborative effort.

Project Management: When does the project really end? Continue to rely on the order and structure of the project management process to tie up the loose ends and transition the new product or service to the regular staff. Support the learning effort by using the new vocabulary of the project and providing consistent, ongoing training.

EXERCISE

Which of the following do you think plays the most important role in making sure that the project release and transition will be a smooth one?

1. The project communication plan

2. The organization's vision and business case shared at all-staff meetings at the beginning of the project

3. Consistent, ongoing training

4. Coordination of all departments affected by the change

5. A reliable bug report

6. The project delivered on time and on budget, meeting all requirements and quality standards

Exercise answer

Sharing the organization's vision and business case at all-staff meetings at the beginning of the project sets the stage for a smooth project release and transition. It sets the standard for all staff communication, coordination between all departments, prepares the staff for the change, and assures training will be provided. Even if there are problems or delays to the project, all staff will know they are part of the vision and therefore, part of the solutions.

45

Collect Lessons Learned
for Future Projects

437

"I'm ready to close out the project," says the Project Manager. "The team has done a great job. We've learned a lot of lessons along the way, especially me. I learned how valuable it is to have a 'not to exceed cost' provision in the vendor contracts—even if I did learn it the hard way!"

The Facilitator nods. "The lessons learned are really gems. Other project teams count on them to know what works and what to avoid. They come to the surface when the atmosphere is positive."

Project documentation is useful in planning future projects

The documentation kept throughout a project not only helps keep the project organized and on schedule, it can also be extremely useful in planning future projects. Other project managers can use your documentation to help with project estimating, risk planning, communication planning, etc.

To be useful in planning future projects, documents need to be complete and up-to-date. These documents become a more valuable resource if they have the estimated targets, the actual results, and an explanation of any variance of 10 percent or more. The documents that are most useful in planning future projects are:

▸ business case
▸ project plan

    deliverables list

    resource requirements/network diagram/activity list

    budget

    quality standards and quality control processes and outcomes (usability testing, scripts, and results; surveys)

    communication plans

    risks and mitigating strategies

    procurement documents and contracts

▸ meeting minutes
▸ lessons learned

Lessons learned help us all improve

The lessons-learned documentation is most likely to help project managers and team members continuously improve. It records the lessons learned throughout the project so you and other teams can avoid the same mistakes or plan for the same successes in the future.

The best way to create the lessons-learned documentation is to have lessons-learned meetings. These can be scheduled throughout a project or at the end of a project (be sure to include early lessons). Keep these points in mind when planning a lessons-learned meeting.

- ▸ The entire team attends the meeting.

- ▸ Team members are encouraged to freely discuss positive and negative aspects of a project and make recommendations on how to eliminate the negative and repeat the positive.

- ▸ The meeting covers every phase of a project. It may be helpful to talk about each phase as a way to organize brainstorming.

- ▸ The focus is on the future. What should be done differently next time? Why?

- ▸ Comments are not personal or directed at individuals.

- ▸ The resulting lessons learned are general enough to be applied to similar projects.

- ▸ Although you might not come out of the meeting with specific recommendations, your lessons learned might help other project managers develop concrete steps for their projects.

Planning a lessons-learned meeting

It can be a challenge for people to talk about mistakes (their own as well as others'). It can even be difficult for them to bring up their successes. As a meeting leader, your challenge is to create a positive environment that encourages open and honest participation so you can collect the lessons learned.

When asked for feedback on a project performance, team members shared what made them comfortable or uncomfortable giving that feedback. Their candid responses are summarized here.

What made participants comfortable about giving feedback	What made participants uncomfortable about giving feedback
(Before the meeting)	(Before the meeting)
—Time in advance to think it over.	—Worry about having what you say used against you or taken in the wrong way.
—A method for anonymous contribution and confidentiality.	—Worry about saying something negative and it getting back to the person.
—The possibility of e-mail, if some are reluctant to share in a group setting.	—Giving feedback to supervisors.
—An informal meeting, perhaps out of the office. Have treats so it feels like a celebration.	
—Planning a brainstorming session.	
(At the meeting)	(At the meeting)
—Setting a positive tone. Talking about how you will see actual improvement in projects down the line. Good to focus on helping future teams.	—Feeling that you are being put on the spot.
—Starting with asking general questions about what went well or things you appreciate.	—Questioning an individual about why a certain decision was made.
—Getting the ball rolling. Using yourself as example. Have leader be the first to say if he made a mistake. Use humor.	—Rehashing a negative.
	—Going around the table and making people talk.
—Owning up to our own mistakes.	—A critical atmosphere—you're thinking you might get shot down.
—When everyone's thoughts were sought out—those who are quiet are given the space and time to speak knowing the team leader is going to listen and act (you know from experience).	—The feeling you are treading on eggshells.
	—Praising yourself.
	—Feeling what you say makes no difference.
—Asking what could we do better next time.	—Pointing out mistakes that won't or can't be fixed because of personalities (defensive?).
—Bringing up the elephant in the room without judgment or argument. (Problems everyone noticed.)	—Pointing out others' mistakes (to them or others).
	—Giving feedback when there isn't much to give because of poor history or notes.
—Telling things I've learned and what's benefited me.	—Variables that are out of your control.

Make the meeting a positive experience

As a meeting leader, here are strategies and tools you can use to make sure you capture the lessons learned and make the meeting a positive experience for your team.

Encourage participation:

▸ Give team advance notice so there is plenty of time for them to review notes and think about them. Make it clear that lessons learned are the most helpful tips for project managers when they are planning a new project.

▸ Share the results from past feedback—write up the notes and circulate them—this can be a final review of items that were recorded throughout the project.

▸ Start by taking a broad review of the project. Express appreciation for accomplishments. Share what other people thought about the project from outside evaluation and from what you have heard others say.

▸ Go around the room to encourage participation. Listen. Let people speak without being interrupted and without a retort.

▸ Separate problem solving from brainstorming. Problem solve at a different meeting.

▸ Be available after the meeting if someone did not feel free to talk at the meeting.

Discuss mistakes:

▸ Use the brainstorming meeting style—all ideas are good ideas. Have an experienced scribe and use flipcharts.

▸ Ask for anonymous feedback before the meeting. The leader can also talk to members individually before the meeting—focus on what can be fixed for the next project.

▸ Share your own examples of lessons learned the hard way as a project manager and what you would fix or avoid.

- Focus on "we," not "you." It's a team effort, and we are all on the same team. This includes the organization as a whole as well as the project team.
- Stay focused on objective lessons rather than personal experiences. Keep the focus on tasks, not people.
- Record what was not expected, such as serendipity; bring up what went really well; opportunities first, what could be improved second.

Create a positive experience:

- Celebrate: go out rather than meet in the office, have food.
- Focus on things that can be fixed for the next project rather than just griping.
- Keep the written record proactive and presented as helpful tips: what to keep; what to avoid.
- Create a place on your intranet for final wrap-up notes.
- Carry lessons and issues forward to your next project.

Report your best ideas

Share the best ideas and give the team feedback on how their ideas were actually used, perhaps in later versions of the project.

In a nutshell

Communication: Feedback—both positive and negative—is valuable to team members who will move on to other projects and to new teams just getting started. Creating a positive atmosphere that supports open and nonjudgmental dialogue will produce the best results. Listening without interrupting is key. For some team members, a private conversation may be appreciated.

Collaboration: Trusting relationships bring out candor, which is most likely to result in suggestions for what could be improved rather than judgments about who should be blamed. Celebrate the team effort of the accomplishment (goals achieved) and focus on how the process can get even better. When were we really collaborating? When were we just cooperating?

Project Management: Keep project documents up-to-date and post where they can be accessed by future project teams. Creating a lessons-learned document by hosting a lessons-learned meeting and providing a positive, brainstorming atmosphere to gather both what went well and what can be improved, is the most helpful means of preserving and passing on the knowledge generated by the project.

EXERCISE

Prepare an agenda for a lessons-learned meeting and create the e-mail you would send inviting the team to the meeting.

Exercise answer

Participants: Team members

Purpose: Share our lessons learned from the Web redesign project

Agenda with time limits:

1. Review of accomplishments of the project. What others have said. (10 min)

2. What went well—what we would keep or do again. Include what was unexpected. (20 min)

3. What could be improved—what we should fix or avoid. (20 min)

4. Our top five "gems" in each category. (10 min)

Handout: Any prior feedback from previous review sessions

Next steps: Where report will be filed

E-mail message to the team:

Congratulations! Sponsor said he's submitting our new Web site for an award, and he's booking us to advise the new team for Version 2. The Web redesign team is celebrating at Darcy's. Let's have ice cream and enjoy some final licks on what lessons we've learned in the project. This is our chance to help the next team leap ahead. Think about what you thought went well and what you would advise be fixed or avoided before the new team starts its work.

46

Release the Team and Start Planning for Future Versions

445

"Is this it?" asks the Project Manager. "I don't know how to let go."

"Acknowledge what the team has accomplished," replies the Facilitator. "You have a record of success. Now go and help other teams achieve their collaborative goals."

Disbanding the team

Anticipating the final meetings and knowing the team will disband can bring a fear of loss or separation to team members. Up until now they have been actively pursing a challenging goal, learning new skills, solving problems, resolving conflicts and, most likely, putting in long hours to get the final pieces of the project in place. Once that is accomplished and closing activities begin, it may be difficult to keep the same level of motivation. Some members may already have moved on to other projects. Some may be hesitant to leave a group of colleagues and an activity that they thoroughly enjoyed.

Preparing the team to disband and helping the members to work through the feeling of loss will help the members as they move to other projects. This table lists some typical negative reactions to anticipated separation and how to respond in a positive manner.

Negative reaction to anticipated separation	Positive response
Anxiety about what will happen next	Share future assignments, if they have been made. Help the team members look forward.
Anger, increased conflict, or sadness expressed as withdrawal	Encourage members to express their feelings.
Lethargy or lack of motivation to complete closing assignments	Maintain enthusiasm and accountability. Continue the review process until all loose ends have been tied up.
Wanting to fix "just one more thing" or add "one more change" or denying that the project is ending	Formally end the project and close it. Explain how these changes may be accomplished outside this project.

Continuing the collaborative goals

The collaborative team effort draws members from different groups or departments in the organization or partnering organizations. The benefits of trust, interdependence, and shared principles learned through working together does not need to, nor should it, end with the project. As team members leave the team, they return to their departments with a higher awareness of what collaboration can accomplish. Challenge team members and expect them to share their skills in collaborative goal setting, conflict resolution, problem solving, accountability, and communication. These skills reinforce alliances and support the strategic initiative of the project, especially if it is bringing change to the organization or department.

The final team meeting

The final team meeting is the time to praise the accomplishments of the team and the members as individuals. More than a celebration, it is the recognition of their contributions to reaching the shared goal, including:

- specific accomplishments
- new skills learned
- victories
- problems solved
- new relationships formed
- "Aha" moments of insight gained or major roadblocks overcome
- praise from others

Performance reviews and official documentation

Project managers may give team members performance reviews at the close of the project. These can be as brief as a note to the person's supervisor or a formal review that is copied for the personnel file. If participation on the team qualifies a member for certification, continued learning credits, or career advancement, see that the proper forms are obtained and filed.

Preparing for the next version

Projects that are being implemented using an agile management approach will be planned and executed in versions. The next version of this project is a new project in itself. It may share the business case, vision, and guiding principles, but it will be planned and implemented as a separate project with its own scope, budget, resources, and quality standards. Start at the beginning by reviewing the business case and vision to align them with any changes to the strategic direction, priorities, funding sources, and market potential that may have occurred.

The first step is to be sure that the earlier project has been officially closed. If not, the project risks becoming an ongoing set of changes and fixes, roles and schedules become confused because of conflicting priorities, and resources are overextended.

It is rare that every team member will continue to the next version. Depending on the priorities of the organization, the skills needed, the availability of resources, and funding, some of the members will be new to the project. Any change in the team will affect the dynamics of the group. The project manager should guide the team to re-form, re-storm, etc. If it is the project manager that changes, the group will be challenged the most to re-form.

In a nutshell ▶ ▶ ▶

Communication: Prepare the team for disbanding by acknowledging that the project is ending and encouraging team members to express their feelings, both the excitement of the success and any anxiety about ending the team. Write formal performance notes to supervisors or hold performance reviews for personnel files. Prepare and file any professional certifications.

Collaboration: The collaborative skills learned throughout the project should be carried by the team members to their departments and organizations to further the strategic initiative, to support the change and build trust, to problem solve, communicate, and to be interdependent, and accountable.

Project Management: Although this is the end of one project, it may signal the beginning of the next version. Close the first so it does not blend into the next, becoming a perpetual project that does not end.

EXERCISE

1. Describe what is the most valuable form of recognition that you would like to receive for a job well done.

2. What do you feel is the most valuable attitude or skill a team member can carry to the next project in the organization or department?

   ▸ ability to respond to change

   ▸ ability to give and accept feedback

   ▸ trust

   ▸ caution that keeps one realistic

   ▸ curiosity that drives questioning and the search for the root causes of problems

   ▸ confidence that motivates and inspires action

   ▸ vision

Epilogue

"70 percent of projects fail. Why do you think that is?" asks the Project Manager. "I'm really glad my project was a success. It had its struggles, though."

"What did you learn that made this project successful?" asks the Facilitator. "What will you take to your next project?"

"Three things," says the Project Manager.

> *"Communication*—I thought it was about what I had to say. It's really about what others hear and if they understand it. That only happens when you take the time to prepare, learn who your audience is and what is important to them.

> *Collaboration*—I thought it was about cooperating and everyone getting along. It's really about building on common ground and resolving conflict. That only happens when you take the time to develop relationships and establish trust.

> *Project Management*—I thought it was about getting organized and doing things right. It's really about people working on the right things at the right time. That only happens when you take the time up front to plan and get the project aligned with the organization's strategic direction."

"Do you think taking this time was worth it?" asks the Facilitator.

"Absolutely," responds the Project Manager. "I only had time to do the project once!"

TIME-SAVERS

Many of the Time-Savers listed below are available for download at the Change Leadership Network's Web site (www.icle.org/cln). To access the files, log in using the user name and password provided when you purchased this book.

Handout: Be a STAR! Guides for Procedural and Navigational Working Styles (Lesson 2)

Handout: Characteristics of a Good Team Member (Lessons 10, 17)

Handout: Definitions of Project Management Planning Terms (Lesson 32)

Handout: Guidelines for Achieving Consensus (Lesson 6)

Handout: Project Activity Dependency Chart (Lesson 22)

Handout: Rules of Conduct for Meetings (Lesson 6, 11)

Handout: Standard Guiding Principles for an Organization (Lesson 13, 18)

Handout: Suggested Icebreakers (Lesson 11)

Handout: The Role of the Team Leader (Lesson 17)

Sample: Executive Summary of the Plan (Lesson 30)

Sample: Gantt Chart (Lesson 24)

Sample: Go/No-Go Decision Matrix (Lesson 30)

Sample: Project Activity List (Lesson 21)

Sample: Project Plan Status Report (Lesson 37)

Sample: Project Time Estimates (Lesson 21)

Sample: Scope Statement (Lesson 19)

Sample: Time Estimates (Lesson 21)

Template: Building a Business Case (Lesson 7)

Template: Meeting Agenda (Lessons 5, 18)

Template: Meeting Notes (Minutes) (Lesson 5, 35)

Template: Project Change Log (Lesson 39)

Template: Project Plan (Lessons 15, 18)

Template: Project Plan/Status Report (Lesson 37)

Template: Work Assignment Sheet (Lesson 35)

Glossary

accept A passive approach to risk management generally used for minor risks. If a project manager accepts a risk, nothing extra is done to prevent it.

acceptor A person involved in a project who is responsible for accepting the final project and deliverables, making sure they meet the project's strategic direction. She is also responsible for making high-level decisions that cannot be made by the project manager.

accommodate A conflict resolution style where one person gives in to the needs of another. Generally, this is seen as a win-lose approach to decision making because one person's needs are met while the other's are not.

action item A task that results from a meeting. It is detailed in the meeting notes, along with who is responsible for it and when it is due.

activity list The specific tasks needed to complete each work package. The activity list is created and used by team members to accurately estimate time, cost, and resources needed for a project.

adjourning The final stage in the team development process in which the project is completed and the team disbands. Adjourning can be difficult for some team members because it signals an upcoming change to their work habits and relationships.

agenda The primary tool for effective meeting management. The agenda identifies the participants, purpose and approach, including topics with time limits, for each meeting. Writing the agenda helps the meeting leader think through the best way to achieve the purpose of the meeting. Sending an agenda at least 24 hours in advance helps team members come to the meeting prepared.

agile project management Agile project management is an approach that focuses on quick turnaround and low overhead. The goal is to deliver the most important product features first, get feedback, and revise or add more features. The quick turnaround and small releases allow organizations to reprioritize and meet high-demand customer needs quicker than projects with longer schedules.

analogous estimating A method of estimating project time that is largely based on experience and past projects. Estimating time in this way is generally quick and lacking in detail. It is most often used at the beginning of a project—during project initiation—when stakeholders are looking for a rough estimate. Analogous estimating typically has low accuracy (+/– 50 percent).

avoid A conflict resolution style where one party chooses to ignore or bury the issue rather than confront it. Avoid is a lose-lose style because the issue is never brought up to be resolved and goals are not met for either party.

This term is also used in risk management to mean eliminating a risk by putting plans in place so that loss does not happen.

baseline The starting point(s) for scope, cost, schedule, and quality against which the process of the project is measured.

bottom-up estimating The most accurate and time-consuming type of estimating. These estimates are created from estimating each activity on an activity list and can be very effective in projects where maintaining time and cost is critical. This type of estimating starts in the planning stage, but continues through the project to keep track of the time and money needed to complete it.

brainstorming A meeting technique that allows participants to generate new ideas without the risk of criticism or debate. In a brainstorming meeting, the goal is to generate a large quantity of ideas without comment on the quality of the ideas.

budget A sum of money or time allocated to a specific project or cause. In project management, a budget is established during the planning process and monitored until the project closes.

business case A document written by the project sponsor to evaluate whether or not a project is worth pursuing. It also serves to collect the important information needed to convey the idea to a larger team. The business case generally includes a high-level view of

- Scope
- Market analysis
- Recommendations from advisors
- Risks/opportunities
- Desired budget (should this be funding source?)
- Desired schedule
- Staffing/skills needed

change leaders Members of an organization who are responsible for leading change.

change log A document used often in project management to track suggested changes, decisions, and due dates.

charge A directive from organization leaders that gives direction to and assigns responsibility for a project or task.

collaboration A method/technique whereby individuals work together and resolve conflict in a way that achieves a common goal. It requires a shared vision and trust between parties. Collaboration results in a win-win solution because all parties are able to achieve their goal. Collaboration often results in strong, long-term working relationships.

compete A conflict resolution style in which individuals or partners try to "win the argument" rather than find a solution that works for all parties. This style is often win-lose because one person gets what they want and the other does not.

compromise A conflict resolution style in which the parties each give up some of their goals to reach a sufficient solution. This is considered a lose-lose approach to conflict resolution because each party gives up something of value and neither party achieves their goals. Compromise is often used to keep forward movement when there is a deadlock on an issue. It is a short-term strategy and the issue will resurface until it is actually resolved.

consensus A method for reaching agreement on important decisions during a project. Consensus occurs when every member of the group says honestly: "My view has been accurately heard by the other members. I will support the decision being recommended even though it may not be my first choice."

constraints Constraints are restrictions put on a project. They often come in the form or funding or resource considerations.

contingencies Percentages of money or time set aside for a project above and beyond the estimated cost and time. Contingencies are used to compensate for unknowns in a project, such as labor shortages, delays, price increases, etc. Contingencies should be created for a project rather than intentionally overestimating (padding) the work.

cooperation Agreeing to share resources, time, cost, etc., without committing to a shared vision. Cooperation fosters avoidance, compromise, accommodation, and competition when parties are faced with conflict.

corrective action A change that is made to bring the project back in line with the schedule, budget, quality, and scope requirements. These changes are generally identified by measuring progress against the project's baseline.

critical path The path through the network diagram that takes the longest time to complete. Delays along this path will most likely extend your deadline and possibly affect other areas of the project. Because completing the activities along the critical path on time and according to specification is so important to meeting the deadline for the project, it is most critical to monitor the activities along this path.

defect repair Changes to the plan that account for the time and cost of reworking a deliverable that did not meet specifications. These changes are typically identified as the quality control process is executed throughout the project.

deliverable The tangible or intangible product of project work that often indicates a significant milestone or end of the project. Interim deliverables are used by project managers to gauge the quality and progress team members are making toward their end goal.

dependency A relationship between project tasks that requires one task to be completed before another can begin. For example, task B is dependent on task A. Therefore, task B cannot be started until A is complete.

duration or calendar time The number of days or weeks it takes to complete a task. This includes downtime. For example, a task may require only 10 hours to complete but is scheduled over 5 days because only two hours are available each day.

enhance A term used during risk and opportunity management to indicate plans have been made to increase the likelihood that an opportunity will occur.

exploit A term used during risk and opportunity management to indicate plans have been made to make sure an opportunity will arise.

facilitator A meeting coach who helps the team work to achieve the meeting's purpose. The facilitator is not usually a regular member of the team. Their function is to advise the team leader and help the team work together where appropriate.

float time The amount of time that a task in a project can be delayed before it causes a delay in the project.

forming The first stage of team development during which team members are introduced to each other and begin to establish trust. Eighty percent of the time should be spent on establishing relationships during the forming stage.

future orientation A collaboration skill that requires collaborators to look to the future when making decisions rather than basing decisions on past assumptions and practices.

gatekeeper A meeting participant tasked with keeping the meeting on time and focused on the agenda.

Go/No-Go An organized method to guide discussion and analysis to determine the feasibility of going ahead, or not, with the project.

groupthink The practice of making decisions without a great deal of analysis or critical thinking or without bringing in outside views. Groupthink is likely to occur in teams when members have worked together for long periods of time, have similar views, would like to maintain harmony, or are uncomfortable questioning the decisions and ideas of others.

guiding principles Organizational standards on which the sponsor, project manager, and team members agree to base decisions.

initiation phase The beginning phase of the project when it is being evaluated for business and strategic need. During this phase, the business case, guiding principles, vision, and key elements are written.

interdependence A collaborative skill that requires collaborators to trust each other. Interdependence acknowledges that all parties in a collaborative effort are responsible for its success.

key elements The deliverables in a project that will bring about strategic advancement.

kickoff meeting The kickoff meeting introduces the team to a project. It focuses on establishing and understanding the vision and what each team member will contribute to the project.

lag time The time after a task is completed before the next task can begin. For example, there is a lag time of two weeks between when concrete is poured for the foundation and construction work can begin on it.

lead time The time one task overlaps with another in the project schedule. For example, you can purchase paint while you wait for plaster walls to be repaired.

lessons learned The results of a meeting held at the end of a project to review what went well in the project and should be repeated during future projects and what should be improved. Lessons learned should be shared to help the entire organization improve at project management.

meeting notes (minutes) A record of who attended a meeting, action items, decisions, and discussion that occurred during a meeting. These minutes are generally saved in a document that can be referred to later. They are distributed within 48 hours of the meeting.

milestone A point in a project that marks a significant achievement, handoff, or turning point. Milestones are often accompanied by deliverables.

mission statement A formal written statement of the purpose of an organization. It can be used to guide decision making during strategic planning and project management.

mitigate Reduce the probability a risk will occur.

navigational learner/navigator A person who has an exploratory working and learning style. The navigator generally is interested in knowing "how this works" and "why is this necessary?" She prefers an overview, is curious about the possibilities, wants to know the context, and needs to know why it is important. The navigator propels your organization forward.

network diagram A diagram that shows the order of activities in a project. The diagram includes each activity, the duration for completion, the resources assigned to it, and the necessary lead or lag time. The network diagram helps manage the activities and the relationship among them as it relates to resource allocation and scheduling.

norming The stage of team development during which team members adopt trust, respect, and teamwork. They develop the ability to make decisions and resolve conflict. Work productivity increases.

parametric estimating A method of estimating that looks at data from many projects to predict the time and cost of similar projects. This method works well if the projects are exactly the same or if differences between projects are clearly understood. The quality of these estimates depends largely on the quality of data.

performing The stage of team development where team members are highly productive and innovative. They resolve conflicts; show a high degree of trust, loyalty, and interdependence; and solve problems quickly and effectively.

preventative action Changes to a plan that prevent an emerging problem or take advantage of an opportunity.

procedural learner A person who has an organized and systematic working and learning style. The procedural learner seeks process, order, directions, and rules. She is efficient and highly productive. She gets your work done.

project manager A person charged with planning, executing, and closing a project according to specified timelines, cost and quality measures.

project plan A document created by the project manager and team that contains the project's scope, work breakdown structure, activity list, network diagram, critical path, communication plan, quality plan, risk and opportunity analysis. The plan may change throughout the project as unknowns are uncovered.

quality plan The document that defines the quality standards—what will be accepted, or not accepted, in the final product. The quality plan answers whether or not the product is finished and if it meets the requirements as specified. The quality plan includes

- ‣ Quality measures (many from the scope statement)
- ‣ Process for checking that quality is on track
- ‣ Assignments and schedule for checking

recorder The meeting participant charged with recording who attended a meeting along with action items, decisions reached, and relevant discussion. The recorder typically sends this information to team members as meeting minutes.

risk management Risk management is the process of identifying possible risks during a project and planning to minimize their impact. Risk management often includes "opportunities management" or considering what opportunities may arise and making plans to exploit them.

root cause The starting point for a series of problems with a product or process. Identifying and eliminating the root cause of a problem is the only way to make sure the problem doesn't recur.

schedule The document that lists and tracks the due dates, cost, resources, and variances of the project deliverables for the project manager. This is the level at which the project manager manages and reports.

scope creep The cumulative effect of additions to projects that were not identified during planning. Scope creep often results in project delays, cost overruns, and poor quality.

scope statement Definition and agreement between the project manager and sponsor on what the project manager promises to deliver.

The scope statement verifies that the project will meet basic strategic objectives. The scope statement includes

▸ Introductory summary paragraph, giving readers a point of reference.

▸ A requirements list that describes the overall project deliverables and key measurements that will be used to gauge success and completion.

▸ Draft of versioning plan, if necessary.

▸ A boundary paragraph that defines what is included and what is not included in the project.

scribe A meeting participant charged with recording discussion items on a flipchart or whiteboard for the team to refer to during the meeting.

share A method of opportunity management that incorporates a partner who is best able to achieve the desired result.

sponsor The person who typically initiates a project by writing the business case and providing funding for the work. Throughout the project, the sponsor is the champion of the work. The sponsor also often serves as the project's acceptor.

stakeholder A person who is affected by or has any interest in the outcome of a project. Stakeholders can include people internal and external to the organization.

storming The stage in team development when team members are adjusting to working with one another. This stage is often accompanied by frustration, animosity, and apathy as team members struggle to find their place on the team and are challenged to give up self-interests and accept the goals of the team. During this stage there is a reluctance to let go of self-interests and a lack of trust among team members. The desired outcome of this stage is trust.

strategic thinking High-level, long-term, and organization-wide planning and decision making that lead to an innovative and advantageous direction or result.

successor A task that follows another in the network diagram. Task B is the successor to task A.

timekeeper A term often used instead of gatekeeper. The timekeeper is responsible for keeping the meeting focused on the time limits as set in the agenda.

transfer A mitigation strategy in risk management that makes another party responsible for assuming a risk. Purchasing insurance or a warranty is an example of transferring a risk.

trigger A warning that an identified potential problem (risk) is about to take place.

variance The difference between the actual result and the projected or baseline result. Variances in the time, cost, or quality of the project deliverables may indicate the project is at risk and action must be taken.

version A planned successive stage of a project. Each version delivers project features managed and implemented as a separate project.

vision A word picture of what the result of a project would be if it were finished and operating today. The goal of the vision is to create a common understanding of the project among the sponsor, project manager, other stakeholders, and team members.

work breakdown structure (WBS) A diagram used in project management that shows the approach that will be taken to complete a project and all of the project's major deliverables. It sets the level of management needed by the project.

Web First Web First is a term used throughout the book to illustrate one of our guiding principles when redesigning our Web site—that what we deliver is not just about content. It is about how it will be delivered and how we will create it. Web First establishes our Web site as the cornerstone of our business. Collaboration and technical knowledge are as important as content knowledge.

win-win The collaborative conflict resolution style. This approach requires all parties involved in a decision to have their goals met.

work package The lowest level in the work breakdown structure. This level is specific enough for the project manager to gauge progress on a project. In general, work packages take between one day and two weeks to complete.

Recommended Reading

Bower, Joseph L., and Clark G. Gilbert. "How Managers' Everyday Decisions Create or Destroy Your Company's Strategy." *Harvard Business Review,* Feb 2007. (Lesson 9)

Brenner, Rick. "How to Say 'No': A Tutorial for Project Managers." Chaco Canyon Consulting, http://www.chacocanyon.com/essays/sayingno.shtml. (Lesson 19)

Buckingham, Marcus, and Curt Coffman. *First, Break All the Rules: What the World's Greatest Managers Do Differently.* New York: Simon & Schuster, 1999. (Lessons 10, 34)

Buckingham, Marcus, and Curt Coffman. *Now, Discover Your Strengths.* New York: Simon & Schuster, 2001. (Lessons 10, 34)

Co-Intelligence Institute's Web site at http://www.co-intelligence.org/P-strategicQing.html. (Lesson 8)

Covey, Stephen R. *The Seven Habits of Highly Effective People: Powerful Lessons in Personal Change.* New York: Fireside, 1989. (Lesson 40)

D'Aprix, Roger, *Communicating for Change: Connecting the Workplace with the Marketplace.* San Francisco, Calif.: Jossey-Bass, 1996. (Lessons 1, 27)

D'Aprix, Roger, *The Credible Company, Communicating with Today's Skeptical Workforce.* San Francisco, Calif.: Jossey-Bass, 2009. (Lessons 1, 27)

Denise, Leo. "Collaboration vs. C-Three (Cooperation, Coordination, and Communication)." *Innovating Reprint,* Vol 7, No 3, Spring 1999. (Lesson 3)

Dent, Stephen M. "Comfort with Change." Chap. 10 in *Partnering Intelligence: Creating Value for Your Business by Building Strong Alliances.* Palo Alto, Calif.: Davies-Black Publishing, 1999. (Lesson 11)

Dent, Stephen M. "Effective Partnering: Collaboration for Change." Partnership Continuum, Inc. http://www.partneringintelligence .com/documents/LeadershipExcellence%20Dec%2006%20article. pdf. (Lesson 4)

Dent, Stephen M. *Partnering Intelligence: Creating Value for Your Business by Building Strong Alliances.* Palo Alto, Calif.: Davies-Black Publishing, 1999. (Lessons 3, 4)

"Drill Down: Breaking Problems Down into Manageable Parts." Mind Tools Ltd., http://www.mindtools.com/pages/article/newTMC _02.htm (details about the 5 Whys and other problem-solving methods). (Lesson 41)

Drucker, Peter F. *Managing in the Next Society.* New York: St. Martin's Press, 2002. (Lesson 42)

Drucker, Peter F. *The Daily Drucker.* New York: HarperCollins Publishers, Inc, 2004. (Lesson 41)

Drucker, Peter F. *The Essential Drucker.* New York: HarperCollins, 2001. (Lesson 40)

Edmondson, Amy. "Do I Dare Say Something?" Harvard Business School. Working Knowledge, http://hbswk.hbs.edu/item/5261.html. (Lesson 35)

Fisher, Roger, Ury, William, and Patton, Bruce. *Getting to Yes: Negotiating Agreement Without Giving In, Second Edition.* New York: Penguin Books, 1991. (Lesson 35)

Goleman, Daniel. *Emotional Intelligence: Why It Can Matter More Than IQ.* New York: Bantam Books, 1995. (Lesson 9)

Goleman, Daniel. 12Manage: The Executive Fast Track. Leadership Styles. http://www.12manage.com/methods_goleman_leadership _styles.html. (Lesson 9)

Goleman, Daniel, Richard E. Boyatzis, and Annie McKee. *Primal Leadership: Realizing the Power of Emotional Intelligence.* Boston: Harvard Business School Press, 2002. (Lesson 9)

Gordon, Jon. *The Energy Bus*. New Jersey: John Wiley & Sons, 2007. (Lesson 10)

Jensen, Bill. *Simplicity, the New Competitive Advantage in a World of More, Better, Faster*. New York: Perseus Publishing, 2000.

Kotter, John P. *A Sense of Urgency*. Boston, Massachusetts: Harvard Business School Press, 2008. (Lessons 1, 27, 39)

Kotter, John P. *Leading Change*. Boston, Massachusetts: Harvard Business School Press, 1996. (Lessons 1, 27, 39)

Kotter, John P., and Rathgeber, Holger. *Our Iceberg Is Melting*. New York: St. Martin's Press, 1996. (Lessons 1, 27, 39)

Leader to Leader Institute. Thought Leaders Gateway, http://www.pfdf.org/knowledgecenter/leaders.aspx. (Lesson 9)

Maslow, Abraham. *Motivation and Personality*. New York: Harper, 1954. Maslow's Hierarchy of Needs has been applied in many business contexts, and numerous references to it can be found on the Internet. (Lesson 11)

McNamara, Carter. "Basic Guidelines to Problem Solving and Decision Making." Free Management Library, http://www.managementhelp.org/prsn_prd/prb_bsc.htm. (Lesson 41)

Michalko, Michael. *Cracking Creativity: The Secrets of Creative Genius*. Berkeley, Calif.: Ten Speed Press, 1998. (Lesson 41)

Mishra, Aneil, and Mishra, Karen. *Trust is Everything: Become the Leader Others Will Follow*. 2008.

Partnership Continuum, Inc. (Stephen M. Dent, founder). Partnering Intelligence. http://www.partneringintelligence.com/; assessment at http://www.partneringintelligence.com/products_assessments_pq.cfm. (Lessons 3, 4)

Shibata, Hidetoshi. "Problem Solving: Definition, Terminology, and Patterns," http://www.mediafrontier.com/Article/PS/PS.htm. (Lesson 41)

Smith, Douglas K., *Taking Charge of Change: 10 Principles for Managing People and Performance,* Reading, Mass., Perseus Books, 1996. (Lesson 1)

Stone, Douglas, Bruce Patton, and Sheila Heen. *Difficult Conversations: How to Discuss What Matters Most.* New York: Penguin Books, 1999. (Lesson 34, 35)

Thomas, K. W., and Kilmann, R. H. *Thomas-Kilmann Conflict Mode Instrument.* Palo Alto, Calif.: XICOM, 1974. (Lessons 1, 3)

Tuckman, Bruce. "Developmental Sequence in Small Groups." *Psychological Bulletin,* Vol 63, No 6, pp 394-99. (Lesson 11)

Turbit, Neville. "Project Quality Planning." Project Perfect, http://www.projectperfect.com.au/downloads/Info/info_project_quality_planning.pdf. (Lesson 26)

Warner, Charles. Chapter 6: Leadership, in *Media Sales Management.* http://mediaselling.us/media_sales.html. (Lesson 9)

Index